Application Development Using ObjectVision

JAMES T. PERRY

University of San Diego

bf

boyd & fraser publishing company

Acquisitions Editor: Anne E. Hamilton
Production Editor: Jean Bermingham
Production Services: Mary Douglas, Rogue Valley Publications
Compositor: Rebecca Evans & Associates
Interior Design: Rebecca Evans & Associates
Cover Design: Kevin Meyers
Manufacturing Coordinator: Tracy Megison

© 1994 by boyd & fraser publishing company
One Corporate Place • Ferncroft Village
Danvers, Massachusetts 01923

International Thomson Publishing
boyd & fraser publishing company is an ITP company.
The ITP trademark is used under license.

Manufactured in the United States of America

Library of Congress Cataloging-in-Publication Data

Perry, James T.
    Application development using objectvision / James T. Perry.
        p. cm.
    Includes index.
    ISBN 0–87709–140–4
    1. Object-oriented programming (Computer science)
    2. ObjectVision. 3. Application software.   I. Title.
    QA76.64.P53   1994
    005.4′3—dc20   93–43455
                                             CIP

1 2 3 4 5 6 7 8 9 10 D 8 7 6 5 4

BRIEF CONTENTS

CONTENTS

7 Creating Menus and Protecting Applications   223

Appendix: ObjectVision Built-in Functions   251

Index   261

DEDICATION

To my stepmother, Virginia "Ena" Perry

PREFACE

This book is designed to support courses on Application Development and Database Development by presenting application development and database linkage using a visual development environment, ObjectVision. ObjectVision operates under Microsoft Corporation's Windows system and provides a graphical development work surface that is easy to use and visually "friendly." This approach increases user productivity and renders prototype systems that can be easily turned into full systems.

Application Development Using ObjectVision can be read and used by those who have little or no application development or database development exposure. You need not be particularly fluent in any programming language or have any prior computer experience to find this text instructive. This book is intended to be used as a supplement to an applications development course or as a stand-alone introduction to Windows application development.

ABOUT OBJECT VISION

ObjectVision is a computer program developed by Borland International, Inc., that provides a graphical, object-oriented environment in which you can create Windows-ready applications. ObjectVision provides an easily learned, intuitive, interactive approach to building applications using a forms metaphor. The visual development environment tools tend to hide the more unpleasant tasks of the Windows application program interface (API).

Information systems students, as well as seasoned applications developers, will welcome this tool. For the student, this text provides the structure and methodology to use ObjectVision to build sophisticated applications without prior programming knowledge. Veteran developers who read this text and become familiar with the techniques presented herein will applaud the availability in ObjectVision of sophisticated linking capabilities, Dynamic Data Exchange functions, and Object Linking and Embedding. ObjectVision makes it easy for both novice and expert to incorporate extant business rules into impressive Windows applications.

ABOUT THE BOOK

The focus of this book is application development in the Windows environment using ObjectVision as the development work surface. Each chapter contains a focus example, with early chapters illustrating simpler applications with not-so-complex interfaces and business rules. Later chapters provide insights into more complex applications linked to several database tables.

DISTINCTIVE FEATURES

Application Development Using ObjectVision has several features that distinguish it from other books on developing applications.

- *Application Development Using ObjectVision* is designed so that the reader can work through the examples in front of a computer or in a non-computer environment.

- Each chapter contains a step-by-step tutorial as well as real-life examples to demonstrate a task.

- Examples are all practical, real-world applications that build incrementally from chapter to chapter.

- Applications take full advantage of the Windows interface, allowing readers to build Windows applications rapidly.

- Although some Windows familiarity is assumed, this text is useful to those with little previous computer experience.

- Every chapter begins with three important elements: a statement of objectives, an overview, and a case. The objectives clearly state what the reader will learn in the chapter. The overview provides a narrative introduction to the material covered in the chapter. The case highlights a practical business problem that is used as an example throughout the chapter.

- Over 140 screen shots are provided to maximize student confidence. The figures match the work the student is completing exactly, and they keep the student on track at every step.

- The text material has been class tested in a variety of situations to ensure its utility.

- Key terms are included in the end-of-chapter material. The key terms highlight terms that were introduced in the chapter.

- Each chapter concludes with a set or review questions to test student comprehension. Review questions include both true/false and multiple choice formats.

- Exercises that require students to create Windows applications using ObjectVision are included at the end of most chapters so that students can use the computer and apply concepts.

- A student data disk containing files and programs to accompany the text is included at the back of the book.

ABOUT THE AUTHOR

Jim Perry is a co-author of several popular trade books and textbooks. They include *Using SuperCalc4, Using SuperCalc5,* and *Understanding Oracle*. In addition, Jim has co-authored *Quattro Pro 1.0/5.0 Projects for Windows, WordPerfect 5.2 Projects for Windows,* and *Paradox 4.0 Projects for Windows*.

Jim is Associate Professor of Information Systems in the School of Business at the University of San Diego. Teaching several Information Systems courses, Jim is able to develop and thoroughly class test the material prior to publication. Jim holds a Ph.D. in computer science from the Pennsylvania State University. He received his Bachelor of Science in mathematics from Purdue University.

ACKNOWLEDGMENTS

In any writing project many people are responsible for bringing the book to completion. The author is only one of a large number of dedicated individuals of the team committed to making the book the best it can be. I wish to acknowledge a few of these people. Martha Stansbury calls on me at the university regularly. She presented my suggestion for this book to the boyd & fraser editors. Throughout the ensuing months, Martha has been supportive and upbeat, as usual. Jim Edwards, my editor and main point of contact at boyd & fraser has been supportive throughout all phases of this project. Finally, thanks to my two graduate students who, at different times, helped me write end-of-chapter exercises and made valuable content and syntax comments. Yio Kei Li designed the Educational Allowance application used in Chapters 1 and 2. Ben Auray, from Paris, France, read the entire manuscript and made valuable suggestions about content and grammar.

I would like to thank the following reviewers who provided valuable comments and suggestions that made the text so much better: Eric Bloom, Boston University; Laura Cooper, College of the Mainland; Kent Foster, Winthrop College;Timothy Heintz, Marquette University; and Gary Schneider, University of San Diego.

As with all my book projects, my wife Nancy has been supportive throughout the process. She has provided that ever-present encouragement at several critical times and has been patient during my less pleasant times. My children, Jessica, Stirling, and Kelly, have periodically supplied me with much needed "attaboys." Kelly, in her wonderfully upbeat style, has told me several times, "you're doing a good job, Dad." Without the support of my wife and children, this book would never have been written.

James T. Perry

INTRODUCTION

OBJECTIVES

Upon completing this chapter, you will understand and be able to describe:

- *The term **visual development environment***

- *The advantages of developing Windows applications with ObjectVision*

- *What comprises the ObjectVision visual development environment*

- *Various objects that are available through Object-Vision to develop applications*

- *The fundamental steps to invoke and use an Object-Vision application*

OVERVIEW

We begin this chapter by looking briefly at several available Windows application development environments, which are known as *visual development environments*. This introduction provides the necessary framework to then explore one of those environments, ObjectVision. The advantages of producing applications with ObjectVision become clear as we take a guided tour of the software. We explore the objects, such as fields and buttons, that are available to application developers. Then we explain the structure and terms used to describe forms—the fundamental end-user interface—and their utility. Finally, we walk through an existing ObjectVision application to learn how to invoke ObjectVision and select an application. You will learn how to navigate a form, the keys, and the mouse actions that are used and how to save and print a form. The chapter closes with an explanation of how to exit to Windows.

After reading this chapter, you will probably conclude ObjectVision provides a clean, intuitive interface that facilitates your developing Windows applications and that presents an intuitive, intelligent, forms-based work surface.

1.1 WINDOWS VISUAL DEVELOPMENT ENVIRONMENTS

In the early days of microcomputing, applications were developed on the PC by following a time-honored recipe: transform designs into a source-program language, compile the source code into object code, link the object code with vendor-supplied libraries, and run the linked application to debug it. When mistakes were revealed by the compiler, the programmer corrected syntax mistakes and recompiled the altered source program. Mistakes observed at execution time—so-called runtime errors—often required a significant amount of detailed study to uncover the logic error(s).

Later, programming language vendors improved the development process by introducing *integrated development environments* (IDE). Borland, a leader in this arena, delivered the first example of IDE with their Turbo Pascal programming language, which comprised a super-fast compiler (Pascal) and an editor/debugger as an integrated unit. When a syntax error was discovered by the compiler, the programmer would be rapidly returned to the editor with the edit cursor pointing to the probable offending source-language statement. A complete language reference manual was included with the software.

The next step in the evolution of development tools and work surfaces was represented by the bevy of interface libraries that provided support in developing attractive, error-proof applications. Database application interface tools were a good example of this evolutionary step. Programmers could describe database interfaces used to retrieve data by "painting" the fields and boxes. One of the problems with this generation of application development environments was that the developer had to specify details like the upper left/lower right coordinates for windows as well as other arcane information. Though helpful, the screen designers and interface libraries were cumbersome and difficult to use.

Microsoft's Windows graphical environment has stimulated a plethora of Windows-capable applications. Programmers quickly recognized the need for a *visual designer*. Today, a Windows visual designer facilitates the development of applications in a graphical (pixel rather than character based) environment. It provides the simple tools for creating drop-down menus, dialog boxes, and standard Windows objects such as title bars, form control-menu boxes, and window borders. Dubbed a *visual development environment* (VDE), this class of application development work surfaces provides an interactive interface design paradigm.

Visual development environments have advanced the state of the art in program development. Much of the difficulty and drudgery of creating a graphical interface, including drop-down menus, radio buttons, and sizable fields, has been eliminated. Exactly what characterizes a VDE? The list of characteristics includes the following:

- A VDE should allow true programming, not simply scripting capabilities.
- You should be able to easily create full-featured Windows interfaces without having to use the Windows API (Application Programming Interface).
- A VDE provides a fully integrated programming environment, allowing you to visually construct interface objects. Additionally, a VDE provides the ability to link objects, much like spreadsheet cells containing formulas that depend on other cells. Some objects contain "triggers" that are tuned to certain events activated by other objects.

Several Windows development products can be classified, either in part or whole, as VDE's. Included in this growing list are Microsoft Visual Basic, Tool-Book, KnowledgePro Windows, Approach, and ObjectVision. Borland's Object-Vision is featured throughout the text, in part because it is easy to use and has a large collection of features that help build forms-based applications quickly. An overview of ObjectVision's features and benefits is presented next.

1.2 WHY DEVELOP APPLICATIONS WITH OBJECTVISION?

ObjectVision is an excellent Windows development tool for nonprogrammers as well as for experienced application developers. It is capable of producing powerful applications. It combines several features into an integrated package, including spreadsheets, forms creation, behind-the-scenes decision trees, and database linkage. These features are displayed in ObjectVision's what-you-see-is-what-you-get (WYSIWYG) form. Nonprogrammers can easily create relatively sophisticated applications visually, without programming, via the simple, intuitive, drop-down menus and the time-saving object bar for selecting objects placed on a form. Three elements, referred to as the "A-B-C's," constitute ObjectVision: (1) the *A*pplication interface, (2) decision trees with intelligent prompting that represent the enterprise's *B*usiness rules, and (3) database *C*onnections that link a form's tables and fields to various data sources.

ObjectVision uses the forms metaphor for Windows applications. That is, a form is the application work surface that end users see when using an application. Because users are already accustomed to dealing with paper forms, electronic forms are just as easy to understand. An ObjectVision form can almost exactly duplicate its paper counterpart. (Section 1.4 shows the structure of a form in more detail.)

Forms help enforce standardization. Thus, a company's rules regarding the format, content, and placement of data can be maintained by a single, consistent form retrieved from a central store. Forms can have a look that is consistent with the company's other forms. Decision trees are particularly important in ensuring that forms and their contents abide by standard input values. Decision trees guide the user through the form and check the manually-input data values.

Users with a wide range of computing skills, including office support personnel, content area experts with little or no programming experience, and skilled application developers, can develop applications. That is probably the most compelling reason to use a visual development environment. You can develop your own applications rapidly without submitting a formal request to the professional design staff or to a programming guru.

Decision trees can be attached to several of the objects placed on the form. The trees are either value trees or event trees. A **value tree** is a graphic logic structure that can calculate a value for the object to which it is attached. It uses familiar spreadsheet functions and additional ObjectVision functions that manipulate forms. A value tree is invisible to the end user and consists of branches that evaluate one or more conditions to determine the value that should be saved in the field. That is analogous to a spreadsheet cell whose contents (the ObjectVision field) are calculated by the cell's stored formula (ObjectVision's value tree). **Event trees** also contain logic branches (binary, yes/no branches). Event trees contain conditions—often called **triggers**—that cause some action to occur. They pass messages and user-defined events up the form hierarchy. No complex calling or return logic is needed. For example, an event tree might be associated with a button labeled QUIT. If the user selects that button and presses the left mouse button, then the application might issue a command that leaves the form and returns to Windows.

Forms are usually saved separately from the values that they display. Saving each value entered in a form, say an invoice form, for all customers whose account is active would waste a lot of disk space. Disk space requirements are decreased when the form is saved separate from the data the form presents. Usually, the information is saved in a database of simple ASCII files. Currently, links can be established to Paradox, Btrieve, and dBASE compatible database tables as well as to delimited ASCII files.

Much corporate information is contained in databases. ObjectVision provides a simple way of connecting application fields and other forms objects to one or more databases. The term **linking** refers to the process of establishing the connection between the ObjectVision form and the database(s). A form user can simply insert, update, delete, or retrieve information through the form as long as the application is connected to a database.

Another important feature unique to ObjectVision is **guided completion**. As you fill in the fields and tables in an application, you are automatically guided only to those fields or table entries that require values. Other dependent fields or table entries—those whose values are derived from other fields—are skipped; their values are calculated and displayed when the requisite fields are completed. ObjectVision continues guiding the user through selected fields until the form is complete. Of course, the user can manually select fields, even dependent ones, to alter the order in which the fields are selected. You select fields with the mouse or by pressing Tab (moving the cursor forward—down and to the right) or Shift-Tab (moving the cursor backward). Fields whose values are calculated from other fields can be overridden. This override interrupts guided completion. You can resume guided completion by selecting the menu choice File | Resume.

ObjectVision accommodates rapid prototyping. You can quickly draw the rough draft of a form, complete with buttons, fields, tables, and other objects. However, this facility is only half the story. Unlike several other VDE's, the prototype can be turned into a working application; thus you can avoid discarding the prototype and subsequently developing the "real thing" from scratch. Incremental development and reusable designs save time.

Borland includes a runtime version of ObjectVision. As a developer, you will appreciate that you can distribute your applications along with the royalty-free runtime version at no extra charge. You do not have to be concerned with fee-per-application charges that other software companies levy. Applications can be protected so that end users are prevented from altering them. This protection is analogous to the security inherent in distributing compiled, machine-code versions of software rather than source-code versions that can be modified or copied.

Finally, applications developed in a Microsoft Windows system can be ported to an OS/2 environment (and vice versa) without change. This transparent migration feature opens up both these major development environments (OS/2 and Windows), enlarging the potential audience of users.

1.3 ANATOMY OF OBJECTVISION'S DEVELOPMENT WORK SURFACE

ObjectVision is invoked in the same way as other Windows applications: by double clicking its program item icon. Managed by Window's Program Manager, program item icons are small pictures that represent applications and files. The pointer will change into an hourglass, indicating that you must wait while the

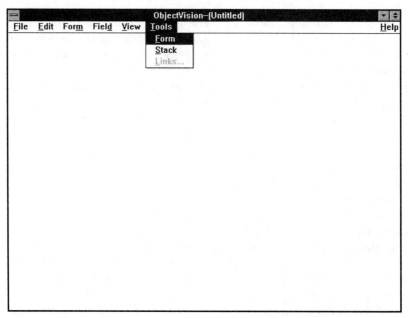

FIGURE 1.1
ObjectVision window

application is launched. Shortly, the first ObjectVision window appears. It is called the "ObjectVision window" (oddly enough). Figure 1.1 shows that window.

Both developers creating applications and end users see the same opening screen with one exception: end users are not shown the Tools menu. This window is particularly important because it is used to invoke ObjectVision's application-building tools.

OVERVIEW OF THE OBJECTVISION WINDOW

Upper left-most in the window is the **control-menu box**. Like other Windows applications, it lets you size or move the window, minimize or maximize it, close it, or switch to another application. The **title bar** shows the name of the application that is active (ObjectVision) followed by a parenthesis and the name of the application or the word *Untitled*. When Untitled appears, it signifies that the application has not yet been named and saved.

As is customary, ObjectVision has the **minimize** and **maximize buttons** in the upper right to minimize the application to an icon or to fill the screen from edge to edge.

An inherent part of ObjectVision, the **menu bar** appears just below the title bar. The menu bar shows ObjectVision's drop-down menus corresponding to classes of commands. When you place the mouse cursor on one of these menus and click, a list of its commands, or action words, is displayed (Figure 1.1 shows the commands for Tools). These commands allow developers access to all tools needed to build an application. The runtime version of ObjectVision, which you can freely distribute to anyone, does not have the Tools menu. That prevents users from invoking Tools commands, which would allow a user (that is, a customer) to alter your application.

Like other Windows products, the *window border* is used to resize the window. When the mouse pointer changes to a double-headed arrow, you can move the mouse to any border edge and drag it to reshape a window. Likewise, you can use the mouse to grab any corner and drag it in any direction to change the vertical and horizontal edges simultaneously.

A BRIEF DESCRIPTION OF THE MENU COMMANDS

All menu commands follow the Microsoft Windows convention that menu commands are light gray (**grayed out**) if they are currently unavailable and are dark black if they are available (see the Tools menu example in Figure 1.1). You can display the commands in each menu by clicking on the menu name. The drop-down menu shows two or more commands. To select one of the available commands, place the mouse cursor over the desired command and click the left mouse button once ("single click"). The menu commands are outlined in the paragraphs that follow.

The menus are arranged left to right in a familiar way. The File menu is located on the far left of the menu bar. File contains commands that create new applications, open existing applications, save applications, print application forms, set up a printer, or exit the application. The commands in File are similar to other Windows products. Initially, all File commands are unavailable except Open, Printer Setup, and Exit.

Edit is the next menu. This drop-down menu contains commands to undo the previous edit operation, cut and paste to and from the Clipboard, copy to the Clipboard, and erase the entire user input for all forms that make up the application (but not the form itself). The commands are Undo, Cut, Copy, Paste, and Clear All. We will discuss these in more detail in succeeding chapters where application development and editing are described.

The Form menu contains two commands: Select and Clear. Select displays a dialog box that contains form names for the current application. You can move to another form and display it. The Clear command erases all user-input values from the current form—the one displayed on the screen.

A form comprises objects such as fields and tables. Thus, it is natural for the Field menu, a subset of a form (the Form menu), to be to the right of the Form menu. The commands Find, Calculate, and Show Tree concern fields and tables. The Find command locates a form and field, first searching the list of object names and then placing the cursor on the form and object. Calculate recomputes the value of a currently selected field by using its underlying "formula," much like the Lotus 1-2-3 Recalculate command does for spreadsheet cells. Show Tree displays the decision tree, if any, associated with the selected field. Decision trees attached to objects are not normally visible to end users.

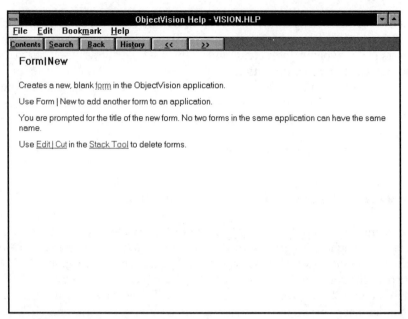

FIGURE 1.2
ObjectVision context-sensitive help example

The View menu has two entries: Screen and Printer. If you select Printer from the View menu (henceforth denoted, for example, in "menu|command" format, such as View|Screen), then the form is displayed on the screen in reduced size. That allows you to see more of the form than otherwise. The Printer command (View|Printer) shows on the screen a rendering of what the form will look like when printed. Similar to WordPerfect's Print Preview command, it gives you an overall idea of where various form elements will show on the form, their relative placement, and so on. In no case is the current form actually printed.

There are three types of help available: object specific, context sensitive, and general. At the most detailed level, you can summon object-specific help on an individual object. Object-specific help is created by the application creator. You can attach help messages to virtually any object, including a field, column, or button. When an end user presses function key F1, help messages created by the application developer appear on the work surface. A field might contain a message about the allowable range of values it can contain.

Context-sensitive help is specific to the current activity, not necessarily to the current object. It is especially helpful for application developers. Pressing F1 while using a particular ObjectVision feature invokes information about that particular feature. For example, developers and end users alike can obtain help about the New command found in the Form menu by clicking on Form and then selecting the New command with the mouse or arrow keys; press F1 and help appears (see Figure 1.2).

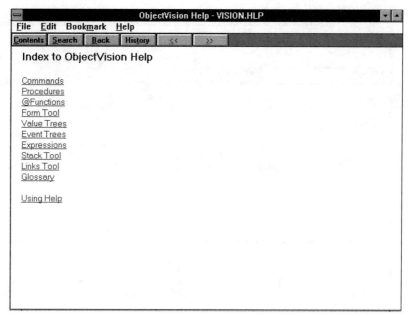

FIGURE 1.3
ObjectVision Windows help index

The most general help is displayed by clicking the Help menu, located flush right in the menu selections. Help displays a list of commands, the first of which is the Index command. Index is helpful when you want to search for an Object-Vision feature but are not sure what it is called. Figure 1.3 shows the help index screen that temporarily replaces the application screen.

1.4 ANATOMY OF AN APPLICATION

An application *form* is the fundamental unit of an application. Users interact with one form at a time, and developers create applications in a form-based paradigm supported by ObjectVision. A form-based approach to visual programming/application development is common among many of the VDE's. Before we begin to build applications, it is important to understand the components of a form and the kinds of objects that can be placed thereon. In this section we first look briefly at a typical form that might be used by various university administrators. The many different form objects that can be placed on a form are discussed. We then describe the several data types that can be used in a form. The extremely versatile, invisible logic elements associated with forms and form objects—trees and database links—are illustrated. Decision trees give their associated objects elegant control logic. Database links provide access to various database types. Finally, we learn about application stacks, an application's largest element.

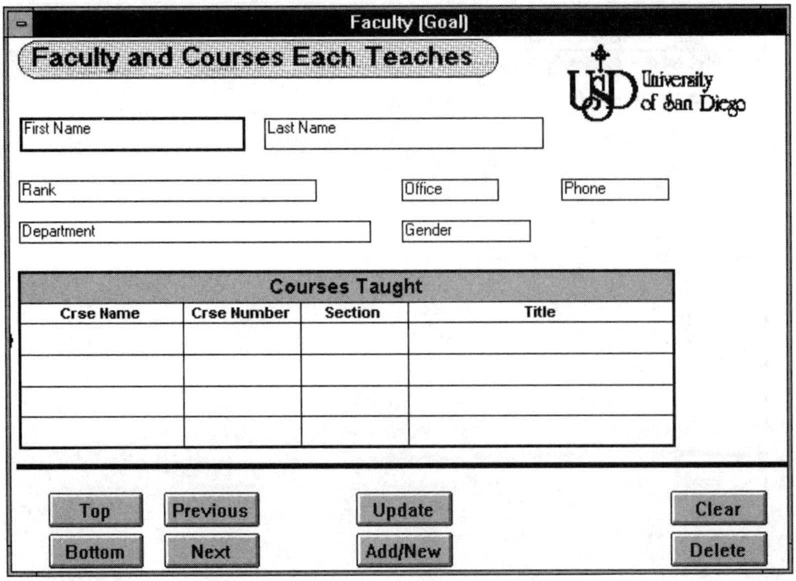

FIGURE 1.4
Example form containing various object types

FORM STRUCTURE

A form is displayed when a user selects a particular application by name. Figure 1.4 is an example typical of those we will discuss. Take a moment to examine it.

The basic structure of the form is similar to ObjectVision's window. Along the top, left to right, are the Form control-menu box, Form title bar, Form Title, and Form Status. The Form control-menu box contains two controls that move and close the application. The **Form Title** not only identifies and names the form but also provides a way for other forms in the application to reference it. Collectively, all the forms in an application are known as a **stack**.

In Figure 1.4, "Faculty" is the form's title. Following the Form Title is the **Form Status**, which shows the current mode of the form. "Goal," enclosed in parentheses to the right of the title, is the form's current mode and indicates the form is the top one in the application's stack. Whenever another form is selected, it moves to the top and temporarily becomes the goal. Besides goal, there are three other possible modes within Form Status: edit, prompt, and complete. Complete indicates that all of the needed data have been entered into a form. Whenever a developer (not an end user) is working on a form with one of the tools, the form's status is edit. Prompt occurs when a user needs to enter a value in a field that is not on a form but is referenced.

Figure 1.5 shows an example of another form, "Add Faculty," which becomes the new goal. Notice that the new goal form does not conceal the previous form, though it can.

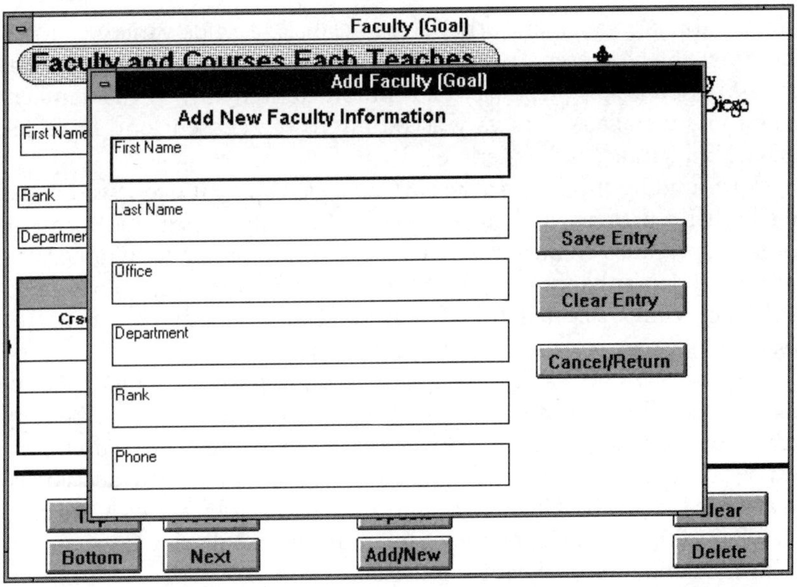

FIGURE 1.5
An application's stack comprising two forms

The Add Faculty form becomes the new goal when a user pushes the Add/New button on the bottom of the Faculty form, indicating a group of information fields is to be entered. Stacks of forms are analogous to stacks of paper forms—when the current form requires a figure that is found on another paper, you turn to the page (form) containing the figure and copy it to the top form. Tax returns are a good example of this type of structure.

The window border surrounds the forms and defines its limits. Applications builders can change the size of the form by dragging any of the borders or the corners. Dragging the right border to the right widens the form; dragging the right border to the left narrows it. By selecting a corner of the form, you can size it in both directions at once. However, end users cannot size a completed form because the requisite menu is missing. That prevents users from modifying the form(s) in an application.

OBJECTS PLACED ON FORMS

Forms built with ObjectVision can contain any number and combination of objects. These objects are what give meaning to the form. Available objects are text, rectangles, fields, graphics, tables, lines, and buttons. Figure 1.4 shows at least one of each of the object types.

The label at the top of the form, "Faculty and Courses Each Teaches," is an example of a *text* object. Text objects label parts of the form, provide help and information, and augment other objects' labels. A wide variety of fonts, sizes, and styles can be chosen. For example, the text labeling the form is MS Sans Serif (font), 14 point (size), bold (style). Fonts are limited only by the number of True Type fonts installed. Sizes vary according to the chosen font. Style selections include bold, italic, and underline.

Surrounding the text is a *rounded rectangle* object. It overlays the text and is filled with a pattern. Rectangles (rounded or square cornered) can enhance a form's appearance and draw a user's attention to particularly important items. In Figure 1.4, it enhances the text title. Various fill patterns, from none (clear) to dark black, can be selected. In addition, you can choose two other characteristics (*properties*) for a rectangle: line width and color.

Several *fields* appear on the Faculty form. **Fields** are one of the most frequently used form objects. There are three ways fields values can be supplied by value trees, or take on values. Field data are filled in directly by a user, their values can be automatically retrieved from databases. Easy-to-create decision trees can be attached to a field. They can monitor values input by the user and ensure that they fall within a range, or they can compute and display a value from other fields much like spreadsheet formulas do.

Notice in Figure 1.4 that the border of the First Name field is different from the others and that it contains a vertical line. That field is the currently *selected field*—the one in which the cursor is located. As you fill in a field and then press Enter, the cursor moves to the next object (for example, another field) in a prescribed order known as *guided completion*. Guided completion selects only fields that need values from the user. Fields that contain value trees, which compute values automatically from other fields, are skipped. The user can override these calculated fields, however.

Many properties can be associated with fields, including value fonts and label fonts, sizes, and colors. Fields in Figure 1.4 contain field names inside the optional borders surrounding them. Fields there are First Name, Last Name, Rank, Office, Phone, Department, and Gender. Field names uniquely identify a field, and they can appear or be hidden. You may wish to hide a field and instead supply a text object to label it in a more meaningful way. The advantage of displaying the field names is that they are created automatically when a field is created. And field names, unlike text objects found near the field, always stay with the field when you move it.

Graphic objects add style and life to a form. You can create them with a variety of graphics packages, including Paintbrush. Figure 1.4 shows a graphic in the upper right that was scanned in from hard copy, manipulated in Paintbrush, and then copied onto the form via the Windows clipboard. Optionally, you can link a graphic image to a Windows graphics program using a technique called OLE, Object Linking and Embedding.

A **table** object comprises one or more columns and rows. Tables act like one object, and columns are similar to fields except that they display more than one value for one named column. Similar to an array, a table is frequently used to display related rows from a database. Figure 1.4 shows a table labeled "Courses Taught" containing four columns and four rows. It displays course names, course numbers, section numbers, and course titles for all courses taught by the professor whose name appears in the Last Name field. All field and table values, except First Name and Last Name, are filled in automatically when the user completes the Last Name field. We describe how this is accomplished in several chapters that follow.

A single *line* object separates the table from the button objects at the bottom of the Faculty form. Line is used to draw simple lines on a form. Line properties are color and width. You can alter a line's length by selecting it (click on any part of the line), clicking on either of its **handles** (the square black boxes at either end of the line), and then dragging the handle to lengthen or shorten the line.

Several **button** objects appear at the bottom of the Faculty form. They are the "verbs" of the form. When a button is pressed (click the left mouse button), it causes an action to occur. A button can be clicked, selected, or deselected. A button always has an event tree. Hidden "behind" a button, an event tree contains the logic comprising conditions and events that take actions, such as closing the current form or application, moving to another form, and sending messages to other objects. Database manipulation buttons labeled Top, Bottom, Previous, and Next select various database records. Top moves to the first row in the database and Bottom moves to the last one. Previous and Next move to records one before and one after the current position, respectively. A virtually unlimited number of buttons can be created to provide a plethora of useful, end-user functions. Buttons eliminate the need for users to know arcane commands in order to trigger common application actions.

DATA TYPES AVAILABLE

A standard variety of field data types are available with ObjectVision. There are four of them: numeric, string, logical, and error. Of these, the first two are most common. Numeric values are real numbers. Exponential format is not supported currently. String-valued fields contain sequences of any characters you can type on the keyboard and are limited to a rather generous 4,096 characters. Field properties, including the data type, can be easily established or changed at any time during the development cycle.

Logical and Error Data Types

Both the logical and error types are returned by expressions associated with fields (called *value trees*—discussed in the next section) or are retrieved from a database. They are not input manually by a user. The logical data type is binary, having true or false (Yes or No) as its range of values.

Character Data Type

There are a variety of ways that control how *character field* typed data is accepted and displayed. These are termed *field type controls* (discussed in detail in later chapters). Field type controls enforce the display and acceptance rules, and they can be set by the developer for each field, independently. The character type controls are General, Alphanumeric, Picture, and Scrolling. General is the default and is suitable for both numeric and text values. Once a value is entered into a General field, ObjectVision converts it. For example, the value 2,123.00 is converted to 2123. Any plus signs, commas, or unnecessary zeros are eliminated.

The Alphanumeric control closely matches the General type except that it allows *any* keyboard character to be input. Further, it does not attempt to convert the input value to another form. An input value such as 2,123.00 remains unaltered when entered. In other words, it is treated as a character string containing eight characters, not as a number.

The Picture control employs a template that ensures a text value conforms to a specific pattern when entered. For example, the picture template for social security numbers might be 999-999-99. A "9" indicates a position where an input digit can be placed; the hyphen is placed in the string automatically, exactly where it appears. Scrolling displays long text values that can be scrolled vertically to be fully seen.

Numeric Data Type

The numeric data accepts numeric values but not characters. Values either input manually or delivered to the field via a calculation or database can be displayed in one of the following forms: Fixed, Percent, Currency, Financial, or Date/Time. Spreadsheet users are familiar with these types, as they correspond to the usual ways spreadsheet cells can be formatted. Which control form is selected is determined by the developer on a field-by-field basis in the same way as character type fields. With the exception of the Date/Time type, all numeric types allow from zero to fifteen decimal places.

Fixed simply controls the number of decimal places that are displayed, from zero to fifteen. No other formatting is either enforced or available other than ensuring that the entry is wholly numeric. Dollar signs and commas are ignored on input and discarded (a convenience for those used to either one).

Percent displays values as a percentage. If 12.34 is entered, then the value is displayed as 1234.00% (assuming 2 decimal places are displayed). Likewise, the value entered as 0.0934 is transformed to 9.34%.

Currency inserts both the currency character and the thousands separator. Henceforth, we refer to them as the dollar sign and comma, respectively, though each can be set in the Windows Control Panel to other characters (for example, Pounds). When a negative value is entered, it is subsequently enclosed in parentheses. Form users can optionally enter both a dollar sign and a comma.

Financial provides the currency separator where needed, though not typed, and encloses negative values in parentheses.

Date/Time displays the date or time format for the value typed. There are several display forms for both time and date, and the exact representation depends on the format chosen. For example, if the date were entered as 8/12/94, the displayed form could be August 12, 1994.

DECISION TREES

Decision trees comprise value trees and event trees, and they represent the hidden "action" associated with selected objects, forms, and stacks. Trees are instructions attached to individual objects that either calculate and display a value or perform a service (action). Value trees can be attached only to fields or columns of a table. Like spreadsheet cell formulas, these trees calculate character or numeric values and display their results in the associated field or column. Event trees are triggered to perform some action by *signals* that are sensed by objects. Once the signal is recognized, the event tree is executed. Not all objects can have value and event trees attached to them. Table 1.1 shows which ObjectVision objects can have either or both tree types associated with them. Some entries may surprise you.

TABLE 1.1
Objects that have decision trees

Object	Types Available for Object	
Stack		Event
Form		Event
Field	Value	Event
Button		Event
Table Column	Value	Event
Text		Event
Rectangles		
Line		
Graphic		Event

All objects can have event trees attached to them except the two rectangle objects and a line object. However, only fields and table columns can have associated value trees. Successive chapters illustrate application building techniques, and you will quickly appreciate how these decision trees play a vital role in a Windows software development environment.

The word *tree* connotes a structure with a single "root" and one or more branches. Similarly, a decision tree (event or value) has that structure. The only structural difference is that a decision tree is drawn upside down—with the root above the branches—unlike nature's trees! Trees are built from nodes connected in various ways. The nodes consist of branch nodes (restricted or unrestricted) and conclusion nodes. Trees are evaluated beginning at the top (root) and working down to various branches. ObjectVision trees are binary—having two branch choices at successively lower levels. At each level, or node, the condition determining which branch to follow is evaluated. Results of that evaluation are either true or false, corresponding to one branch or another. Once a "true" condition results, ObjectVision ignores the conditions that follow in the tree. The depth of any particular series of nodes along a logic branch is unlimited. That is, a tree can be arbitrarily complex.

Value Trees

Value trees calculate the value displayed in a field to which the tree is attached. Values from other fields in the application—on the same form or on other forms in the stack—can be used in the tree to deliver the result. In addition, information from external databases *linked* to the application and appearing in one or more fields can be used. Finally, the expressions and conditions that appear in a tree can make use of the hundreds of ObjectVision built-in functions or user-defined functions.

Value trees can be arbitrarily complex and have several branches that represent different results. Each possible result is stored in a branch of the tree. Or, value trees can contain no branches at all. In that case, the value tree consists of a single expression containing references to other ObjectVision fields and ObjectVision functions. For both value trees with branches and those without, each expression that provides the value for a field is called a **conclusion**. An example of a value tree with three branches is shown in Figure 1.6, and it illustrates a simple value tree containing a restricted branch node and several condition and conclusion nodes. A conclusion node corresponds to a true result from a condition evaluation for its branch. That is the value displayed if the associated condition is true.

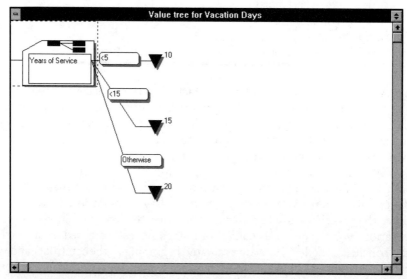

FIGURE 1.6
Value tree with branching based on a field's value

The value tree is one of many in an example application called "Employee" (described fully in Chapter 2). Among other fields is one that computes a given employee's allowed vacation days. The previous value tree, whose logic is displayed in Figure 1.6, computes a value which is displayed in a field called "Vacation Days." Dependent on one other field in the form, labeled "Years of Service," the tree determines which of three possible values is returned to the Vacation Days field.

In Figure 1.6, the Years of Service field is compared to the first condition (<5). If the employee has been at the company less than five years (true value), then the value 10 is returned for the value tree and no further nodes are examined. However, if not true, then the next condition is examined: is length of service less than 15 years? In any case, Vacation Days cannot be undefined, as the value tree deals with *all* possible cases. That is, if all previous tests fail (none of the above are true), then the Otherwise condition—one that is the last node and is always true—unfailingly returns the value or expression shown in the conclusion node (20 years in our example).

Value trees, invisible to a user, provide a tremendous amount of power for an application developer. We have a great deal more to say about them in subsequent chapters.

Event Trees

An event tree causes an action to be executed based on the occurrence of an event. A frequent event is when a user presses the left mouse button (referred to as a *click* event). The objects in Table 1.1 with the event indicator in the right column can all cause actions to occur when triggered by an event. Event trees are similar to value trees in that they are attached to objects and they contain condition and conclusion nodes. An event may immediately lead to actions being taken or may be passed to other nodes for evaluation. Figure 1.7 shows an example of a simple event tree. That particular tree is attached to the Add/New button of the Faculty application illustrated in Figure 1.4.

When the user clicks on the Add/New button to add a new faculty member, it generates a click event that is detected by the Add/New button event tree. Specifically, the click event appears in a condition node. Subsequently, because click is true, the series of steps that follow the node are executed. They clear the fields in the faculty form (@CLEAR . . .) and bring the add faculty form to the top of the stack (@FORMSELECT . . .). Event tree conclusion nodes, the action part of the event tree, can contain ObjectVision built-in functions, user-defined functions, commands, and a variety of elements. All of the statements in conclusion nodes have a common trait: they are executable (not expressions resulting in values).

Event trees allow the processing of **asynchronous events**—events that occur unpredictably. Event trees are one of the most powerful elements of the ObjectVision development environment and allow a degree of visual "programming" that is easy to understand and master. Much time is devoted to discussing both value and event trees throughout the text. In addition, we will show examples of event trees placed in stacks (the highest level), forms, and other objects.

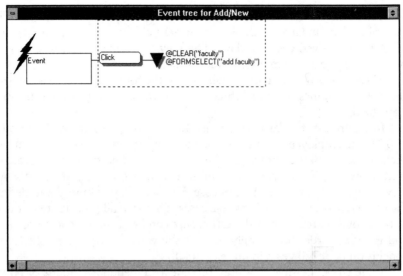

FIGURE 1.7
Event tree implementing an action

STACKS

ObjectVision applications always have at least one form. Most applications have several forms, which collectively are called a *stack*. Forms piled on top of each other physically resemble a stack of papers. The stack concept resembles a three-dimensional spreadsheet, with which most people are familiar. Recall that Figure 1.5 shows an example of a two-form stack.

Stacks, like most other objects in the ObjectVision paradigm, can have a *stack event tree*. A stack event tree contains the logic that is to be executed every time an application is run. Its effect is global. That is, a stack event tree applies to all forms in the stack. Not every stack has an event tree, although we will see that a stack event tree is a logical place to position all application-wide initialization activities and to introduce any user-created functions. A one-form stack is still a stack. Think of the terms *stack* and *application* as synonymous. Whenever we refer to a stack, we mean the topmost, fundamental structure of an application.

DATABASE CONNECTIONS

Databases hold data about customers, inventory, scheduled airline routes, tax and wages, and so on. One of the problems application developers, especially novices, face is retrieving all that data and turning it into information. Briefly, the problem is that it is difficult to query typical database systems without knowing the often arcane database access language.

That problem is ubiquitous, but ObjectVision provides a smooth, seamless path for accessing database information. It is equipped with an easy-to-use set of tools that help link the fields and tables of a form to database entries. One or more fields can be linked to a corresponding number of database fields. When the application is opened, it can be set up to deliver automatically one or more values from specified databases. Likewise, it is easy to include database insert, update, sort, and delete capabilities to end users via the use of special purpose buttons containing event trees with database-exclusive functions. In a matter of moments, you can create a form that gets its input values from (1) the user, (2) a value tree that calculates the value, (3) and a database field. Several applications found later in the book make extensive use of database linkages and describe how database interfaces are created.

1.5 SOME FUNDAMENTAL OBJECTVISION OPERATIONS

Before moving to the next chapter, we present a few of the frequently used, fundamental ObjectVision operations and commands. These commands establish a firm foundation for creating applications and provide a "taste" of a typical visual development environment. This section introduces how to invoke Object-Vision, select, alter, or save an application, print an application's forms, work on multiple applications, and exit to Windows. First, we explain how to launch the ObjectVision application development environment.

INVOKING OBJECTVISION

From Windows' Program Manager, click on the ObjectVision icon. The opening screen shown in Figure 1.8 is displayed. The Tools menu on the menu bar is available for developers to create and maintain applications. That menu choice is omitted from runtime ObjectVision to preclude users from altering your applications.

Click the File menu. Three choices are highlighted (as is customary, dimmed menu items are not available in a given context). From top to bottom, menu command choices are Open, Printer Setup, and Exit. Click on Printer Setup (discussed later) to establish printing details. Click on Exit to return to Windows. To build a form from scratch—to create an application—select the Tools menu. Click the Open command to initiate the sequence to load an ObjectVision application.

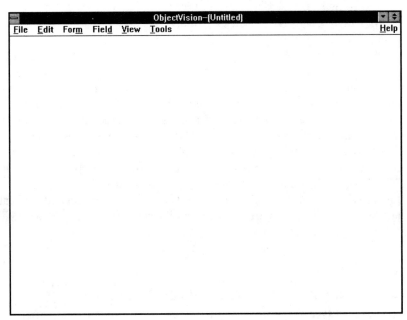

FIGURE 1.8
ObjectVision's opening screen

SELECTING AN APPLICATION

The Open command in the File menu is the gateway to loading existing applications. After clicking Open, the Open File dialog box appears (see Figure 1.9). Specify the filename of the application you want and then click OK.

You can either use the mouse to select an application or type in the name following the File Name prompt. The Open File dialog box acts like any other Windows dialog box: You can use the mouse or the keyboard to select files. If the application was saved with a password, a series of asterisks is displayed instead of the password. In that case, type in the correct password to open the application.

Alternately, you can use your mouse to select a different disk or directory (choose [..] to move up the directory tree) until one or more ObjectVision application file names are displayed. All ObjectVision application files have the secondary file name "OVD." When you choose a file name by double clicking it, it is loaded and then fills the screen.

Three buttons appear throughout ObjectVision's many dialog boxes: OK, Help, and Cancel. OK generally signifies that the completed dialog box or its selected choices are correct. Help displays context-sensitive help. Cancel closes the current dialog box, makes no changes, and returns to the form from where the dialog box was invoked. Pressing OK in the Open File dialog box is equivalent to double clicking the highlighted file name or pressing Enter after typing the file name.

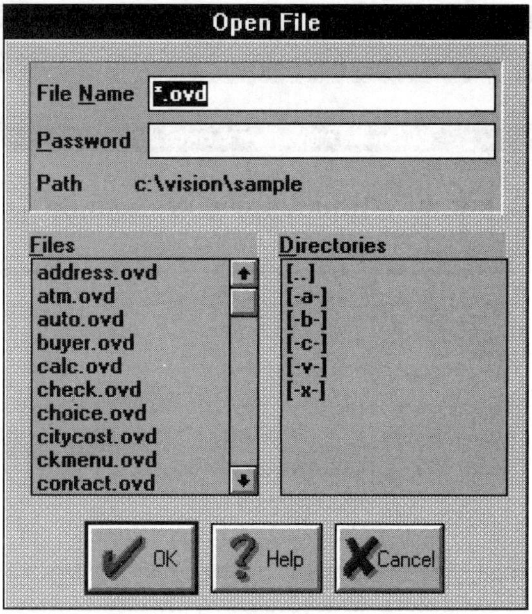

FIGURE 1.9
Application choices in the Open File dialog box

ALTERING AN APPLICATION

Windows application developers will find the ability of ObjectVision to alter an application of the greatest interest. In fact, it is the most complex and rewarding feature of ObjectVision. Altering an application comprises all instructions and procedures that are used to create an application. Those Windows applications users who have ObjectVision runtime can invoke your applications and use them repeatedly. However, they cannot create or alter applications because their runtime version lacks the key that unlocks the development/editing door: the Tools menu.

Developers have unrestricted access to the Tools menu. One important command in the Tools menu is Form. After clicking Tools and then the Form command, you can begin creating a new application. Similarly, after selecting an application via the Open File dialog box, press Tools and then Form (frequently abbreviated "Tools|Form") to edit the evolving application. Figure 1.10 shows a finished form we will revisit—a simple employee educational allowance form.

The form in Figure 1.10 contains a graphic and several field objects and shows the Name field with solid square boxes at each corner. These object handles indicate the current position of the cursor—the highlighted object. They appear only while editing an application, not during form completion by end users. Handles are used to size the object, something a user cannot do. Later, we will see that the highlighted object's properties can be amended by simply clicking the right mouse button. An object can be moved about the form by dragging

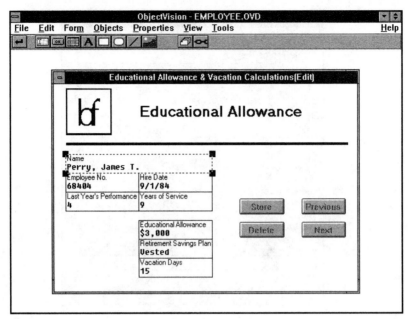

FIGURE 1.10
Editing an application

it. (Whenever the term *drag* is used, that means you click on an object and keep the left mouse depressed while moving the selected object.) A new object can be highlighted by using the mouse or the Tab and Shift-Tab keys. The Enter key does not move to another object on the form, though Enter is used frequently to confirm choices. Arrow keys can also be used to move around the form while editing it. Frequently, we refer to the act of selecting another object—whether in edit mode or not—as moving the **focus**.

Just below the menu bar is the **object bar**. On it are small icons that save time. Left to right, the object bar shows icons for each of the frequently used objects: field, button, table, text, square and rounded rectangles, line, and graphic. Rightmost are two special object icons: stack and link.

By using the object bar, objects can be selected quickly without referencing the menu bar. After clicking on an icon, you move it onto the form and click to "drop" it in place.

There is a great deal to learn about editing applications with ObjectVision. The many aspects of editing are presented in the ensuing chapters.

PRINTING AN APPLICATION

One of the principal outputs from an application is often the printed form. Though some clients may be satisfied exclusively with viewing and manipulat-

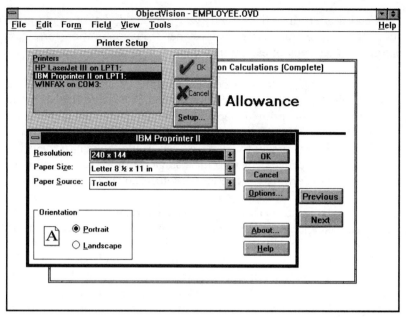

FIGURE 1.11
Printer Setup dialog boxes

ing information on the screen, others may want a hard copy for their files. A printed copy may be a reminder about standard form for data or it may be used to document an application. ObjectVision provides several ways to print an application. A single form, containing its present values, can be printed. Or all forms of a given application can be printed, with each printed form resembling what you see on the screen (without the border or ObjectVision title and menu bars, however). In addition, you can print a form repeatedly, once for each associated database row that displays in the form (called a **linked** database).

Before printing, check which printer is selected. Selecting File | Printer Setup (File menu, Printer Setup command) brings up a list of printers from which to choose. Note that any printer names displayed therein are those that have been established through Windows via the Control Panel Printers icon. Adding or deleting printers is done from Windows, not ObjectVision. Figure 1.11 shows an example of the Printer Setup dialog box and a Printer-specific (an IBM Proprinter II in the example) Setup dialog box. If no printer-specific changes are needed, then simply double click on the desired printer from the list (or use the arrow keys).

You can print a form, including all values in fields, from the File menu. Select File | Print Form to print the currently displayed form. If the active form is associated with a database, make sure that the proper database record values are displayed in the form before printing, as what is shown on the screen is precisely printed by this command.

Selecting File | Print All is a handy way to print all the forms in a given application, thus serving as part of a developer's documentation for a completed application. One copy of each form (Figure 1.5 shows two forms of an application, for example) is printed.

Whenever a form's table or field objects are supplied with data from databases, the File | Print Link choice can be selected. An advantage is that multiple copies of the form are printed, one for each of the associated database rows. For example, Figure 1.4 shows an empty form that is linked to a database. Each of over fifty employee rows in the database can be individually retrieved into this form. It would be convenient to print a single form for each employee, which occurs when File | Print Link is chosen. Of course, an application such as the simple form in Figure 1.10 has no database links, so the File | Print Link choice is grayed-out, which means it cannot be selected. Forms containing tables linked to databases likewise print one for each associated database row that loads into a table row.

There is yet one aspect of printing that is not addressed in the File | Print commands: decision tree printing. Windows application producers will be interested in printing some or all of the decision trees. After all, decision trees hold the invisible evaluation logic and trigger mechanisms that provide sophistication to the application. Without value and event trees, an ObjectVision application is an inanimate form—a flat screen that is nice to look at but that is devoid of inherent "intelligence."

A tree must be displayed on the screen before it, or any other tree from the application, can be printed. (For now, do not be concerned about how decision trees are displayed on screen. That will be described later). With a tree (value of event) displayed, press File menu and a different set of commands are displayed (see Figure 1.12).

The displayed or current tree can be printed by selecting File | Print Tree. All event and logic trees can be printed by choosing the File | Print All command. Note that the effect of this is different from the same command in a different context. When viewing a form, not a tree, the File | Print All will behave as before by printing all forms. In the context of a tree display, all trees are printed.

SAVING AN ALTERED APPLICATION

During application development an application should be saved periodically to avoid recreating a large portion of it (should your computer loose power, for example). When an application is complete and all the forms and decision trees have been printed and saved with other documentation, be sure the final version is saved. ObjectVision displays a warning if you try to Exit an application without first saving it. Select File | Save to save the altered application under the current application file name. Or, select File | Save As to specify another file or disk.

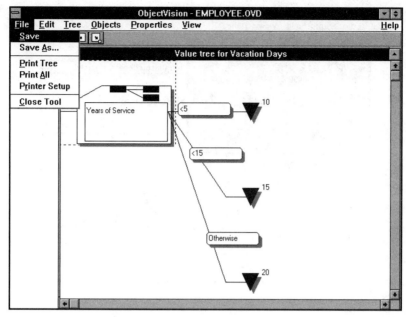

FIGURE 1.12
Printing one or more decision trees

WORKING ON MULTIPLE APPLICATIONS SIMULTANEOUSLY

It is convenient to have multiple applications on the Windows work surface simultaneously. Perhaps, for example, several applications are related to one another. Or maybe you just want to copy the same form and function of one ObjectVision application to a new, evolving one. In either case, it is convenient to have more than one application available at the same time. Currently, Object-Vision can manage only one application at a time. A simple trick to get around that limitation is to invoke *multiple instances* of ObjectVision. That is, from the Program Manager, click on the ObjectVision icon more than once. There is a limit to the number of ObjectVision tasks that can run at once, but at least two can be made available simultaneously so that you can bounce between two Object-Vision applications during development (for example, to clone objects between the applications). This workaround is fine if you want a few ObjectVision applications to be available; however, it does consume a large amount of (memory) resources and does not accommodate very many ObjectVision instances at once.

EXITING TO WINDOWS

Whether developing Windows applications or using them, ObjectVision users exit an application by selecting the Exit command from the File menu. Control

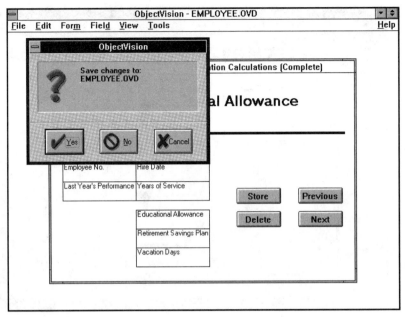

FIGURE 1.13
Exit warning message

normally returns immediately to the Windows Program Manager. However, if changes have been made—either in the developing application or in an end-user form—ObjectVision first signals that the application has changed. Figure 1.13 shows an example of the warning issued. This feature minimizes the chances of inadvertently losing the (hours of) changes made to an application.

S U M M A R Y

You have learned a little about the short history of how visual development environments evolved from humble roots. One of those mature development environments is ObjectVision. The purpose of this chapter has been to familiarize you with the look and feel of ObjectVision by illustrating some applications and introducing a few fundamental commands. You know how to invoke Object-Vision and select an application from a displayed list of applications. Additionally, you have learned how to execute the File menu commands that print and save your applications. Many new terms unique to ObjectVision have been introduced in this chapter. As you read ensuing chapters, important terms will reappear and you will become more familiar with them.

KEY TERMS

Asynchronous events Events that occur unpredictably, at random times.

Button ObjectVision object that, when pressed, starts an action.

Conclusion Part of a decision tree that determines a result of an object's tree. A conclusion is the last node in a tree branch for each of the tree's branches.

Condition Part of a decision tree that determines which branch of a tree is selected next. It contains logic resulting in the values True or False.

Control-menu box Located in the upper left corner of the window, it can be used to resize, move, maximize, minimize, and close windows or to switch to other applications.

Decision tree A graphical display of calculations and actions. Similar to flowcharts, decision trees evaluate a condition and then, based on the result, perform the next branch or conclusion.

Dimmed menu item (see "Grayed-out menu item").

Drop-down menu The style of Windows menu that drops down from the menu bar to reveal a list of commands.

Event tree A type of decision tree used to recognize an event and initiate an action.

Field A uniquely named object that contains a value either entered by a user, calculated from a decision tree, or provided by a database link.

Focus The current location of the cursor. Often, the focus is noted by a dashed line around the object. The arrow keys and the Tab key can be used to change the focus without selecting an object.

Form status Current condition of the form, found in the form's title bar to the right of the title. It can be any of the following: Goal, Complete, Prompt, or Edit.

Form title Title of the active form as displayed in the title bar.

Graphic One of the types of objects that can be incorporated into a form. Programs such as Paintbrush produce graphic objects as output.

Grayed-out menu item A menu item whose light appearance indicates that it cannot be selected in the current context.

Guided completion Action invoked while filling out a form in which only a field requiring user input is selected after Enter is pressed. As a result, the application user saves time and effort.

Handles While using the Form Tool, the small black squares appearing in the corners of the selected object or at the ends of a selected line. By selecting and dragging a handle, the developer can resize an object.

Linking The process of establishing the logical connection through which database and external file values are associated with ObjectVision fields and tables.

Maximize button The button in the upper right of a form window that enlarges the active window to the entire screen. Double clicking on the title bar will toggle between full screen and normal size.

Menu bar The bar containing menu selections that allow developers full access to all the tools needed to build an application. The menu bar is located at the top of the window.

Minimize button The button in the upper right of a form window that reduces the active ObjectVision window to an icon.

Object bar The bar just below the menu bar that contains graphic buttons representing the objects that can be placed on a form. Clicking on an object bar icon places the corresponding object on a form.

Stack All forms of an application, collectively. The terms *application* and *stack* are synonymous in an ObjectVision environment.

Table An object containing multiple values organized as one or more rows with one or more columns.

Title bar The bar at the top of each active form displaying the form's name (title).

Trigger An event or signal that causes an action to occur in some event tree of an application.

Value tree A decision tree that calculates and returns a value for the field to which it is attached.

REVIEW QUESTIONS

True or False Questions

1. **T F** Program runtime errors occur at execution time, whereas syntax errors are recognized by the program compiler.

2. **T F** ObjectVision is an example of a visual development environment product.

3. **T F** Application developers must have broad experience in programming before using a visual development environment tool to create forms.

4. **T F** The feature called "guided completion" means that a program developer must include explicit end-user instructions about which form fields should be filled in first.

5. **T F** Any field of a form can have an attached but hidden value tree.

6. **T F** Event trees are reserved for use with buttons only.

7. **T F** An application can have more than one form. This collection of forms is called a *stack*.

8. **T F** Two or more objects, such as a field and a line, can be grouped together and then moved about as a unit.

9. **T F** Information can be delivered to a form by two sources: manual (user) input or value trees.

10. **T F** A runtime version of ObjectVision is available for end users. Users are unable to alter an ObjectVision application using the runtime version.

Multiple Choice Questions

1. Which of the following is *not* an ObjectVision object that can be placed on a form?
   a. field
   b. table
   c. line
   d. link

2. Which ObjectVision menu item is missing from the runtime version?
   a. file
   b. tools
   c. view
   d. edit

3. Only two objects can have value trees. Besides the field, what is the other?
   a. text
   b. button
   c. table column
   d. stack

4. Value tree nodes have two building blocks that produce branches and (ultimately) results: conditions and
   a. conclusions
   b. functions
   c. branches
   d. events

USING A FORM-BASED APPLICATION

OVERVIEW

The focus of this chapter is on *using* a form so that you can become more familiar with the ObjectVision application development platform. By using a form and the ObjectVision menus we lay the groundwork for subsequent chapters that describe form design and creation. A common business case and a corresponding form are presented and discussed throughout the chapter.

The chapter first examines the importance of designers creating and pretesting a mock-up, or prototype, form. By using a prototype, a developer can determine whether field placement is appropriate and whether the form's look is intuitive to the projected user audience. We then review selecting and launching an application. Form navigation is then discussed, both to present *how* to move about an ObjectVision form and *why* a particular arrangement of objects may be better than another. We examine how databases are integrated into many applications, and we discuss how databases are attached to applications and their associated fields. Derived or calculated fields and the value trees delivering those values are also presented. Finally, we discuss field properties and how they are established, value and event trees, and how databases are linked to fields. Having completed this chapter, you should be ready to proceed to designing and implementing your own application form.

CASE: EMPLOYEE EDUCATIONAL ALLOWANCE

You are employed by the Best and Final Company, which produces high-quality sheet metal products for the aerospace industry. Best and Final is a small company with less than 150 employees. The company has one facility that houses both manufacturing and corporate administration. As the lead analyst in the Information Systems Department, you have been asked to help automate a part of the human resources office. The human resources manager would like to move the personnel administration activities from the cumbersome mainframe system to a PC. In particular, she would like you to develop a Windows-based system that will make the administration of employee benefits easier. To get started, you and the human resources manager agree to design and prototype a benefits review form-based interface that resembles the currently used paper forms. Presently, each employee's educational allowance, retirement vestment status, and vacation days are calculated manually. This form is to be automated, incorporating Best and Final's business rules concerning those three benefits.

2.1 INTRODUCTION

The above case is typical of a business situation in which a systems analyst is assigned the task of creating PC-based software. The benefits review module is part of a larger system that will aid management decision making because the interface—a form—renders that task easier, more intuitive, and less subject to error.

In this chapter we examine a form developed with ObjectVision that satisfies the human resource manager's requirements for determining selected employees' benefits. At this point it is beneficial to examine a finished form to understand how the parts of it relate and interact. You can build your own applications in part by borrowing objects and techniques uncovered in the analysis of a working form. A secondary benefit of examining a finished form is that you place yourself in the end-user's shoes. Traversing a form from the user's perspective provides valuable insights when forms are later developed. An unwieldy form is quickly obvious when the application developer switches to the end-user role.

AN OVERVIEW OF THE FORM

An uncomplicated form, when put together carefully, can satisfy the human resource manager's needs. Figure 2.1 shows an example of such a form. It contains five objects: a graphic, a line, text, fields, and buttons.

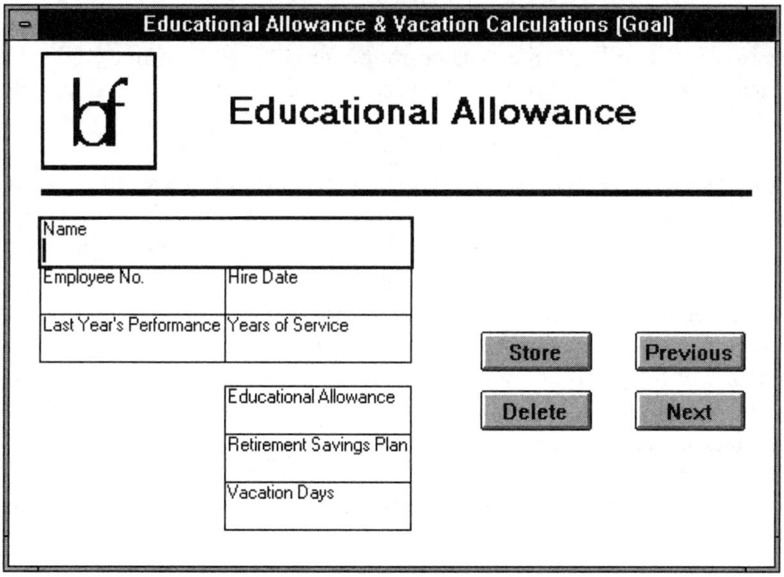

FIGURE 2.1
Employee benefits form

The upper left corner of the benefits form contains a graphic with the company's logo (actually, it is Boyd & Fraser's logo borrowed for this example). To the right of the logo is the text object, "Educational Allowance." A line object is visible below the graphic and text objects that visually separates the form into two segments and provides an attractive heading. Fields appear below the line on the left half of the form. They include a Name field, Employee No. field, and others through and including the Vacation Days field. The eight fields constitute the employee data, part of which is automatically calculated and part of which is input manually. Buttons appearing in the lower right portion of the form provide the user with a way to interact with an underlying database system that can hold employee information for countless employee records. The database system is linked to the employee benefits application, although the database is initially devoid of records—the record of an individual employee's data entered into the form.

DOES THE FORM MEET THE REQUIREMENTS?

How does the proposed benefits form meet the requirements of the human resources manager? Four of the fields are manually entered: Name, Employee No., Hire Date, and Last Year's Performance. The latter is an integer from 1 (below average) to 5 (superior) assigned by an employee's supervisor. The performance rating affects some of the benefits as per company policy (the rules are described later). The remaining four fields, Years of Service through Vacation Days, are automatically derived from formulas involving both the Hire Date and Performance fields. These calculated fields, similar in nature to spreadsheet cells, are precisely what the human resource manager wants: automatically calculated educational allowance, retirement vesting status, and vacation days values.

EXAMPLE BUSINESS RULES IMPLEMENTED IN THE FORM

Each form created by an application developer will reflect business rules in some fashion. It is no different with the benefits form in our example. Before going further we will examine the rules implemented by the example form. Later we will see how these rules are incorporated into the form.

One of the business rules prescribes how much money is given to an employee for reimbursement of education expenses. The rule is shown in Table 2.1. Two factors determine the dollar amount of an employee's educational allowance: the number of years with the company (tenure) and the employee's performance rating. Tenure is the primary factor followed by performance within the longevity constraints. Notice that if employees have been with the company more than nine years, performance rating is no longer a deciding factor (seniority has its privileges!). For example, this company's policy states that the annual educational allowance is $1,500 for an employee having a rating of 4 and having worked less than 5 years with the company.

TABLE 2.1
Educational allowance rules

Annual Educational Allowance		
Tenure (years)	*Performance Rating*	*Educational Allowance*
1 to 4	1	$0
	2	$500
	3	$1,000
	4	$1,500
	5	$2,000
5 to 9	1	$0
	2	$1,000
	3	$2,000
	4	$3,000
	5	$4,000
10 or more	(n/a)	$5,000

Two other benefits business rules are implemented in the form: earned vacation days and retirement savings plan status. Both these rules are more simple than educational allowance, as each depends on only one factor or variable. Number of vacation days is a function of an employee's tenure with the company. Those with the company from 1 to 4 years get 10 vacation days. Those with 5 to 14 years of service earn 15 vacation days. And anyone having worked for the company more than 15 years receives 20 vacation days. The retirement savings plan status is also a simple rule. Employees are not vested until they have worked more than 4 years. That is, once they have worked for five years, they are vested. How these rules are implemented—incorporated into the form—will be presented later.

2.2 SELECTING AN APPLICATION

Chapter 1 described briefly how to select an ObjectVision application. A quick review is in order. After double clicking the ObjectVision icon shown in one of

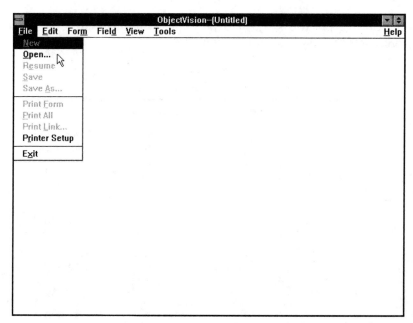

FIGURE 2.2
Selecting File|Open to open an application

the Program Manager's groups, the opening screen (shown in Figure 1.8) is displayed. Click the File menu and the available file commands are displayed. Remember, grayed-out (or dimmed) commands cannot be selected. Only the bold menu items can be activated (see Figure 2.2).

The arrow points to the Open command. Click Open and a list of applications (those with the OVD secondary name) is displayed in the Open File dialog box (see Figure 1.9 for an example). Different directories or different disk devices can be selected from the Directories display on the right side of the dialog box in the usual way. The selection "[..]" provides a way to move up the current directory tree to the node's parent. You can use the scroll bar to the right of the Files display to view file names below or above the display frame. When you find the desired application, place the mouse on its name and double click. The application will launch and display its first form.

Executing an application will help you to understand how the commands work. At this point, select, for example, the application EMPLOYEE.OVD (the educational allowance application being discussed here) and duplicate the activity presented in the text by trying it on the educational allowance application.

At any point when you wish to choose another application, simply select the File menu (click on File) and select the Exit command (see Figure 2.3). Or select the Open command from the File menu to choose another application to run. If the application has changed and you choose either to exit ObjectVision altogether or to select a new application, a Warning dialog box is displayed (shown in Figure 1.13) so that you have one more chance to save the changed application.

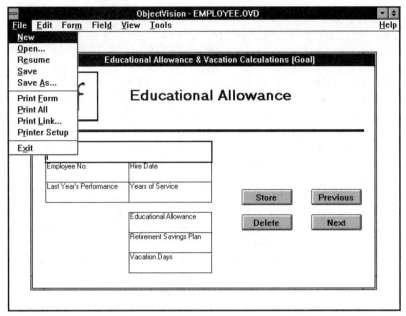

FIGURE 2.3
The File menu

At the top of the form is the title "Educational Allowance & Vacation Calculations" followed by the status "Goal." The latter indicates that the form is incomplete.

2.3 NAVIGATING A FORM

Entering data and moving from field to field is easy in ObjectVision. A few basic keystrokes are all that need be remembered. The mouse is very useful when it comes to activating any buttons and jumping randomly from field to field, but for basic data entry the keyboard is most useful. When filling in forms, then, it is best to stick with the keyboard. The keys used to enter data, move from object to object, scroll a form, and modify data are described next.

MOVING FROM FIELD TO FIELD

After an application is opened, the cursor (sometimes called the *focus*) usually is resting within the first field. For example, if you open the EMPLOYEE application, the focus appears in the Name field in the form of an I-beam (see Figure 2.1). Data appropriate to a field is typed in. Once completed, a field is stored and the cursor is moved to another by pressing one of several keys.

Most often, you type in a field's value and then press Enter to complete it. That causes the cursor to move to the next field *requiring* a value. Fields requiring a value are those whose values are input manually. In contrast, fields whose value is automatically calculated are those that contain value trees or those that have values delivered by a database. In the EMPLOYEE application, four of the fields require values to be entered manually. The remaining four fields—Years of Service, Educational Allowance, Retirement Savings Plan, and Vacation Days—are automatically calculated by their value trees, hidden from view, from formulas using some of the manually input field values. The values for these four fields appear automatically once the associated independent variables, upon which the value trees depend, are filled in by a user. So, it is best to use the Enter key to move from one field to the next because that method utilizes *guided completion*. Only the fields requiring values are "visited" by the cursor if Enter is pushed to move on.

Alternately, the Tab key can be pressed to move the cursor from one field to another. However, Tab visits fields in the same way. It moves from left to right, top down through the entire form, disregarding any notion of required versus automatic values. In other words, if you pressed Tab after entering Name, Employee No., and so on, the cursor would visit the first five fields and then move to the Store and Previous buttons. Subsequently, the cursor would move through the remaining fields: Educational Allowance, Retirement Savings Plan, and Vacation Days. Pressing Tab from the Vacation Days field moves the cursor back to the top field, Name. This latter action is commonly referred to as a **wrap around**.

Try entering data in the fields by using both Enter and Tab at the end of each field. First experiment by filling in the following values, beginning with the Name field, and pressing Enter after each:

Name:	`William Gates`
Employee No.:	`12345`
Hire Date:	`6/7/91`
Last Year's Performance:	`3`

Notice that after the Hire Date field is completed, three fields take on values: Years of Service, Retirement Savings Plan, and Vacation Days. Those fields need not be filled in, as their values are wholly derived from the "seniority" value, Hire Date. Figure 2.4 shows the example form just after a value for Hire Date has been entered.

Correcting mistakes in a field or in another object is done with a few, simple keystrokes. For example, by pressing and holding the Alt key and simultaneously pressing the Backspace key, the cursor backs up to the previous field and restores any previous value. (Throughout the text a two-key sequence like the previous one is noted with a hyphen. For example, Alt-Backspace indicates the previous action.) Mistakes made while in the midst of completing a field can be corrected by pressing Esc to clear the field and start over. Otherwise, you can use the Back-

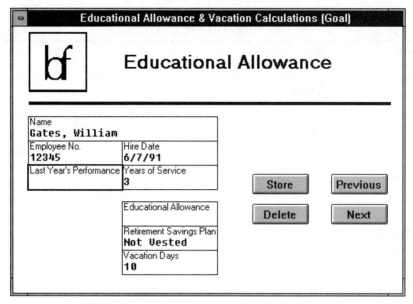

FIGURE 2.4
Example of fields calculated automatically

space key to erase the entry letter by letter from the right. Though the arrow keys do not move the cursor from field to field, they can be used to move non-destructively left or right in a field or table column. Similarly, Home moves immediately to the first position in a field, while End moves to the right of the rightmost character in a field.

The Tab key can be used to complete a field and move to the next object, though we do not recommend using that key (use Enter, instead). Tab is convenient, though, to move quickly from object to object across and down a form. Press Shift-Tab (press and hold Shift and tap Tab) to move from object to object in reverse order.

Somewhat surprisingly, neither Tab nor Enter have any effect on buttons. In particular, after all of the required fields in the Employee application are complete, pressing Tab or Enter a few more times places the focus on the Store button. Press either Tab or Enter. No action occurs, but the cursor moves to the right, stopping on the Previous button. Presumably the buttons appearing in Employee have some purpose other than looking interesting on the form! There are two ways to press them: press the left mouse button or use the keyboard. Press the Spacebar whenever the focus is on a button to activate that button. In this case, a mouse is preferable to using the keyboard. Table 2.2 summarizes the keystrokes that are used while filling in a form. The rows are presented in approximate order, top to bottom, corresponding to the more frequently used keys.

TABLE 2.2
Form data input action keystrokes

Keystroke	Description
Enter	Enters a value into a field; moves to the next field *requiring* input (guided completion).
Alt-Backspace	Backs up to the previous field and restores any previous value. Works only if pressed immediately after pressing Enter or Tab.
Tab	Enters a value into a field and moves to the next field. Movement is left to right, top to bottom. Every field is visited.
Shift-Tab	Goes to the previous field. Movement is reverse of Tab: right to left, bottom to top. Every field is visited.
Spacebar	Activates a selected button.
Shift-Enter	Enters a value in a cell, exits the table object, and then selects the next field not in the table.
Esc	Removes a typed value from a field during input. Has no effect if data had been entered.
Ctrl-PgUp Ctrl-PgDn	Scrolls a form horizontally.
PgUp or PgDn	Scrolls a form vertically.
F1	Function key invokes object level help specific to the currently selected object. Otherwise, ObjectVision general help is displayed.

GUIDED COMPLETION

It is important that you arrange fields so that users fill in data in a natural, obvious way. If ObjectVision is being used to automate an extant paper form, perhaps the fields should appear in the same order as the paper form. Or if the top to bottom order of the paper form fields appears to be counterproductive based on observation, then alter the fields so they appear in a convenient order. Your attention is focused on the order in which fields are selected as you fill in field values.

ObjectVision automatically determines the order in which field objects are selected. Selection begins, in general, from the object in the top left of the form and then proceeds left to right and top down until it reaches the bottom right of the form. The order in which fields are selected is based on the position of each field's bottom right corner. (Remember that as you design forms and position fields!) Visualize each field by the position of its lower right corner. Scanning from left to right and top down (the way you would read a book), the first field selected is the one whose lower right corner is encountered first.

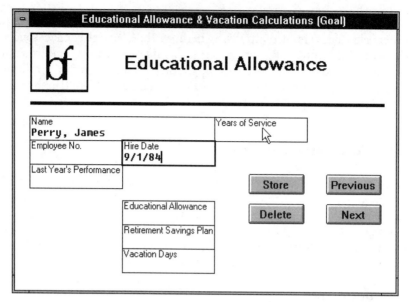

FIGURE 2.5
Guided completion skipping to required field

Not every field object is selected during guided completion, however. Only fields that require values from the user are selected. The expression "fields that require values" refers to fields upon which other fields depend, much like the notion of a spreadsheet formula that references other spreadsheet cells. If guided completion encounters a field in the usual left to right, top down flow that contains a calculation, then any fields required to satisfy the calculated field are selected in turn.

A given calculated field displays a value the moment all its referenced fields have obtained values. In other words, fields with value trees are skipped in favor of fields that feed into those value trees. If one or more fields referenced in a value tree is omitted from the form, a default form appears temporarily in which the required value is entered. For example, suppose the Educational Allowance form were altered so that the Years of Service field was relocated directly to the right of the Name field. As you can guess, Years of Service is a calculated value that references the Hire Date field and the current date. After filling in the Name field, guided completion moves the cursor to the Hire Date field, temporarily skipping Years of Service and Employee No. The arrow in Figure 2.5 indicates the calculated field skipped in favor of Hire Date (the cursor is at the end of the date).

Why is Years of Service skipped? Because it cannot take on a value until the value of Hire Date is filled in. Once Hire Date has a value, Years of Service displays a value and guided completion moves the cursor to the Employee No. field.

Guided completion is suspended when the mouse is clicked or the Tab key is pressed to select a field. Subsequently, fields are selected in the expected left to right, top down order, regardless of whether or not calculated fields requiring other field values are encountered. Sometimes, there may be good reasons to alter the form fill-in order. Perhaps a previous value is incorrect and it should be changed immediately before continuing. Guided completion can be resumed following its suspension by executing the Resume command found in the File menu (File | Resume).

FILLING IN FIELD VALUES

Fields are filled in manually by typing an appropriate value and pressing Enter. As stated before, the cursor moves to the next required value via guided completion rules. For example, if a typographical error ("typo") occurs and a nonnumeric value is entered among a series of digits for the Employee No. field, then an error message is issued. Each field provides a high degree of context-sensitive value checking. Fields contain field type and format information.

Field Data Types

Fields in the Educational Allowance form, as well as in any other ObjectVision form you may construct or use, are constrained to accept only particular values. The Name field seems rather simple: any keyboard character can be entered. Other fields, such as Employee No. and Hire Date, accept a restricted set of characters. Values of the wrong type for a particular field are rejected with an attendant warning message. There are two fundamental data types for fields: numeric and character. A developer establishes the data type for each field. A field's data type along with several other of its characteristics can be examined and changed through the **property inspector**. The property inspector is invoked when the cursor is within a field and the right mouse button is pressed. (Details about this facility are presented later in this chapter). Whenever a field is created, it takes on the default data type, which is character.

Numeric Fields

Numeric fields restrict the data entered to digits, sign, decimal point, and a few other characters. Alphabetic characters are rejected when part of a numeric field. All fields in the Educational Allowance form except Name and Retirement Savings Plan are numeric. Interestingly, Hire Date is considered a numeric field. In particular, numeric data comprises the following six subtypes: fixed, percent, financial, currency, date, and time. Which of these numeric types is chosen determines what characters can be entered into a given field. For example, a date field can contain any of the digits—barring an illegal date—and slash (/) characters in the appropriate positions. Likewise, time values contain colons to separate hours, minutes, and seconds. These six numeric variations also serve to format an entered number to display with dollar signs, commas, percent signs,

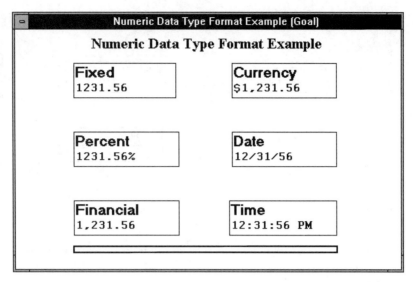

FIGURE 2.6
Numeric field examples

and so on. Figure 2.6 illustrates numeric field types. Each field's name indicates its type for easy reference.

The value 1231.56 has been entered for the Fixed, Currency, and Financial fields; 12.3156 was entered in the Percent field. The Date and Time fields were entered as you see them, with slashes and colons explicitly typed in the respective fields. Notice, for example, that a comma is inserted when needed in a Financial field. A dollar sign and insertion commas are displayed automatically in currency data. Selection and formatting details of numeric types are presented later in the discussion of the property inspector.

What happens in a form when you press Enter repeatedly, visiting each of the Educational Allowance form fields in turn? Try it. Open the Educational Allowance form inside ObjectVision or, if ObjectVision is displayed, execute the command File|Open and select the application. Interestingly, when Enter is pressed with no other keystrokes, each field appears to contain nothing. However, after Hire Date is completed (Enter, only, is pressed), an unrealistically large value (93 or greater) is displayed for Years of Service. In addition, the Educational Allowance field shows "$5,000" and the Retirement Savings Plan shows "Vested." This exercise confirms that null values in numeric fields are interpreted as zeros in calculations. On the other hand, walking through all the fields by pressing Tab has no effect on the dependent, calculated fields. Tab leaves all fields untouched. Keep these differences in mind as you use forms. Later we will see how to prevent null entries from playing tricks with the value trees of other fields.

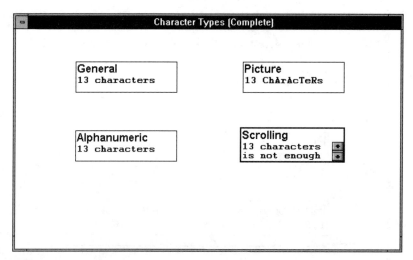

FIGURE 2.7
Character field examples

Character Fields

Character data comprises virtually anything you can type on the keyboard (no Ctrl- or Alt- combinations allowed). Four variants of the character are available: general, picture, alphanumeric, and scrolling. Figure 2.7 shows a character string displayed in the four field types. Each data type is identified by its field name.

When a field is created, it is initially assigned the default type character and the general format type. General is suitable for displaying both numeric and text values. ObjectVision will attempt to convert numeric values after they are entered into a general field. Alphanumeric character data fields accept any keyboard character, similar to general fields, but a value is not converted. Picture character data provides the developer with a large number of ways to format entered character strings and numbers. Formatting characters, including !, @, and #, stand for positions in a field. They cause each character to be converted to uppercase or lowercase letters, or they force a particular position to accept only digits. Notice in Figure 2.7 that the word *character* contains alternating lowercase and uppercase letters. That is because the underlying picture (a lot like COBOL's PICTURE statement) specifies the following format string:

```
##^!@!@!@!@!@
```

The caret shown in the third position stands for a blank. All characters in the picture field are entered in lowercase. The picture string converts the letters automatically. In addition, the length of the picture string limits input values to that length. Table 2.3 lists all of the picture elements for your convenience.

TABLE 2.3
Character type picture string elements

Picture Element	Description
#	Accept only a digit
?	Accept only a letter (lower- or uppercase)
&	Accept only a letter; convert to uppercase
@	Accept any character
!	Accept any character; convert to uppercase
;	Take next character literally
{} [] , =	Reserved for future use

Other characters can be entered in a picture string. They are literally inserted in the field each time. For example you might want a social security number picture string to be ###-##-####. Hyphens can be inserted conveniently that way. When the special characters in Table 2.3 are to be inserted literally, precede each with the semicolon. The meanings of each of the symbols should be obvious.

Scrolling character type fields are especially useful for representing long entries. Notice that a scroll bar appears on the right of the field, indicating that text can be scrolled vertically by pressing the up or down arrow keys.

Field Type Checking

When a value is entered that does not agree with the field's data type an error message is generated. For example, entering the character string **December** (to the left of the mouse arrow) into the Hire Date field raises the error condition shown in Figure 2.8. Though date/time type fields accommodate a wide variety of entries for dates, the month alone is insufficient and thus incorrect. Note, however, that dates such as the following are all equivalent and are correctly converted to the field's selected format: December 7, 1994; 12/07/94; Dec 07, 94; and 12-07-94. Data validation is also performed for several of the other data types. Of course, the general type accepts any characters and is thus exempt from data entry errors. Table 2.4 lists the data types for each field in the Educational Allowance application.

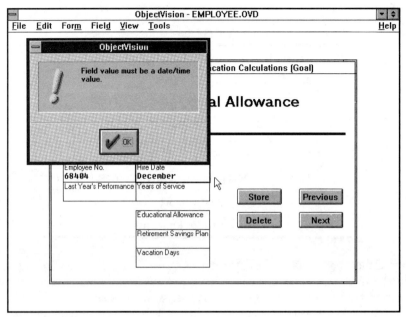

FIGURE 2.8
Example field data entry error

TABLE 2.4
Data types in the Educational Allowance application

Field	Data Type
Name	General
Employee No.	Fixed, zero decimal places,
Hire Date	Date/Time
Last Year's Performance	Fixed, zero decimal places
Years of Service	General
Educational Allowance	Currency, zero decimal places
Retirement Savings Plan	General
Vacation Days	Fixed, zero decimal places

OVERRIDING CALCULATED FIELDS

End users can override a calculated field by simply moving to that field and entering the alternate value. When a field's value is overridden, the field displays a dot pattern as a visual signal that the value is not necessarily generated by the field's value tree. A developer can prevent individual fields from being overridden by setting a field's protection attributes in a particular way (discussed later). An overridden field's default calculated value can be restored by executing the command Field|Calculate. Overriding calculated values is used frequently and provides a mechanism for users to enter information for the occasional exceptional cases.

2.4 ACCESSING DATABASES FROM A FORM

Most significant applications make use of a database. Most Windows applications can benefit from that extra dimension. Of course, the Educational Allowance form can be used like a spreadsheet: the human resources manager enters a person's data into the input fields and the benefits are calculated automatically. Then the employee and the human resources manager can review the employee's benefits and be done with it! If another employee stops by the human resources office, then different data is entered in fields and answers again appear in the calculated fields. It would eventually save time, however, if the calculations were saved somewhere so they could be retrieved again for next year's review.

WHY HAVE A DATABASE, ANYWAY?

ObjectVision forms have no "memory." That is, apart from the data entered into a form and saved, an ObjectVision application, by itself, cannot retrieve information that may have been previously entered into a form. An obvious solution to the lack of storage—or memory—for an application is to store information in a simple file or a more sophisticated structure such as a database. ObjectVision does not have a database file format of its own, which is good. Instead of using an internal, proprietary database system inaccessible to all other software, ObjectVision connects easily to any of several popular databases. Support is provided to access Paradox, dBASE, and Novell Btrieve files. In addition, ObjectVision can both store and retrieve information from flat, ASCII files. Of course, like other Windows applications, ObjectVision supports the Windows Dynamic Data Exchange (DDE) protocol. DDE provides a seamless and familiar way to exchange data with other Windows applications. ObjectVision's support for full Object Linking and Embedding (OLE) technology provides an even more versatile way to access not only data but also the product that manipulates the data.

An ObjectVision form is not limited in power and can retrieve and display data from multiple database systems and multiple database files. For example, a single form might link to a Paradox table, a dBASE IV file, and a Btrieve file. Thus, with database access capability, application fields and tables can be filled in automatically with database-supplied data. Those people developing applications that link to databases can specify whether the linkage is strictly retrieval, storage, or both. Therefore, an application's "memory" is created when a form's fields and table values are saved in a database.

Having a database accessible to an ObjectVision application means that information can be saved, rather than discarded, whenever a user wishes. In the case of the Educational Allowance application, this capability provides the potential for saving all of the employees' data values as they are entered and saved. The human resources manager then has the ability to recall any employee's record when a periodic review is conducted, thereby saving time and effort.

WHAT IS A DATABASE?

A database is a collection of interrelated data items that can be processed by one or several applications. A **database system** comprises a database (the data) and database management system software. The latter handles all database access—including information retrieval, alteration, and storage—in a transparent way. Transparency allows an application to request the database management system to retrieve or store information even though the application does not know any details about how the information is stored or where it is located. All of those details are the responsibility of the database management system. So it is with ObjectVision. Applications that require data from a source other than the user or a calculated result ask the database system to supply information, if any, for selected fields in a form.

The benefits of using a database with ObjectVision applications accrue to both small and large companies. Retyping the Educational Allowance form anew each year for each of the employees in our hypothetical company, Best and Final, would be a chore as well as a waste of valuable time. On the other hand, if we employ a database to archive the data from previous years, then only a small amount of data for new employees will need to be typed. An employee's record can be recalled by pressing an ObjectVision button supplied in the application. Relevant fields are automatically filled in from corresponding database fields. Only field changes need be typed in to update an employee's record.

LINKING FORMS TO DATABASES

In our example form, information to be saved in the database comes from four fields, the *independent* information from which the remaining form fields are derived: Name, Employee No., Hire Date, and Last Year's Performance. Among these four values stored in the database, it is likely that only an employee's performance rating may vary from time to time. Other fields should remain constant. Thus, very little information on the form need be updated annually.

The mechanism for establishing the relationship between the form's fields and the underlying database is called a *link*. A link is the logical mechanism for connecting ObjectVision application fields and tables to database tables external to the application. Links between a form's objects and database structures provide database access, including the ability to retrieve, alter, delete, and preserve values to a database. The links serve as conduits through which data flows back and forth between application and database(s) as needed. An application can have a single link relating multiple fields to a single database, or it can have several links relating multiple fields to several databases.

Though not evident, the Educational Allowance application has a single link establishing connections between form fields and database fields. Links are made of connections that can be individually set up to pass information from the database to the application, from the application to the database, or both. These connections are called **read**, **write**, and both, respectively. Read connections supply a form's fields with data that is rarely altered in the database. Information remains relatively constant over the life of the application. Having a write connection between a form field and a database field means that information entered into a form can be saved permanently in a database. Having both read and write connections between form and database fields provides a two-way street. Data can flow, on command, back and forth between form and database.

The Educational Allowance application provides both read and write connections. That means an end user can retrieve employee data from a previous review, examine it, change it if necessary, and write it back to the database to save it. Values are exchanged between the form and the underlying database through the buttons shown on the form (see Figure 2.5). There are many other database actions that can be initiated with buttons, but only these four are used in the example. Other actions are described in subsequent chapters.

BUTTONS AND DATABASE ACCESS

For such a simple application as the Educational Allowance form, four database action buttons are sufficient for interaction with a database. Information that has been entered on the form can be saved with the Store button. After the user has entered the four requisite fields, the dependent fields display values automatically and the cursor moves to the Store button. It has been placed among the four buttons in that upper left position because it is likely that a completed form will be saved. In addition, guided completion picks the Store button first. Under normal circumstances, the user merely presses the left mouse button to activate the store process that saves the current screen's critical fields in the database. On the other hand, if the form users were more likely to perform some other action most of the time (such as, delete), then the button corresponding to the frequent activity should be placed in the upper left position.

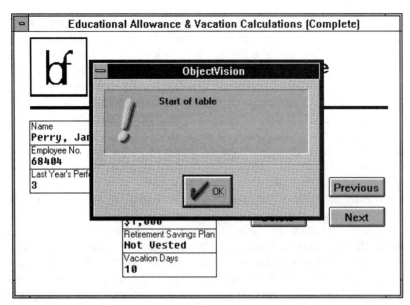

FIGURE 2.9
A database warning message

The Store button stores the current form's fields of Name, Employee No., Hire Date, and Last Year's Performance in similarly named fields in the database. For this example, we have used a Paradox database called EMPLOYEE.DB with fields labeled Name, Identification, Hire Date, and Performance. Relationships between the database fields and the form fields should be obvious. Note that the database can employ field names that do not match those of the form.

Employee's names are used to keep the database in order. Thus, employee Smith would appear after employee Perry. If the Store button is pressed before information is entered, the empty fields can be saved to the database anyway. Only one occurrence of an "empty" employee record will be saved, however.

Erroneous database **records**, copies of incorrect form data stored in the database, can be purged by clicking the Delete button. The record corresponding to the currently displayed employee information is then deleted from the database. The procedure to delete a record consists of two steps: first locate the record in the database then click Delete.

Both the Previous and Next buttons are used to scroll through and view individual database records via the form. When you click Next, the subsequent database record is fetched and the fields are filled in—four are derived from the database and the three remaining are calculated from database data. Similarly, clicking Previous retrieves the employee record that precedes the current one and displays its contents in the form. Clicking either Previous or Next enough times brings you to the end of the database, to either the first or the last record. Clicking (pressing) the Next or Previous button once more displays a message indicating that you cannot move farther in the current direction. Figure 2.9 shows such a message.

Correcting or changing stored data is a straightforward process. First search for the erroneous record in the database by repeatedly clicking the Next or Previous buttons. When the form displays the employee data to be corrected, use the mouse, tab, or enter keys to move to the field(s) to be changed. After the data has been corrected, click the left mouse button to save the corrected record.

There are many other database action buttons that can be used in a form, but we have reviewed all that are needed for this application. The next section describes how actions are assigned to buttons as well as how dependent fields are able to calculate automatically the results that they display. By peeling back the surface of a form's object, we will see just how easy it is to specify both value and event trees and assign them to various objects.

2.5 BENEATH THE SURFACE OF A FORM

Windows applications developed with ObjectVision can consist of fields, tables, and text arranged aesthetically to resemble the actual paper forms of a business. However, an application with fields that are filled in manually has little more functionality and utility than a word-processed document. Windows applications in general, and those developed with ObjectVision in particular, take on a much higher functionality when they contain help that is embedded, dependent value fields that are automatically calculated, and field values that can be retrieved from a data store. These features reside one layer below the visible, ostensibly simple, form objects.

Beneath the surface of most ObjectVision applications are decision trees, customized properties, object level help, and database links. Decision trees cause actions to occur when a button object, such as the Store button, is clicked. An object's properties control every aspect of how information is formatted. Object-level help makes available context-sensitive help. And database links provide the vehicle to deliver information between the application work surface and a database.

Not every application has all of the preceding features but most have a rich assortment of them. The Educational Allowance application is no exception. The following sections describe the field properties, field help, decision trees, and database links found within our example application. Relatively simple examples of these features have been implemented to help explain concepts without unnecessary complexity being introduced. First we examine how a developer assigns various properties to the fields in the application. Then we show how to incorporate help into the application so that a user can better understand what information is supplied for individual fields. We then examine the decision trees, both value and event, that are used to calculate and display values or that cause actions to take place. Finally, we show how a database is linked and used with the Educational Allowance application to store and retrieve information.

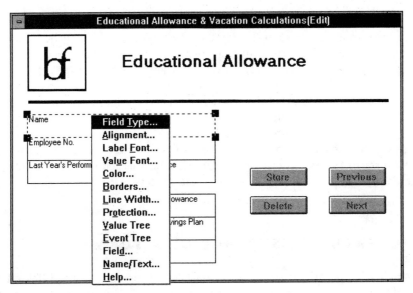

FIGURE 2.10
Properties of a sample field

FIELD PROPERTIES

ObjectVision developers—from the novice to the expert—can assign each object (text, table rows, fields, and so on) unique **properties** that both aid the end user and reduce development time. Depending on the object type, various properties can be selected that govern the way data is displayed, the color and font of the data, and whether or not decision trees are attached to the object.

Two methods are available for inspecting or changing an object's properties. First you must be editing the form. To do so select Tool|Form. Then move the focus (with either the mouse or the keyboard) to the object to be inspected. (An object has the focus when it is surrounded by square handles.) One way to view an object's properties is to select the Object command of the Properties menu (Properties|Object). A list of object properties is displayed for the selected object(s). Alternatively, you can use the **property inspector** by clicking the *right* mouse button when the cursor is on the selected object. You can select multiple objects whose properties you wish to inspect or change by holding down either the Ctrl or the Shift key as you click the left mouse button. The property inspector lists properties of an object and allows you to modify each one. Figure 2.10 shows the several properties that can be customized for a field from our featured application.

Field Type

Some properties will be unavailable if several objects have been selected prior to invoking the property inspector. For example, the Name/Text property is dimmed during multiple-field property inspection operations because it would

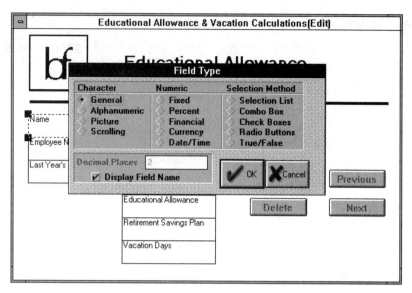

FIGURE 2.11
Field Type dialog box

not make sense to assign the same name to more than one object. The Field Type property establishes the appropriate data type for the object. Only fields and tables have this property. Figure 2.11 shows the choices available when you click Field Type from the list.

Several diamond-shaped radio buttons are available under Selection Method. (Radio buttons provide a group of mutually exclusive choices. Select one and another is deselected.) Data type choices occupy the first two columns, from General to Date/Time. Move the mouse to one of these and click. Depending on the one selected, other choices appear that affect what data can be entered. For example, if Fixed is selected, only numeric data can be entered. Selecting any of the types from the Numeric column subsequently allows you to select, independently, the number of decimal places (the Decimal Places choice is displayed toward the bottom of the dialog box). Selecting one of the four character types causes the Decimal Places choice to remain gray (unavailable). Subsequent menus are displayed for some format choices. For example, if Date/Time is selected, then several date and time formats are displayed.

The Field Type dialog box provides a rich variety of data types and allows you to choose from several data formatting options. Finally, the Display Field Name check box is checked by default, indicating that field names appear inside their fields on a form. All the field names appear in our example because they are convenient and meaningful. Other times you may wish to omit names from a field box and instead use a text object to label objects.

Alignment, Label Font, and Value Font

The second field property shown in Figure 2.10 is the **Alignment property**, which determines the relative position of an object's text within its display area.

Alignment choices are left, center, right, and justified. Both text and numbers can be aligned in any of the four ways.

A variety of fonts can be assigned to both an object's label and its value, or contents. **Label Font** is used to assign a font (typeface) and point size to an object's label. **Value Font** assigns a font and size for field and table values. The number and sizes of fonts available are dependent on Windows. If you have installed True Type fonts, for example, the list of fonts is much more extensive than the default fonts available with the standard Windows package.

Color

Individual colors can be selected for an object through the *Color* choice of the property inspector. You can select standard colors or custom colors for an object's label, value, background, and border. Black is the default color for the label, value, and border, and white is the background's default color. A border can be eliminated altogether from most objects, or it can be masked by selecting a color matching the one that surrounds the object.

Borders

Borders around objects can enhance their appearance and provide a visual boundary between fields. Clicking the Borders selection of the property inspector displays the Borders dialog box. Five check boxes appear, corresponding to the four sides of a field and the entire perimeter. Choose from Outline (the entire outside), or Left, Right, Top, and Bottom. Any combination of the latter four can be checked. For all sides, simply check Outline. Click once on any box and a check appears within it. Check a second time and it is unchecked. Press either OK to confirm the settings or Cancel to leave them in their former state.

Line Width

Line Width governs the width of lines surrounding some objects. The width of the border surrounding a field, for example, can be one of four line widths ranging from thin (default) to very thick. The larger sizes can be used to emphasize important fields. Like other dialog boxes, the Line Width dialog box provides the confirming OK button as well as a Cancel button if you wish to nullify a line width change.

Protection

Values automatically calculated and displayed, such as the field Years of Service in the highlighted application, can be protected so that their values cannot be overridden. Normally, a user can override a field's value by simply selecting the field and entering a value. However, a developer may wish to safeguard some values from alteration. The **Protection** property restricts users from entering

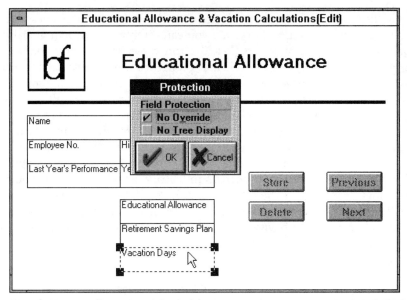

FIGURE 2.12
Protection dialog box

values into a field. For example, the human resources manager may need to change an employee's calculated educational allowance value for reasons not anticipated by the application developer. Such a calculated field would remain unprotected. On the other hand, company policy may preclude anyone except the president from manually altering a Vacation Days field. The latter can be protected from alteration. Figure 2.12 illustrates invoking the Protection dialog box for a field in the Educational Allowance application. Notice that the No Override box has been checked to preclude changing the calculated value. Protection makes sense only for objects having value trees.

Field

The Field property allows you to change the name of a field. It is similar to the Name/Text property (below).

The next two properties, value and event trees, are more important than those properties discussed so far (see Figure 2.10). Because they are so important, a separate section is devoted to them.

Name/Text

Selecting the Name/Text property allows you to change an object's name or edit the text in a text object. A field name change percolates throughout an application, including anywhere it is used in decision trees and in copies of the field in other forms of the stack. Thus, when an object's name is changed, all its dependent references are changed as well.

The ObjectVision system is installed with a set of default values for each of the preceding properties. However, you can establish your own global default values for each class of objects (field, button, table, and so on) so that each new object you create has the new default properties. This global default feature is particularly handy when you wish to create several objects having some core set of identical properties. It is simple to establish your own default properties on all but the button object. Click a button on the object bar with the *right* mouse button, set the default properties of that object through the property inspector, and press the OK button in the property inspector. All of the properties you set become the default for all objects of that type (such as, fields) throughout the application. You can reset properties to factory default values by choosing the Defaults command in the Objects menu (select Objects|Defaults). Table 2.5 shows all objects and the corresponding properties that can be set for each. Notice that some objects have very few properties, whereas others have several that you can customize.

TABLE 2.5
Objects and their properties

	Button	Cell	Column	Field	Graphic	Line	Rectangles	Table	Text
Alignment			✓	✓					✓
Borders				✓	✓		✓		✓
Color		✓	✓	✓	✓	✓	✓	✓	✓
Event Tree	✓		✓	✓	✓				✓
Field			✓	✓					
Field Type			✓	✓					
Help	✓		✓	✓					
Label Font			✓	✓				✓	✓
Line Width				✓	✓	✓	✓	✓	✓
Name/Text	✓		✓	✓				✓	✓
Protection			✓	✓					
Scroll Bar								✓	
Value Font		✓		✓					
Value Tree			✓	✓					

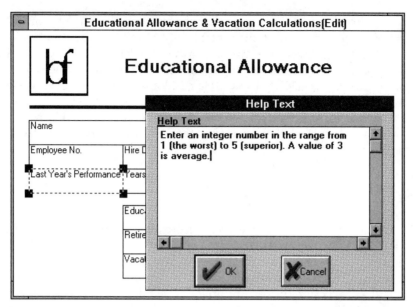

FIGURE 2.13
Creating help text for a field

CUSTOM, OBJECT-LEVEL HELP

Online help is provided by ObjectVision so that the application developers can review tutorial and reference information about all aspects of ObjectVision, from its functions to how to create a new form. The F1 function key provides that help. End users who invoke Windows applications also should be able to call upon your help when needed. The F1 function key can be used to display your stack, form, and object-level help messages. Help can be created for three types of objects: fields, table columns, and buttons. With very little additional effort, you can build help messages into each object that appears on your application forms. Then when users forget what sort of information can be entered in a given field (for example, Last Year's Performance), they can move the focus to that field and press the help key, F1. Your help message is displayed. If you have not packaged help with the field, then ObjectVision simply displays the not-so-helpful field name as the help message. It is much more helpful to tell the user what the range of valid field values are, for example, for the performance field. That way the user will know that "superior" is not one of the acceptable entries for performance.

Custom-help text is included with an object by invoking the property inspector for the highlighted object and selecting Help (see Figure 2.10). A Help Text dialog box appears in which you type your help text. You must press Ctrl-Enter whenever you want to continue text on another line. If you press Enter, that activates the Help Text dialog box OK button, indicating that you have completed the help text. Figure 2.13 shows an example of how to add help text to the Last Year's Performance field. The figure shows the Help Text dialog box just prior to pressing Enter to complete the operation. The text I-beam is to the right of the period in the second sentence.

When help is invoked by the user (form completion mode), the message is displayed in a dialog box with the field name and the word *help* (such as, "Last Year's Performance help"). Close the Help dialog box by either double clicking on the Control-menu or pressing Esc. The Help text disappears, and the focus remains on the object for which help was invoked. Another way to provide introductory or general help is to place it on a separate form that is part of the application's stack of forms.

DECISION TREES

Decision trees are a graphical method of depicting decision-making processes. For a particular situation, people evaluate a set of alternative actions and choose one. Decision trees are represented graphically and represent business rules with their branching alternatives and results, called *conclusions*. Using decision trees is particularly easy because they are intuitive and self-documenting. As noted before, decision trees comprise two types: value trees and event trees. Together these trees give applications the ability to calculate and deliver values automatically and to spring into action when one or more conditions occur.

Value Trees

A value tree is a decision logic tree represented graphically. It computes the value of a field object based on information found in other fields or table cells. It comprises branching nodes, conditions, and conclusions. A branching node of the tree evaluates a condition. The result determines which of several branches is taken next. Branches eventually terminate in conclusions. Similar to spreadsheet formulas, value trees deliver values to fields and affect the path of guided completion. Fields whose value depends on other objects in the application contain value trees. The conclusion nodes of the trees contain the set of possible values that are calculated and displayed.

As we saw earlier, value trees are found in four fields in the Educational Allowance application: Years of Service, Educational Allowance, Retirement Savings Plan, and Vacation Days. Figure 2.14 shows the value tree for the Vacation Days field. It contains the business rule describing how an employee's vacation days are calculated. In the upper left corner is the value tree's branching node, a box referencing the field Years of Service. Three branches emanate from it, representing the three conditions, or cases, recognized by the rule. The first condition encountered contains the expression <5 and indicates that the expression

    Years of Service < 5

is to be evaluated. If the expression is true (the employee has worked less than five years for the company), then the value displayed is found in the triangle

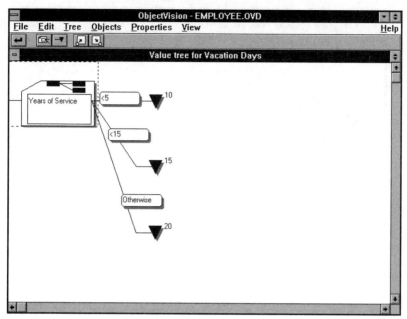

FIGURE 2.14
Value tree containing a branching node

conclusion node—the value 10. Ten would be displayed in the Vacation Days field in this case.

If the previous condition is not true, then the remaining cases are evaluated in order of their appearance from top to bottom in the tree. Next, the condition

```
Years of Service < 15
```

is evaluated and the value **15** is calculated and displayed if true. The last condition is special. The condition Otherwise is the "if all else fails" catchall condition. It is always placed last (lowest) in the series of branches for a particular node because its conclusion node is the result when all previous tests fail. In other words, it applies to all employees who have worked fifteen years or more.

Carefully observe how the conditions are arranged. If the condition **<15** were placed first followed by the condition **<5**, then **<15** would be chosen for new employees as well as those that have worked up to 14 years! Conditions are arranged in either increasing or decreasing order (change the relational operator to greater than (>) if arranged in decreasing order of longevity). In any case, check the logic to ensure that early cases in the value tree make it possible to reach cases farther down the tree.

Not all value trees contain branch nodes. Some are similar to familiar spreadsheet formulas that unconditionally calculate a value given one or more values from other sources in the application. An example of this type is the value tree for the Years of Service field. Its contents are shown in Figure 2.15. The triangle

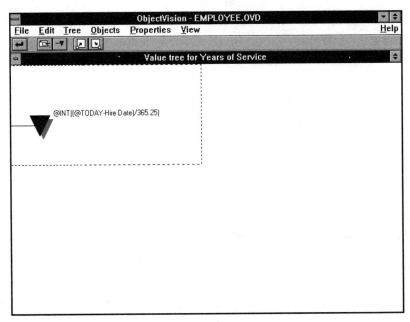

FIGURE 2.15
Value tree not containing a branching node

stands for a conclusion node. Indeed, the value tree is solely a conclusion node. To its right is the expression, not a constant like the previous figure, that computes the elapsed time between an employee's hire date and the present date—the number of years the employee has worked for the company. The formula is a bit more complicated than just a simple difference. In fact, we have used ObjectVision built-in functions in addition to standard mathematical operators. The formula is:

```
@INT((@TODAY-Hire Date)/365.25)
```

Both @INT and @TODAY are ObjectVision functions. Their names are familiar to spreadsheet users because they are identically named in Quattro Pro, Lotus 1-2-3, and a plethora of other spreadsheet products. Today's date (@TODAY) minus the employee's Hire Date field value yields elapsed *days*. Dividing that number by the approximate days in a year (the fraction takes care of leap year) gives us a number that we truncate to the nearest year (zero decimal places) with the @INT function. The result is longevity in years. Once the value for Hire Date has been entered, this formula can complete its calculations and display the result in its associated Years of Service field.

The property inspector reveals whether or not a field has a value tree. When you right click on a field having a value tree, the property inspector shows a check mark next to the Value Tree property in the list of properties.

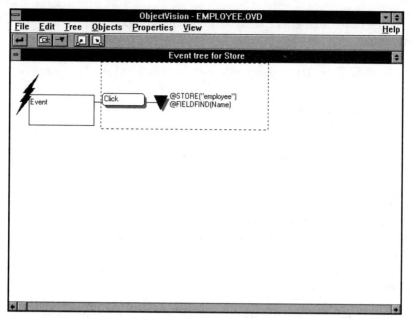

FIGURE 2.16
Store button event tree

Event Trees

An event tree causes an action to occur based on a prescribed event occurring. All objects except rectangles and lines can have an associated event tree (see Table 1.1). Additionally, an event tree can be attached to a form and the entire application (called a *stack* event tree). An event tree is created by clicking on the property inspector for a selected object (or by selecting the Object command in the Properties menu) and defining the event's logic tree. Similar in form to a value tree, an event may lead directly to a conclusion node that performs some action, or it may pass through a series of nodes before reaching a conclusion node. Figure 2.16 reveals the Store button event tree.

The event tree shows what action occurs when a user "presses" (clicks) the Store button, thus activating it. The event tree shown in Figure 2.16 comprises an event that will trigger the action and the actions taken when the event occurs. In our example, the event tree springs into action when it detects the click event—when a user presses the left mouse button of the Store button. The conclusion node shows two steps that collectively represent the action that takes place when a click is detected.

The Store button, along with the other three buttons, cause some interaction to occur between the application and a database that contains a permanent record of the employees' forms. Clicking on Store causes the information entered into the form to be saved in a database. It provides a self-evident, easily understood way for a nonexpert to save information in a database.

The two statements found in the conclusion node are executed when Store is clicked.

- @STORE("employee"), which stores the form information in the database
- @FIELDFIND(Name), which moves the focus (cursor) directly to the Name field in preparation for the next employee

Both statements are special database functions that we will discuss in detail later. There are several other database-specific event functions. The Previous, Delete, and Next, buttons all contain event trees also activated by the click event (when you select a button and click the left mouse button). Each has a conclusion node containing a single database event function that performs the function indicated by the button names. Previous moves to the previous database record and displays corresponding information in appropriate form fields. Next moves to the successor record and displays its fields in the form. Delete removes a database record.

You edit an event tree just as you edit a value tree. Click the right mouse button of the desired object (button, in our case), click Event Tree in the property inspector, and click the right button on the conclusion to be edited. Double click the control-menu to close the Edit window. We will spend a great deal of time on the process of editing event trees, so be assured that these details will be discussed thoroughly. The important point here is that event trees "listen" for particular signals and, upon recognizing them, execute one or more statements stored in the conclusion of a branch of an event tree.

DATABASE LINKS

The Database link feature is one of ObjectVision's most significant capabilities. While value trees deliver automatically calculated information from other sources within the application, database links deliver information to fields from databases outside the application. The most significant feature of database links is that centralized, consistent data can be maintained by a database system and simultaneously delivered to many independent applications. Unlike spreadsheet information, each ObjectVision application accessing the central database can access the same, up-to-date data. It is constantly maintained so that, for example, the ObjectVision application looking at today's sales data is always accurate.

The Educational Allowance application has connections—database links—to a large amount of externally stored and maintained employee database information. Four field values are stored in the database for each employee: Name, Employee No., Hire Date, and Last Year's Performance. Over a period of a year, records for all employees in the company, entered through the form, will be stored in a database. Subsequent benefits and performance reviews may take

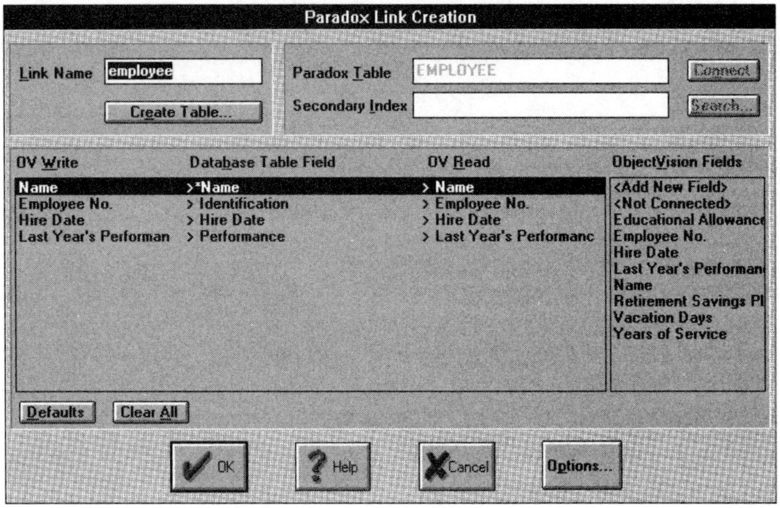

FIGURE 2.17
Establishing links to a Paradox database

advantage of the stored information. Once an employee's record is stored, it can be easily recalled. The four fields are filled in automatically from the two-way link created to both store and retrieve data from a database. In our example, the information is stored in a Paradox database. Several other databases are supported. An application can simultaneously access information from multiple database products, bringing together common information from disparate sources.

Linkages between ObjectVision form fields and database elements are established by selecting the Links command from the Tools menu (Tools | Links). Alternately, press the Links button on the object bar. The Data Links dialog box (shown in Chapter 5) is displayed. Because the Educational Allowance application has a link, its name (employee) is displayed. Selecting the Modify button leads to the Link Creation dialog box, shown in Figure 2.17.

Details are not important here. Merely observe in the figure that there are three columns in the center of the dialog box. The OV Write and OV Read columns list field names from the application, which can be written to read from (respectively) the database. The middle column lists database column names (the term "field names" is used synonymously by some database publishers) found in the database. An application name and database name are linked when they appear in a row in the dialog box. For example, the Paradox database EMPLOYEE has a column named Performance that corresponds to the Educational Allowance field named Last Year's Performance. The asterisk next to the Name column indicates that the Paradox table is ordered (indexed) on that field. A path is established between each application field and its corresponding database column through which data is delivered back and forth between the two on demand.

SUMMARY

You have learned more about ObjectVision by examining the details of a simple form that satisfies some needs of a small business. Form navigation has been described.

ObjectVision's several data types have been discussed, and we have shown that the property inspector is invoked to format fields and column entries to restrict the range of values that can be entered. Key features in ObjectVision are its decision trees and its ability to link to a wide variety of database systems. Decision trees embody business rules, providing logic trees that comprise arbitrarily complex condition/conclusion pairs from which a result is calculated.

Database links provide the path between an application and one or more databases. Database values are delivered to ObjectVision fields and tables, and information in forms can be written into the database.

KEY TERMS

Alignment property Determines the relative position of an object's text within its display area. Alignment can be left, center, right, or justified. It is accessed via the property inspector.

Database system A collection of programs that allows stored data to be integrated, reduces data duplication, and allows even complicated objects to be easily represented, retrieved, and maintained.

Label Font property Establishes the typeface and point size of an object's label. It is accessed via the property inspector.

Line Width property Establishes one of four different widths for a line object or the border surrounding an object. It is accessed through the property inspector.

Properties Attributes that are defined for objects through the Form Tool (used by developers, not end users). Several properties can be established for some objects, whereas a line has only two properties that can be manipulated.

Property inspector In the Form Tool, you can inspect and alter the properties assigned to one or more objects. By clicking the object or group of objects with the right mouse button, the inspector lists all the properties from which to select.

Protection property A property that can only be assigned to a field and a table column. Protection prevents users from changing the field or column value or viewing an object's tree.

Read connection A read connection is one of the two types of database links. It allows a database field value to be delivered to a field or column in an application (read from the database).

Record A single row of a database that contains information about a single, unique entity such as an employee or a purchase order line item.

Value Font property A property that establishes the typeface and size of an object's displayed value (not its label). The property inspector allows you to set the font, size, and other characteristics based on the available Windows fonts.

Wrap around Used in this context to describe the path that the cursor takes when Tab or Enter is repeatedly pressed. It eventually returns to the initial position, having traveled to each field and then back.

Write connection A write connection is one of the two types of database links. It allows an application to write an object's value into a database.

REVIEW QUESTIONS

True or False Questions

1. **T F** An event tree calculates a value that is displayed by the field or column.

2. **T F** Business rules can often be represented by event trees and value trees.

3. **T F** Guided completion moves the cursor from field to field, selecting independent fields before selecting those that depend on them.

4. **T F** The Tab key can be used with guided completion to move from one object requiring input to the next.

5. **T F** A value can be entered into a field even though it has a value tree. The calculated value is *overridden*.

6. **T F** Values entered in a field can be restricted to numeric only, for example, by selecting any of the numeric data types from the Field Type dialog box.

7. **T F** ObjectVision applications can store data only in an ObjectVision proprietary database.

8. **T F** Help can be associated with various form objects so that a user need only press function key F1 to obtain object-specific help.

9. **T F** Few applications make use of the Link facility providing access to one or more databases.

10. **T F** Only two properties of a line object can be altered, its color and width.

Multiple Choice Questions

1. All objects have properties that can be changed. Of those, which object has the largest number of properties that can be customized?
   a. table
   b. cell
   c. field
   d. text
   e. graphic

2. Which key can be pressed, in place of the left mouse button, to activate a button?
   a. tab
   b. enter
   c. shift-enter
   d. spacebar
   e. none of the above

3. Event trees contain branch nodes, conclusion nodes, and what other type of node?
   a. conditional
   b. evaluation
   c. answer
   d. condition
   e. variable

4. Which dialog box is invoked when you want to prevent a field value from being overridden?
   a. Override dialog box
   b. Privilege dialog box
   c. Field dialog box
   d. Protection dialog box
   e. Attributes dialog box

5. The @TODAY function can be used in an expression to calculated elapsed time. Which formula will compute the number of days between today's date and a date stored in a field called BIRTHDAY?
   a. (TODAY-BIRTHDAY)/365.25
   b. @TODAY-BIRTHDAY
   c. (@INT-BIRTHDAY)/TODAY
   d. (@TODAY-BIRTHDAY)/365.25
   e. BIRTHDAY-@TODAY

DESIGNING AND IMPLEMENTING AN APPLICATION

OBJECTIVES

This chapter describes how to design and build a Windows application with ObjectVision from the ground up. While Chapter 2 introduced you to a prebuilt application, this chapter actively involves you in the process of creating an application that incorporates many of the powerhouse features provided by ObjectVision. In this chapter you will learn the following:

- *The basic design guidelines for effective form layout*

- *Why it is important to build a prototype and to check the flow of a form from a user perspective*

- *How to select and place fields and other objects on the form*

- *How to modify objects' attributes to affect display form and enforce data range limits*

- *What roles value and event trees play in a form and how to attach them to objects*

- *How buttons can provide simple controls for a user and how to select and customize them*

OVERVIEW

This chapter explains an application from its design to its initial prototype to its completion. First we ensure that the application's goals and objectives are precise and list several important questions that must be answered before moving on. Next we examine important form layout guidelines, which help to avoid forms that look too cluttered, intimidating, or are in other ways counterproductive. Once these guidelines are understood, we discuss selection and placement of information objects on the form. Here we use ObjectVision to select fields, text, lines, and other objects. We begin to construct the form carefully as we work through the chapter.

After objects are in place on the form, their individual properties are modified to suit our needs. Decision trees, both value and event, are added to selected objects, and we add a button to the form. Some of the many ObjectVision built-in functions are described, as they are most often used in the logic of decision trees. You will see how simply and elegantly these work to enhance the application. Keeping our end users in mind, we add both object-specific and general help to the application.

After you have finished reading this chapter, you will know how to create a complete, useful form. Because you are encouraged to create the form as you read, you should have a good understanding of the steps involved in interacting with ObjectVision to create the full-featured form. Central to this chapter is its example application, which is described next.

CASE: FACULTY INFORMATION FORM

You are employed by the Academic Computing Department of a small, private university, the University of San Diego. Currently, information about faculty and staff is kept on a minicomputer. However, access to the remote minicomputer is not convenient. Moreover, faculty information displayed by the computer is far too detailed and cumbersome. The provost has asked you to perform two major tasks. First, you are to move the faculty information from the minicomputer to a microcomputer based system—a local area network. Second, and more importantly, you are asked to design a Windows-based application that allows selected users to display and update faculty information. The application should be attractive, intuitive, and easy to use.

Your first goal is to design a form that contains a subset of the information required by the administration. Once the prototype form has been approved, you can proceed to design the form's logic, add other forms as needed, and finally link the form to the newly downloaded faculty database system. For the present, you concentrate on developing a single form system. Later, you will develop other forms and link the application to a database.

3.1 INTRODUCTION

Designing an application system that will be both useful and acceptable to the user population is a goal that you, the application developer, should establish from a project's inception. The egocentric design style of the past has given way to a sincere desire to accommodate skills and needs of end users. This section outlines some important points to consider as you create a new application.

Both form and function are equally important in a form-based application's success. A wonderfully complete application satisfying the functional requirements will fail miserably if the information is cluttered and difficult to extract. Correspondingly, a pleasant form with well-placed fields and a generally pleasant appearance will not pass users' acceptance tests if crucial information is absent or difficult to locate. Though you are not expected to be a screen design expert, you can greatly increase your application's chances for success if you keep the end users and their needs in mind. One of the most important ways to ensure that you are solving the end users' information needs is to involve selected users early and often in the project. The following are some important points to bear in mind.

- Never forget the users' needs. Frequently ask yourself "Is this design directly and effectively providing a solution for my target audience?"
- Actively involve the user in the initial design specification and repeatedly seek user feedback on your design.
- Both form and function are important in any software application, but especially so in a Windows-based application.
- Produce a prototype of the application quickly to allow the user an early glimpse of the application as you envision it.
- Consider how much latitude users will be allowed when they enter information into the form.
- Make sure sufficient on-line help is available for the intended audience. Sophisticated users need less help and are annoyed when it gets in the way. Novices need quite a bit more help.
- Survey the users periodically, once the application is in place, to ascertain their likes and dislikes. (You may wish to seek the help of professionals in writing the survey instrument.)

An important part of the application design process is the design of the form itself. After all, the applications interface—a form for those designing with Object-Vision—is a user's major contact with the application. A highly sophisticated application is given low marks if the human interface (the form) is difficult to use. Screen design minimally involves the following processes:

- Determine what information should appear on each form (and, what should not!).

- Establish the fundamental format(s) of the selected information fields.
- Decide where to position the objects on a form.
- Produce a prototype as quickly as possible (limited functionality).
- Have a representative end-user group evaluate your design and refine it if necessary.

The next section discusses one of the preceding aspects of design, object placement on a form.

3.2 FORM LAYOUT GUIDELINES

Two important metrics used to judge a screen or form's design are its aesthetics and its usability. Aesthetics is a subjective measure of the overall visual appeal of a form. Usability refers to how easy it is for a user to maneuver through the form or forms. A form with high marks in usability should be easy for a user to grasp quickly. Additionally, a form should allow a user to understand implicitly how to proceed through it. Following a few suggestions for good layout will help you design attractive, intuitive, and visually appealing forms.

Place important information in the upper left corner of a form. The western world reads top down, left to right. Similarly, we are accustomed to scanning screens beginning in the upper left corner. Our eyes generally move from upper left corner to lower right. Because of that flow pattern the upper left corner takes on heightened significance and is a good place to position important information such as a customer's last name or a client's identification number. Similarly, the lower right corner is a natural location for any final or "continue" instructions. It is where we look just before turning a book's page.

Dividing the screen into separate logical horizontal and vertical zones enhances a screen's readability and contributes to its usability. When using multiple forms in an application, consider placing certain types of information in the same part of the screen. A user then knows, in advance, what types of information to expect in particular part of a form for subsequent forms of an application. That shortens an end user's learning time, and the user becomes familiar with an application more quickly.

Careful use of color can contribute to the aesthetics and usability of a form. Generally, hot and warm colors (red, yellow, orange) attract a user's eyes more readily than do cool ones (brown, blue, green). Cool colors serve well in background areas, while warmer colors draw the user's attention and are good choices for foreground items. Above all, do not use too many colors or garish color combinations, because either will tend to distract the end user. The message will be lost in a sea of color!

Text should be a mixture of uppercase and lowercase letters. Capital letters appear to shout at the reader. Use fonts sparingly. Your choice of typeface (fonts) depends on several factors, such as the intended audience and the type of information in the form, and can be used to enhance your message. However, limit the number of fonts appearing on a single form to two or three. Any more than that can be distracting and may clutter the form.

The preceding are some of the most important form layout considerations. A business often has additional rules about the appearance and placement of company logos and other rules affecting the design of your application's forms. Be sure to adhere to any company policies that may affect both layout and privacy issues before building the application.

3.3 BUILDING A PROTOTYPE FORM

Recall that in designing a prototype form you must consider what information is required on the form, what format should be used to display the information, and where various fields should be placed. Once those decisions are made, you can produce a prototype and subsequently have it evaluated by the end users. First we will examine what information is required.

Talking to your end users (customers, clients) is one of the simplest and most direct ways to determine their information needs. After interviewing several of them, you can determine a common subset of information. The initial prototype form for our case study should contain the faculty information fields: last name, first name, department or administrative unit, phone number, office number, academic rank (such as Assistant Professor). It should also contain the six confidential fields that only selected people should be able to view: birth date, hire date, tenure date (or empty if not tenured), annual salary, gender, and years of service. You anticipate that you can later add other information on other forms, including a list of courses taught by each faculty member. However, that can wait until the basic form is designed, prototyped, and approved by your users.

The sections that follow lead you, step by step, through an example of creating a prototype form—rapid prototyping—that can be evaluated early in its development by the end-user audience. First we launch ObjectVision, create a new form, and place fields on the form.

3.4 CREATING A NEW FORM

Before we begin creating our first application, it is important to examine several key features of a form. Figure 3.1 illustrates these features.

The application title bar displays the ObjectVision program name followed by the **file name** of the application on which you are working. If you are creating a new form the file name is "Untitled" and is enclosed in parentheses. On either end of the title bar are buttons described later. The menu bar is located below the

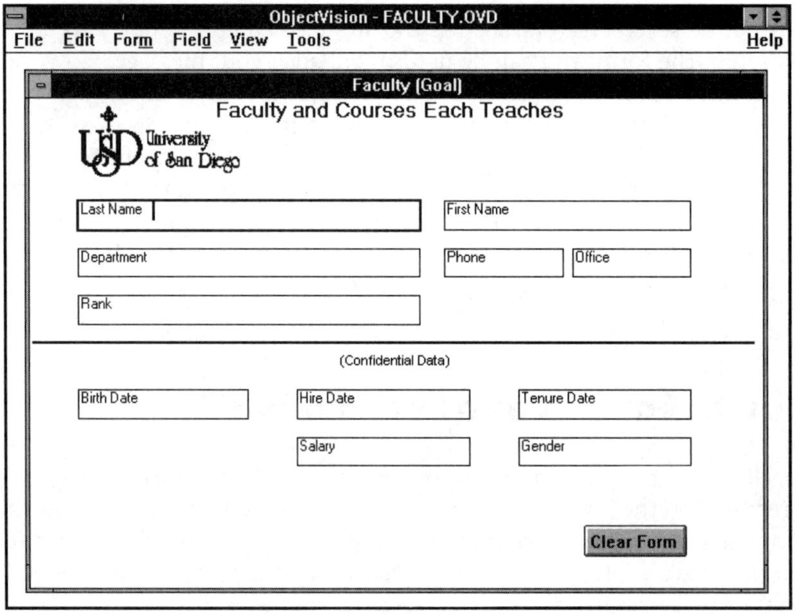

FIGURE 3.1
ObjectVision application and one form

title bar. The form is found inside the ObjectVision window below the menu bar. At the top is the form name, "Faculty," and its status, "Goal," enclosed in parentheses. There are four possible form *modes*, or status conditions, and the current mode is indicated to the right of a form's name. The four modes are complete, edit, goal, and prompt.

- **Complete mode** indicates that all fields and table objects of the application have values.

- **Edit mode** means that you are using the Tools|Form commands. This mode is used to design applications.

- **Goal mode** is assigned to the top form in a stack comprising an application. It is the form that the application user completes.

- **Prompt mode** occurs when a value is required from a field located in a form other than the current one. When that occurs, the form containing the required field is displayed, and the form is given the prompt status. If the field is not found in *any* of the application's forms, then a Scratchpad form is displayed that prompts the user for the required value. Once the missing value is entered, the original form is redisplayed with its "Goal" mode.

For convenience and simplicity, we will frequently use the term *design mode* in place of edit mode because an application programmer or developer is designing a form. Similarly, we will often use the term *browse mode* to refer to any of the other three modes—complete, goal, or prompt—that can be invoked by a user. When necessary in various examples, we will distinguish which mode of the three is applicable.

Application developers create applications by first entering design (edit) mode. Unlike end users who operate strictly in browse mode, you can create, erase, and size objects, assign object characteristics, and invoke the entire range of ObjectVision commands. Application users may *use* your completed applications, but they cannot alter them with the runtime version of ObjectVision. This custom, royalty-free form of ObjectVision lacks a crucial menu and associated special commands that allow entry into design mode. This book examines application development from the developer's viewpoint, and thus assumes you have access to the standard version of ObjectVision.

After starting Windows, invoke ObjectVision by double clicking its icon. Next click the Maximize button located on the top right corner of the Object-Vision window. That will enlarge the window to fill the screen. Next enter design mode by clicking the Tools menu and then selecting the Form command. By convention, that command sequence is indicated with the notation "Tools|Form." If you were editing an existing form, you would *not* select Tools|Form. You would instead load the application you wish to modify by selecting the File menu. Then you would click the Open command. This frequently used method is presented in detail later.

SIZING A NEW FORM

Because the application and thus a form is new, ObjectVision displays the Form Name dialog box shown in Figure 3.2 when you click the Form command. The form name "Faculty" is entered. When the name is complete, click OK or press Enter. The Faculty form appears as a somewhat small rectangle in the Object-Vision window. Its size can be altered to accommodate the objects you want to appear and can be larger than the screen. When you choose Tools|Form, the Form Tool *object bar* is displayed. It appears just below the menu bar and provides quick, one-click access to actions otherwise available on the menu bar.

You will probably want to enlarge the form before working on it. You can reduce or enlarge the size of a form by dragging any of its borders with the mouse. For example, you can drag a left or right border to increase or decrease a form's width. Likewise, you can change a form's height by dragging the top or bottom borders. A form's height and width can both be changed at once by positioning the pointer in a corner of a form. When the pointer changes to a double-headed arrow, drag the form's corner to change both dimensions simultaneously. Figure 3.3 shows a form being enlarged by dragging its corner. The shadowlike border suggests the new form size when the mouse button is released.

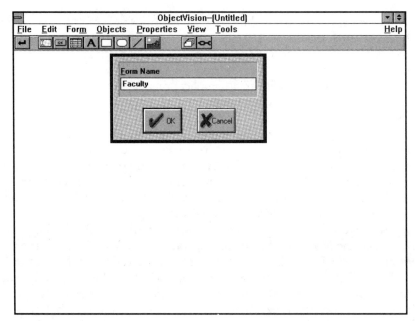

FIGURE 3.2
Entering the new form's name on the Form Name dialog box

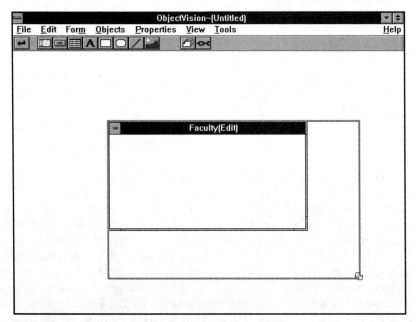

FIGURE 3.3
Enlarging the form by dragging a corner

The corner-dragging method expands a form only to the size of the screen. That may not be large enough for your application. To extend a form beyond the constraints of the computer screen, place an object in it and extend that object *beyond* the form window. As you do so, the form expands to accommodate the object. We will see just how to do this later.

Examine the object bar shown in Figure 3.3. As we saw in Chapter 1, the object bar contains the Return icon on the left, followed by eight object icons. To the right of these icons are the Stack icon and the Links icon. The eight objects provide a quick way to select any of the eight ObjectVision objects and place them on a form. They are, left to right, field, button, table, text, filled rectangle, rounded rectangle, line, and graphic. The meaning of the eight objects as well as the Stack and Links icons is summarized in Table 3.1.

TABLE 3.1
Object bar icons and their meanings

Object Bar Icon	Description
Field	An object that can receive an input value.
Button	An object that can cause an action to occur when clicked.
Table	An object with one or more columns and one or more rows that can receive input values. Each column can act as one object of a set of related objects.
Text	An object comprising one or more text characters. This object cannot be altered by a user. It can label forms or areas within a form.
Filled Rectangle	An object that enhances the appearance of a form. It cannot receive any input values, and it cannot be altered.
Rounded Rectangle	An object that is identical to the filled rectangle, except that its corners are rounded.
Line	An object that creates a straight line in a form.
Graphic	An object that is created by some other means and imported into a form. It cannot be modified by a user.
Return	Not an object; it closes design (edit) mode and returns to browse mode.
Stack	Not an object; when clicked it enters the Stack Tool. It subsequently displays the application stack, which lists an application's forms, their names, and their relative order in the stack.
Links	Not an object; when clicked it opens the Link Tool, which allows you to establish connections between a form's fields and table columns and database data files.

USING THE RULER AND CHOOSING A GRID SIZE

You can use ObjectVision's built-in ruler to size a form exactly. Both a horizontal and a vertical ruler are available in design mode. The three calibrations you can choose are inches, centimeters, and characters (the default metric). Displaying the ruler inside a form is easy. First be sure you are in design mode (execute the Form command in the Tools menu) and then follow the steps listed below.

1. Select View | Ruler (View menu, Ruler command) from the menu bar. The Ruler Preferences dialog box, shown in Figure 3.4, appears.

2. Check the Top and Left boxes to place a ruler in the top and left of the form (either or both can be selected).

3. For inches, check the Inches box.

4. Click OK to complete the ruler display process. Otherwise, click Cancel to abort.

Having rulers displayed in the form can be helpful when you want to align objects on the same mark. As you will see later, any selected object's dimensions are indicated by a shadow on the ruler. Aligning objects and standardizing their lengths is much easier with rulers. When finished with either or both rulers, simply invoke View | Ruler again and uncheck the ruler choices. During development, it is preferred to have rulers available.

When you place objects on a form, they can be moved in discrete increments on an invisible **grid**. When you place an object on a form, it will "snap" to the closest grid points. There are three levels of grid granularity: coarse, medium, and fine. Coarse, the default, is a grid whose points are one character apart. The medium grid points are one-half character apart, and the fine grid points are one-quarter character (both horizontally and vertically) apart. It is usually best to leave the grid at its default coarse setting until you want to put the fine, finishing touches on a form. It is more difficult, for instance, to align objects when the fine grid is active, as the differences in positions are measured in one-quarter characters and are almost imperceptible.

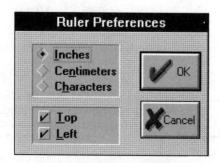

FIGURE 3.4
Ruler Preferences dialog box

FIGURE 3.5
Grid Style dialog box

Change the grid setting by selecting the Grid command in the View menu (View|Grid). Then select the appropriate grid size by clicking one of the radio-style buttons (called *radio* because "pushing" one button "pops out" any other button that might be pushed in at the time—just like radio station selection buttons). Figure 3.5 shows the Grid Style dialog box. As with other ObjectVision dialog boxes, click OK to confirm your choices and leave the dialog box.

CREATING A FIELD

Fields are one of the two objects that accept input from the user. The other object is a table. Fields are one of the main form-building block objects, and adding them to a form is straightforward. Because adding a field is a design activity, not something an application user would want to do, you must be in design (edit) mode to select a new field (choose Tools|Form to enter design mode). There are two equivalent ways to select a field: either select Field from the Objects menu on the menu bar or select the Field icon from the object bar. The steps are summarized next.

1. Make sure you are in edit mode.
2. Click the Field icon found on the object bar. (The default field name is shown in the Field Name dialog box.) See Figure 3.6.
3. Type the name of the field, including spaces and other special characters, in place of the suggested default name. For our example, enter the field name Last Name and then click OK. The arrow pointer changes to a crosshair with a miniature Field icon to the right and below it (the Field cursor).
4. Move the Field cursor where you want the field to be. Do that by positioning its upper left corner. Click and then drag the cursor to where you want the lower right corner of the field. Notice that the field's perimeter is dotted and there are handles at the field's corners. Figure 3.7 shows the Last Name field being placed on the form. Notice we make use of the rulers to place the field.

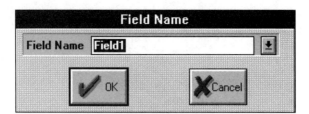

FIGURE 3.6
Field Name dialog box

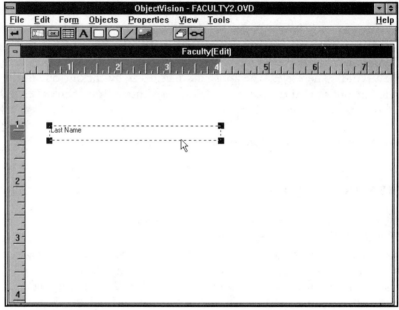

FIGURE 3.7
Positioning a field

Repeat the previous four steps to add the following fields: First Name, Department, Phone, Office, and Rank. Figure 3.8 shows an example of the form after the six fields are created. Their exact position is not significant. However, their relative position *is* important. The Last Name field should be the first, upper left field.

Sizing a Field

A field can be resized in edit mode, only. Select the field you want to resize (click on it) so that the four handles appear. When the arrow pointer is sufficiently close to one of the field handles, it changes to a black square resembling a handle. Click and drag the field handle to change its size in any direction. A field's size will "snap" to the nearest grid coordinates when you release the mouse button.

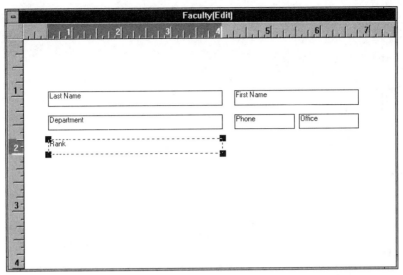

FIGURE 3.8
Six fields of the Faculty form in place

A field's size determines how much information it can hold. To see if a field is long enough, switch back into browse mode and enter digits until you can enter no more. If there is not enough space, then switch to edit mode and lengthen the field to accommodate more characters. In addition, the selected font for a field affects how many digits it can hold. A Helvetica 14 point font occupies more space per character than a Times Roman 10 point font. That means, for a given size field, a Helvetica 14 point font field will hold fewer characters than the same field with a 10 point font. Fonts are selected via the property inspector described later. Remember these points (ha!) when you size fields and establish their positions.

Moving a Field

Fields can easily be rearranged on a form. To move a field, first select it by clicking the left mouse button. When the four handles appear, position the arrow pointer inside the field and then click and drag it to the new location. As you move it, the arrow changes to a crosshair and the field handles disappear temporarily. Be sure to not drag a handle, as that will resize the field but will not move it.

CHECKING A FORM'S DATA INPUT FLOW

It is important to leave design mode periodically and check the form for functionality and suitability from the end user's perspective. That way, you can always check that your form design is on target and will serve your users well. One important consideration is the data input flow inherent in your form—the natural path from field to field that is followed when a user inputs data. This data

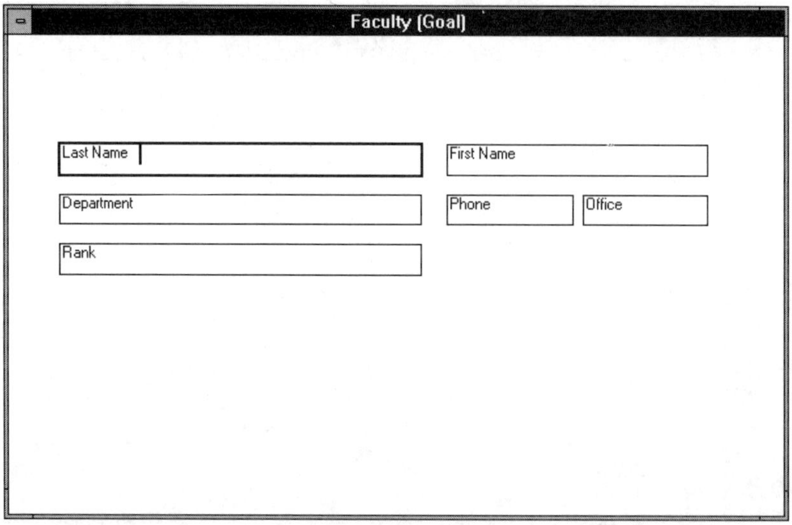

FIGURE 3.9
Checking information flow in Goal mode

input flow can be natural and comfortable, or it can be awkward and counterintuitive. As a form developer, always strive for the former.

You can check the default order in which fields are visited by ObjectVision's guided completion by entering goal mode (press the Enter icon on the object bar or execute the Close Tool command of the File menu). Then move to the first selected field by executing the Edit|Clear All command. Then execute the Resume command of the File menu (File|Resume) before entering data. Edit|Clear All clears the form of any residual data that might be in fields. File|Resume places the cursor at the first entry point of the form. Figure 3.9 shows the cleared form with the input cursor in the first of several fields to be entered. Your form should look approximately like the one shown.

Enter a value in the Last Name field and press Enter to follow the input flow. You see that the First Name field is selected next. Enter information for this field and press Enter. Continue this way for each of the remaining fields and be sure that the field selection order is satisfactory and natural. If it is not, then fields can be rearranged to facilitate a specific entry order. Recall that guided completion is based, in part, on the location of the lower right corner of each field and proceeds from upper left to lower right based on that corner of each field.

ADDING TEXT, LINE, AND GRAPHICS OBJECTS

Text, lines, and graphics can enhance the appearance of a form and provide helpful visual cues to those using your forms. Each of these objects is described next.

Text Objects

Text can be used to label a form, an area of a form, or provide helpful instructions to users. Text objects are different from field labels and are not associated with fields, tables, or any other objects. Furthermore, text objects cannot be altered or filled in by a user as can fields. There are a wide variety of fonts and text display characteristics from which to choose for text objects. Fonts available depend on those installed in Windows on your machine.

Text can be used in lieu of field labels if you want more control over their placement. A field label is displayed in one place in a field. You cannot, for example, choose to place the field label above the field or to its right. However, you can use text labels to accomplish that goal—field label placement choices. To do so, suppress the Field Label display (one of the properties of a field discussed later) and then select a text object. Type whatever text you would like to place near the field and then position it anywhere near or in the field that suits you.

We will use a single text object in our faculty example to label the Faculty form. We can place an attractive title near the top of the form that indicates the form's use. Insert a title on the top of the form by following the sequence below.

1. Select (click) the Text icon from the object bar (see Figure 3.10).

2. Type in the desired text in the Text Value dialog box, then press Enter or click OK when the text is correct. If you want to move to a new line, press Ctrl-Enter (hold Ctrl and tap the Enter key). If you simply press Enter, then the dialog box closes (see Figure 3.11).

Text icon

FIGURE 3.10
The Text icon on the object bar

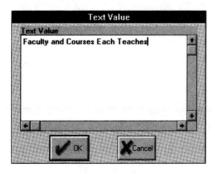

FIGURE 3.11
Text Value dialog box

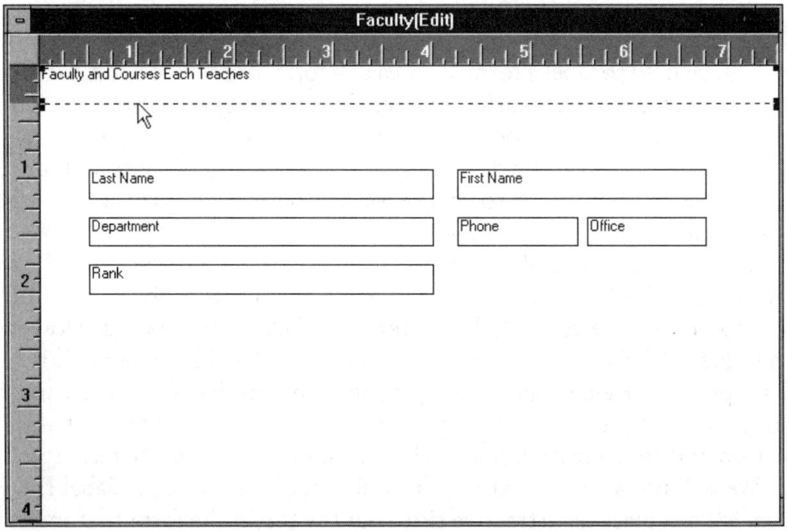

FIGURE 3.12
Sized text on the form

3. Position the special text cursor so that the crosshair is in the upper left corner of the form and click the left mouse button. Notice that as you position the Text icon, vertical and horizontal lines appear on the ruler (if present) to indicate the precise location of the text's upper left corner.

4. Resize the text as desired, using any of the four handles appearing at the four corners. You can move the text by simply dragging it anywhere but at the corners. For maximum visibility, we stretch the text box so that it is full length (about 7.5 inches long if you use the ruler) and one-quarter inch high (see Figure 3.12).

The text font size really is not correct. It should be larger and, perhaps, bolder. We will make both font and style changes to the text later in this chapter. For now, focus on simply placing objects on the form.

Line Objects

You can use lines to separate parts of a form or to give it a more interesting appearance. To draw a horizontal line across a form, follow these steps:

1. Click the Line icon located on the object bar (see Figure 3.13). The line cursor is displayed: a small crosshair with the Line icon to the right.

2. Move the icon to the left margin so that the crosshair is opposite the 2.25 inch mark on the vertical ruler.

3. Drag the crosshair to the right margin (to the 7.5 inch mark on the vertical ruler). Make sure the line is straight and spans the entire form from left to right. Release the left mouse button.

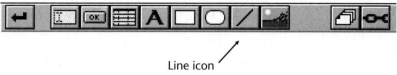

Line icon

FIGURE 3.13
The Line icon on the object bar

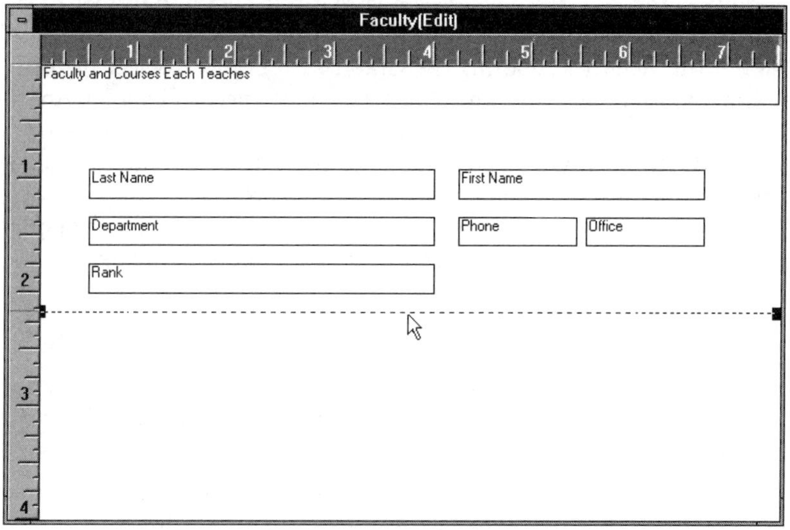

FIGURE 3.14
Horizontal line with handles

A dashed line resembling that shown in Figure 3.14 appears between the line handles. Like field handles, they can be used to shorten or lengthen the line. In addition, you can drag one of the handles to change the line's orientation (to a vertical line, for example).

Graphic Objects

ObjectVision forms can include graphic files produced from a variety of programs. The graphic types that can be incorporated include:

- Windows bitmap files: A Windows bitmap file, which has the secondary file name of .BMP, can be created in Paintbrush or in other Windows graphics applications.

- Windows metafiles: When you use other Windows programs that save files in the bitmap format (the files have the secondary file name .BMP), you can copy them to the Windows Clipboard. Files copied to the Clipboard are automatically converted to a special metafile format. These files have the file name extension of .WMF and can be used by ObjectVision.

- ObjectVision graphic files: These files have a secondary file name of .OVG and can be imported into an ObjectVision form.

Images can be either monochrome or color. When printed, ObjectVision prints an image that is consistent with your printer.

You can add a graphic to your form to dress it up or perhaps add a bit of flash. To add a metafile or bitmap graphic to an ObjectVision form, first copy it to the Windows Clipboard (this process converts it to a common format that Object-Vision can accept). Then place the object from the Clipboard into an Object-Vision form by either choosing the Graphic icon on the object bar or selecting the Graphic command from the Objects menu (Objects|Graphic). Another way to incorporate graphics into a form is to use Window's Object Linking and Embedding (OLE) facility. The advantages of using this alternate technique to incorporate graphics are beyond the scope of this text.

The following steps illustrate how to incorporate a Paintbrush graphic image into a form—in particular, into the Faculty form we are developing.

Create a Paintbrush graphic:

1. Open the Program Manager's Accessories group. Double click the Paintbrush icon to open it. The Paintbrush window displays. Click the Maximize button to fill the screen.

2. Use any of the Paintbrush tools to create a "painting"—your own Rembrandt. (We use the Airbrush, Paint Roller, and Brush tools to create a facsimile of the University of San Diego logo.)

Place the graphic on the Windows Clipboard:

3. Click the Pick Tool icon and drag the selection "rubber band" to enclose the graphic.

4. Choose Edit|Copy. This copies the enclosed image to the Clipboard.

5. Save the image only if you want to modify or change it later. Otherwise, simply exit Paintbrush (File|Exit).

Place the graphic into the ObjectVision form:

6. Open ObjectVision, making it the current window on the work surface. Make sure the form is in design mode, if necessary (select the Form Tool).

7. Choose Objects|Graphic or click the Graphic icon found on the object bar. Enter dialog box displays (see Figure 3.15). Click Yes to indicate you want to import the graphic from the Clipboard.

8. The Save Clipboard Graphic As dialog box appears in which you specify the .OVG file name under which the graphic is to be saved. Enter any name of your choice—for example, enter USDLOGO.OVG as we have in Figure 3.16—and then press Enter or click OK. The graphic is named and saved.

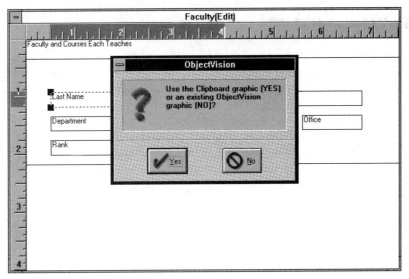

FIGURE 3.15
Use Clipboard Graphic dialog box

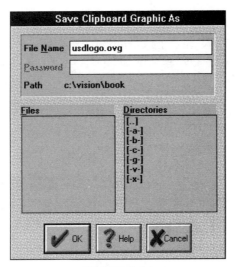

FIGURE 3.16
Save Clipboard Graphic As dialog box

9. The graphic crosshair pointer appears. Position the graphic in the upper left corner of the ObjectVision form and click to place it permanently. The graphic appears.

10. To resize the graphic, drag any of the four handles that appear around it.

A border now surrounds the graphic. Later we will see how to remove the borders.

3.5 SAVING AN APPLICATION

We have designed a good bit of the Faculty form up to this point. Now is a good time to save the partially complete application so that we have a copy on disk. It is always a good idea periodically to save any in-process applications you have altered. We follow a simple rule: save your work every 15 to 20 minutes. A shorter time interval is probably too much; a longer interval risks losing a lot of work. Your time is too valuable to risk losing the efforts of more than 30 minutes.

You can save an application, which includes all its forms, by executing either the Save or Save As commands found in the File menu. File|Save allows you to save the currently displayed application to the same file name that you specified to open the file. Save As allows you to save the current application to a new or different file name. The previously saved version, if any, remains unchanged. If you save the file with Save As and it already exists, a dialog box appears asking you whether or not you wish to overwrite the existing file.

To save the current application with the file name Faculty (all ObjectVision applications are given the secondary name OVD automatically when they are saved), execute the following steps:

1. Execute File|Save. Because the file has never been saved before on disk, the Save File As dialog box is displayed in which you enter a file name (see Figure 3.17). Notice the current path shown is c:\vision, and the File Name box displays a generic file name in reverse video. Whenever an item in any text box is shown in reverse video, it is completely replaced when you type the first letter.

2. Move the mouse pointer to the Directories box and double click the directory, [sample]. The current path changes to c:\vision\sample, and the File Name is no longer in reverse video.

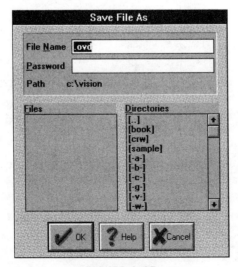

FIGURE 3.17
Save File As dialog box

3. Type the new file name in the File Name text box: `Faculty`. Then press Enter or click OK to complete the file-saving process.

The file is saved with the file name FACULTY.OVD. The ObjectVision title bar also displays the new file name.

3.6 MODIFYING OBJECTS' PROPERTIES

You may want to change the appearance or other characteristics of various objects for aesthetic reasons. The objects we have created so far (fields, text, a graphic, and a line) have taken on default characteristics, called **properties**, which govern how they look. In addition, some properties assigned only to fields also control what information may be entered into the fields (see Figures 2.6, 2.7, and 2.8). ObjectVision provides default settings for the properties of each type of object. These default settings are automatically established for objects you create. Of course, you may change the settings for individual objects by selecting the object and then clicking the right mouse button. A list of the object's alterable properties is displayed by the property inspector (for example, see Figure 2.10). Of course, forms and stacks also have properties which you may set.

This section describes how to change selected properties of the objects we have placed on our Faculty form. We discuss how to change default object properties at the end of this section. First we learn how to change a text object's properties.

ALTERING TEXT PROPERTIES

Text objects have a number of properties that can be changed. At the top of our Faculty form is the text label "Faculty and Courses Each Teaches" (see Figure 3.14). It is surrounded by a thin border, and the text is a bit too small and anemic. Furthermore, we would like the form title to be centered on the form. To inspect and change these properties first load the application you recently saved (it is called FACULTY.OVD). Make sure you are in edit mode (execute Tools|Form, if not) and then select the text title. Invoke the property inspector by clicking the right mouse button or execute the Object command in the Properties menu (Properties|Object). A list of properties associated with text objects appears (see Figure 3.18).

First change the text alignment so that it is centered in the text box: choose Alignment (click it). The Field Value Alignment dialog box appears. Four alignment check boxes are displayed: Left, Right, Center, and Justified. Select the Center check box and press Enter or click OK. The property inspector disappears, and the title is now centered.

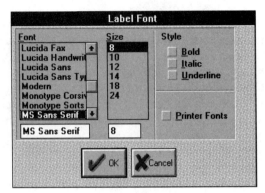

FIGURE 3.18
Text properties

FIGURE 3.19
Label Font dialog box

Next we will enlarge the text so that it is a bit easier to read. Invoke the property inspector once again (right click the Text object). To enlarge the text, select Label Font. A list of available typefaces and styles appears in the Label Font dialog box (see Figure 3.19). Typefaces from which you can choose are found in the Font box, and font sizes for each typeface are displayed in the Size box. Pick a font such as MS Sans Serif and select a size of 12 points or larger. Also check the Bold check box to emphasize the title. Click OK to finalize these selections.

Here is a well-hidden fact about ObjectVision text type sizes: You may specify a wide variety of font sizes—more than are indicated in the Label Font dialog box. Point sizes from 4 to 127 can be specified for most fonts. For instance, three font sizes are listed in the Label Font dialog box when you select Courier: 10, 12, and 15. However, you can select from a range of point sizes by typing a value from 4 (very small) to 127 (you can see it from a satellite) in the Size text box. Experiment with these sizes. Select a text typeface and then manually enter a font size and press Enter. Keep trying until you find a size that pleases you.

The last change to the title is to remove its border. A border appears around text objects by default, although we will see how to alter this global default. Invoke the property inspector once more and select Borders. A Borders dialog box appears with five, self-evident choices (see Figure 3.20). Notice that Outline is currently selected. Deselect Outline by clicking it and press Enter to remove the border.

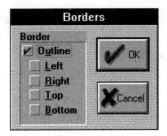

FIGURE 3.20
Borders dialog box

Other text characteristics that can be changed are color, line width (for border lines), and the text itself with the Name/Text option. The event tree property does not affect the appearance of text. Rather, it assigns an action to an object. These actions are described in Section 3.7.

CHANGING LINE PROPERTIES

Only two properties are associated with a line: color and width. As it now appears, the line is a bit too thin. Change its width by selecting the line and right clicking it. The two properties choices Color and Line Width are displayed. Click Line Width to see the choices.

The current line width is enclosed in a rectangle. In our case, the thinnest line is selected. There are four line thickness choices. Make the line somewhat thicker by selecting the second thinnest line by clicking it (a rectangle will surround your choice). Press Enter or click OK to confirm your choice. The line now appears less anemic and is better for separating the top half of the form from the bottom.

You could also change the color of the line by selecting the Color property and then clicking on one of several available colors in the palette. Remember, however, that the color will be translated to a shade of gray on a monochrome printer or screen.

CHANGING GRAPHIC PROPERTIES

Recall that we incorporated a graphic into the upper left corner of the Faculty form. We created it using Paintbrush and subsequently copied it to the form via the Windows Clipboard. The graphic you created and placed on the form is surrounded by a border that can be removed if you desire. Three properties are associated with a graphic: color, borders, and line width. To change one of these, click on the graphic while still in design or edit mode and invoke the property inspector with the right mouse button. The Borders dialog box (see Figure 3.20) appears, and you can uncheck the Outline choice to remove the border surrounding the graphic. Press OK to go back to design mode. Figure 3.21 shows our Faculty

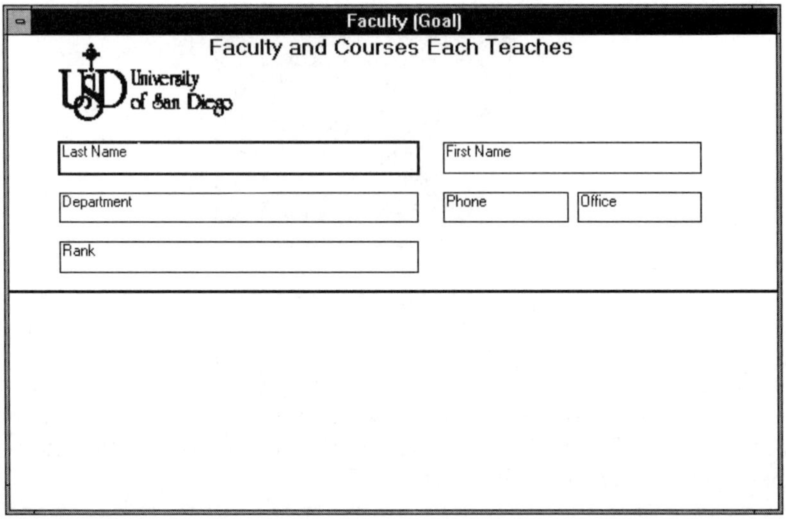

FIGURE 3.21
Faculty form after changing selected properties

form (with the USD logo graphic) after making the preceding changes to the text
title, line, and graphic.

CHANGING SELECTED FIELD PROPERTIES

In all likelihood, you will want to customize the properties assigned to Object-
Vision fields. There are 11 properties that may be set for fields in addition to
specifying either a value tree or an event tree for fields. Like other objects, field
properties are set by selecting a field and right clicking the mouse. Here are the
field properties that can be set: field type, alignment, label font, value font, color,
borders, line width, protection, field, name/text, and help. Table 2.5 contains a
list of objects and the properties that can be set for each. The property inspector
displays the preceding properties, and Figure 2.10 shows an example of that property list. Few properties are altered in the Faculty example. Most are left at their
ObjectVision default values. However, some are different. The following is a
summary of the field properties specifically set for selected fields.

All fields have the same label and value fonts: label fonts are 12 point MS
Sans Serif, and value fonts are 12 point Courier. Only the Field Type and Help
properties vary from their default settings. Last Name, First Name, and Department fields are character strings, and their field types remain the default, General. However Phone, Office, and Rank are different. Each type is described next.

The Phone field holds an internal number that can be dialed without the
usual prefix if dialed on campus. That field is therefore restricted to four digits
(not four characters, but digits). Constraining the input values is easy. Right click

the Phone field to display its properties and then select Field Type from the list. Then do the following:

1. In the Field Type dialog box, check the Picture check box and click OK. That constrains the input to a fixed type and length.

2. The Picture String dialog appears. Enter the picture #### and press OK. Wherever a pound sign appears in the picture string, a digit—and only a digit—can be entered. Because there are four pound signs, only four digits can be input for the Phone field.

The Office field is similar to the Phone field except only three digits can be entered. Repeat for the Office field the process above to set the input type to three digits (enter only three pound signs in the Picture String dialog box).

Rank is a field whose values are limited to four choices in our example. From the least to the greatest, they are Instructor, Assistant Professor, Associate Professor, and Professor. A special field type called a **selection list** is ideal for this type of situation. When a selection list is encountered as the form is being completed, a drop-down list of the possible choices is displayed. A small number of possible choices is available (and each choice should be spelled correctly). Setting up a list of allowed choices frees the user from typing. A user simply clicks on one of the four allowed values for rank and the Rank field is filled in. Set up the Rank field this way (make sure you are in edit mode):

1. Select the Rank field and right click the mouse to display the properties.

2. Click Field Type.

3. Check the Selection List found in the Selection Method column of the Field Type dialog box and click OK. The Expected List dialog box is displayed (see Figure 3.22).

4. Enter the rank Instructor and click OK to add it to the list.

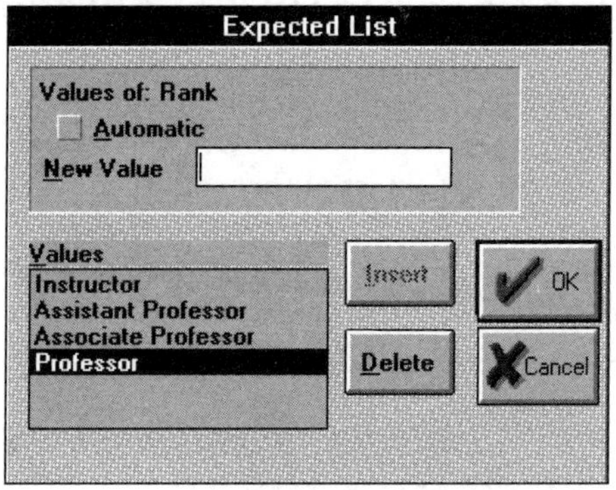

FIGURE 3.22
Expected List dialog box

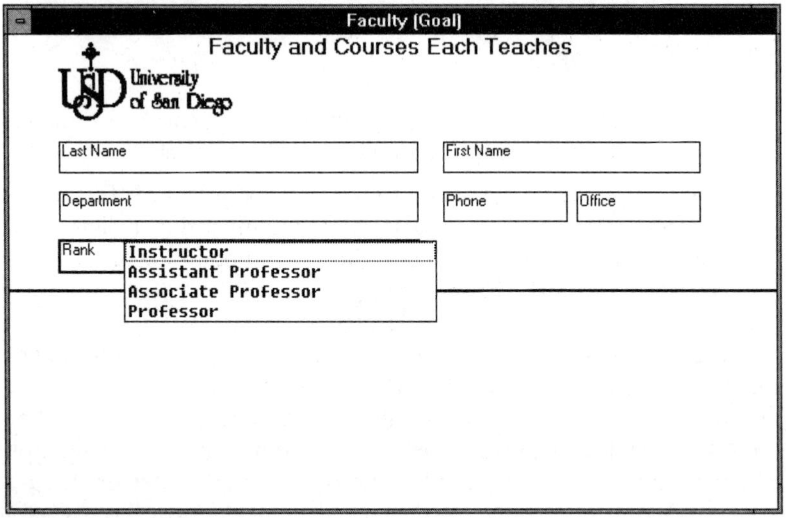

FIGURE 3.23
Selection List field example

5. Repeat step 4, entering each of the following ranks: `Assistant Professor`, `Associate Professor`, and `Professor`. Click OK an additional time to close the Expected List dialog box.

After you set the Rank field to a Selection List type and fill in the allowed list values, it will always display those values in a drop-down list that appears whenever the cursor selects the Rank field. Figure 3.23 shows the field's form when it is selected. Notice the dashed line surrounds the first of the list members. Use the mouse to select a value or use the arrow keys to move the dashed line up and down the list.

ESTABLISHING OBJECT DEFAULT PROPERTIES

If you change the same properties of an object very often, you can save time by changing that object's default properties. Once you establish default properties for an object type, every new object of that same type will have those properties. For example, if most of the field objects you create are numeric, it would save time to set that as the default. You can assign your own default properties to any object on the object bar except a button. Here is one way to redefine object default properties:

1. Click an object bar button, such as Field, with the *right* mouse button. The property inspector appears for that object.

2. Set any new default properties, such as alignment, field type, and color, just as you would for an individual object. Once set, these properties be-

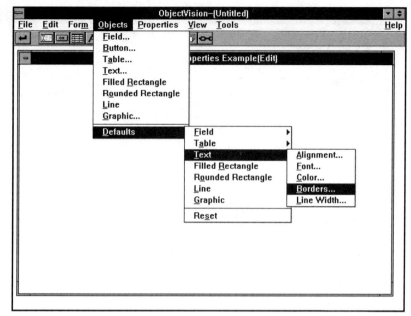

FIGURE 3.24
Changing default properties of an object

come the new defaults for any objects of that type that you create and will remain in effect until changed.

Alternatively, you can set property default values by choosing the Defaults command from the Objects menu (Objects|Defaults). A list is displayed of objects whose properties you can change. Then you can select any object and ObjectVision displays a list of the properties that you can alter. For example, you can create text objects without borders by selecting Text. A list of options, shown in Figure 3.24, appears. Then, select Borders from the list and change the option.

If you find that you want to reset all property values to their original defaults—the way ObjectVision was originally configured—then choose the Defaults command from the Objects menu and select Reset (Objects|Defaults|Reset, see Figure 3.24).

ADDING THE REMAINING FIELDS

To fill out the Faculty form, we need to add six more fields. Because these fields are confidential, they are placed below the line we drew earlier. A small label is placed just below the line indicating the confidential nature of the additional fields: Birth Date, Hire Date, Tenure Date, Gender, Salary, and Years of Service. All of these are assigned custom field types other than the default type. In addition, the Years of Service field will require no manual entry at all because it will be constructed as a calculated field. Here is how to modify the form.

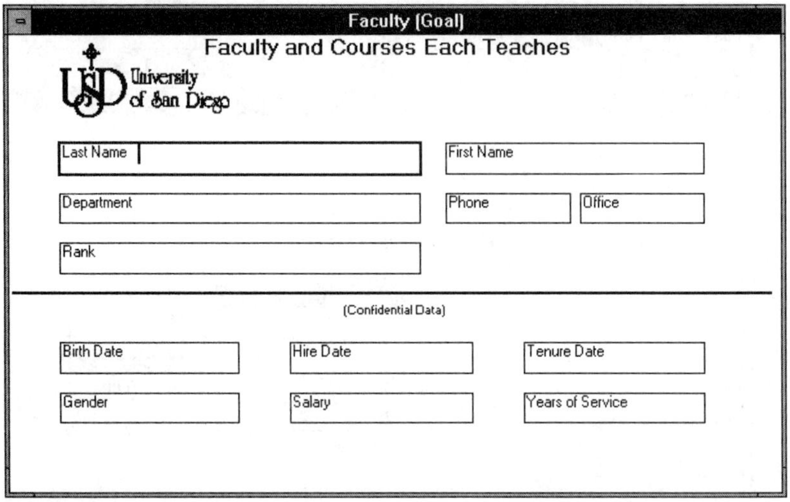

FIGURE 3.25
Faculty form with all fields

First create the text object "(Confidential Data)" and center it, left to right, on the form. A convenient trick to center a text object is to stretch it so that it spans the width of the form; then click the Center check box of the Alignment property. Set the text font to Arial 8 point so that it is not obtrusive.

Next add the six fields to the form:

1. Click the field object on the object bar and name the field appropriately.

2. Size the field to about 1.5 inches long by 0.25 inches high. If you find it difficult to size the field to these exact dimensions, check the Grid Style dialog box (click the View menu to find the Grid command) and make sure that the grid is set to Medium. (A course grid makes it more difficult to fine-tune the position of objects.)

3. Repeat steps 2 and 3 until you have added all six fields.

Figure 3.25 gives an idea of the size and position of these new fields. Use it as a guideline.

Now the formats of the fields (their field type property) can be altered. First change the field types for the three new date fields: Birth Date, Hire Date, and Tenure Date. Each one is changed by following these steps:

1. Select a field and right click the mouse to display the property inspector.

2. Click Field Type on the list.

3. Click the Date/Time radio button in the Field Type dialog box and then click OK. The Date Type dialog box appears.

4. Several date and time forms appear in the list. Select the first one (month/day/year format) and press OK.

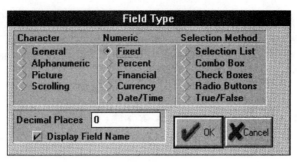

FIGURE 3.26
Field Type dialog box

Fields labeled Gender, Salary, and Years of Service can be assigned new field types. The two choices for gender can be shown in a selection list. Though it is simple for a user to type in "M" or "Male" for instance, a selection list confines a field's values to a standard, consistent set. It is impossible to introduce into a gender field variants in spelling or capitalization if the user is presented a drop-down list of choices from which to select.

Using the steps shown before, change the Gender field type to Selection List and enter the two values F and M (capitalize them so they stand out in the list). Move to the Salary field and set its type to Currency with zero decimal places (whole dollar amounts are sufficient). Then change the Years of Service field to the Fixed data type with zero decimal places. Figure 3.26 shows the Field Type dialog box that appears when you select Field Type from the list displayed by the property inspector.

Years of Service is different from the other fields in the Faculty application in one significant way—it is a calculated field whose value is automatically determined by a formula. Unlike the other fields, users need not supply a value for that field, though they may **override** the calculated value. The next section describes how to create this special property as well as others.

3.7 INCORPORATING DECISION TREES

Chapter 2 introduced you to decision trees, both value trees and event trees. In this section, we add a few of each type to our Faculty application. A value tree will be attached to the Years of Service field so that the field's value can be calculated and displayed. Event trees cause actions to occur in response to trigger events.

An event tree attached to an entire application is called a **stack event tree**. It springs into action whenever an application is opened or closed. Individual forms within a stack can have event trees, called **form event trees**, that cause one or more actions to take place when a form is opened or closed. More frequently, however, event trees are associated with buttons found on individual forms. A labeled button can be clicked with the mouse when needed to perform activities like closing a form, choosing a new record from a database, or clearing a form. We add button and attendant event trees to our form to clear it when necessary. This facilitates retyping information or entering new information. First, however, we will create a value tree.

ADDING A VALUE TREE TO A FIELD

Recall the three sources from which fields can receive their values: user input, a calculation based on other values, or an external link to a stored value. Value trees implement the second way of placing values in fields—by calculating them. Much like a spreadsheet, value trees contain logic that can test conditions and determine which of several alternate values to calculate and display.

Value trees comprise branches, conditions, and conclusions. The branches of a value tree contain the conditional logic, and the "leaves" contain expressions that compute a field's value. In the Faculty application, we have a simple example of a value tree: the Years of Service field. Though an end user could determine how many years an employee has worked for the university, it is not necessary to go through all that work. All the information needed to *calculate* that value either is in the Faculty form or is available from the computer. Years of Service is simply the number of whole years that have elapsed between an employee's hire date and the current date. A formula can be constructed that determines that number by using the Hire Date field value and the current date available from the computer's internal clock. If you are familiar with any of the popular spreadsheet products, then you may know how to write the formula calculating the elapsed years.

Like spreadsheet products, ObjectVision has a large number of **built-in functions** that simplify formula writing. Nearly every function available in popular spreadsheets like Quattro Pro, Lotus 1-2-3, and Excel is also available in ObjectVision. Several additional functions necessary to implement actions and database manipulation are also included in the ObjectVision functions. Fortunately, ObjectVision's names for the most of the functions are the same as their spreadsheet cousins. When a value tree is associated with a field, its value is calculated and displayed as soon as all of the fields it references have values. For example, a value tree attached to Years of Service will display a value only after a user fills in the Hire Date field. The system time, of course, is immediately available and need not be manually supplied. Here is how to build the requisite value tree.

1. Choose Tools | Form if necessary to open the Form Tool.
2. Click the Years of Service field with the right mouse button. That allows you to inspect its properties and change them.
3. Choose Value Tree from the list. The Value tree for Years of Service dialog box appears. The value tree is empty, because we are creating a *new* tree for the field.

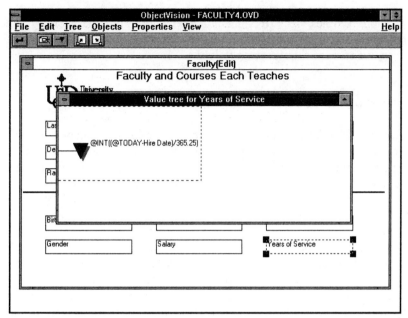

FIGURE 3.27
A simple value tree for Years of Service

4. Click the Conclusion button on the object bar. It is the one that is a tri-angle with a line to its left. The Conclusion for Years of Service dialog box appears.

5. In the dialog box enter the following formula:

   `@INT((@TODAY-Hire Date)/365.25)`

   Press Enter or click OK to indicate the conclusion is complete and can be stored in the value tree. Figure 3.27 shows the dialog box with the completed value tree formula.

6. Double click the control-menu box in the upper left corner of the dialog box to close it and return to the form.

In the formula for the Years of Service value tree, two ObjectVision built-in functions are used, @INT and @TODAY. The @TODAY function in the expression

`(@TODAY-Hire Date)/365.25`

returns the current date. Subtracting from it the Hire Date field value yields the number of elapsed days. Dividing that value by the average number of days in a year gives the number of years (with decimal places) of employment. Finally, the @INT function ensures that any fractional years are discarded, leaving an integer answer (for example, 3.6 years is reduced to 3 complete years of employment). A complete list of ObjectVision built-in functions is given in the Appendix.

More complex value trees, including ones containing decision logic and several alternate conclusion nodes, can be constructed. We will illustrate more complex value trees in chapters that follow.

ADDING A BUTTON TO A FORM

You can add buttons to your form that can cause some action or series of actions to occur. For example, buttons provide a simple way for users to move to another form in an application, store a completed form on disk, or retrieve the next database record. A button object is inanimate until an event tree is attached to it. An event tree gives life to a button by defining actions that are initiated when the button is "pushed." Without an event tree, nothing happens when the button is pushed.

We will add a button to perform a simple task: clear all fields of the Faculty form and return the cursor to the first field. It can be selected when a user wishes to start the form from the beginning due to a large number of errors in various fields. Or, a user might want to restore the form to its original, empty state before saving it on disk. As usual, the form must be in edit mode before you can add a button to it. Follow these steps to add the button object to the Faculty form:

1. Open the Faculty form and then select Tools|Form to place it in edit mode.
2. Click the Button icon on the object bar (or select Button from the Objects menu). The Button Name dialog box appears.
3. Type Clear Form to name the button. It replaces the default name, Button1.
4. Click OK or press Enter to accept the button name. A button crosshair appears.
5. Using the mouse, position the crosshair where you want the upper left corner of the button to be.
6. Click and drag the crosshair to the right and down to where you want the right corner to be. The button should be approximately 1.25 inches long. You can click and drag any handle to resize the button.
7. Click and drag the button to position it in the lower right corner of the Faculty form.

Now we have a button on the form that will be used to clear it. However, it is inert. A nonempty event tree must be attached to the button for it to be functional.

Attaching an Event Tree to a Button

Next we create the event tree that is attached to the Clear Form button in the Faculty form. When pushed, the button and its associated event tree will clear

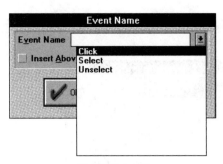

FIGURE 3.28
Event Name dialog box

all fields on the form with an ObjectVision built-in function just made for that purpose: @CLEARALL. Then the form cursor—or focus—will be moved to the first field on the form with another built-in function, @RESUME. These two functions accomplish the same thing as the commands Edit|Clear All and File|Resume, respectively. However, we do not want the user to have to activate those two menu commands manually. They are conveniently packaged into the Clear Form button, so the user need only click it to clear the form.

To create an event tree for a button that is already on the form, do the following:

1. Click the Clear All button on the Faculty form.

2. Right click the mouse button to display the button object properties that may be altered. There are three properties: Event Tree, Name/Text, and Help.

3. Choose Event Tree. An empty event tree for the Clear Form button appears. For easier viewing, click the Maximize button located to the right of the title bar. The event tree for the Clear Form button fills the window.

4. Click the Conclusion icon on the Event Tree button bar. (It is the inverted blue triangle that is the third icon from the left.) The Event Name dialog box displays.

5. Click the Combo Box icon found to the right of the Event Name text box. A list of available events is displayed (see Figure 3.28).

6. Choose Click from the list of events to which the button will respond. Click is placed in the Event Name text box.

7. Click OK or press Enter to confirm that choice. The Action for Clear Form dialog box appears. Into this text box type the action step or series of steps that occur when the button is pushed. There are two actions we want the button to perform: (1) clear the form and (2) move the cursor to the first field.

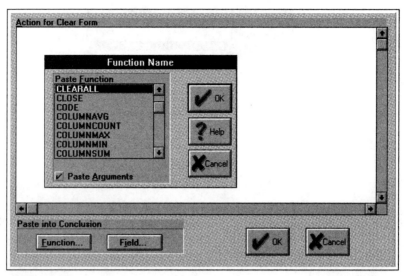

FIGURE 3.29
Action for Clear Form dialog box

8. Click the Function button in the Paste into Conclusion box to display an alphabetical listing of ObjectVision functions (see Figure 3.29).

You can scroll through the list of functions with the scroll bar by clicking the arrows or by dragging the scroll bar box. Clicking advances the pointer to the next function.

9. Locate the CLEARALL function. Click the Paste Arguments check box (left, bottom of the dialog box), and then click the CLEARALL function.

10. Click OK to place the function into the event tree.

Now we are ready to place the second and final action function, @RESUME, in the event tree.

11. Press Ctrl-Enter to move the cursor to the next line in the Action for Clear Form dialog box. If you press Enter instead of Ctrl-Enter, the dialog box closes and the event tree is redisplayed. So remember the Ctrl-Enter method of moving to a new line.

12. Repeat steps 9 and 10, but search for the RESUME function.

13. Click OK to display the completed event tree (see Figure 3.30).

14. Finally, close the event tree by double clicking its control box or by clicking the Return icon on the button bar.

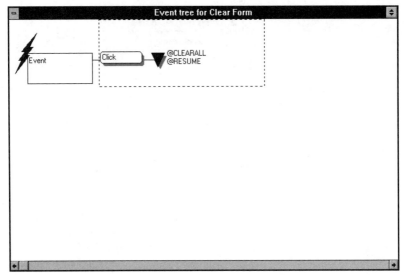

FIGURE 3.30
Completed Clear Form event tree

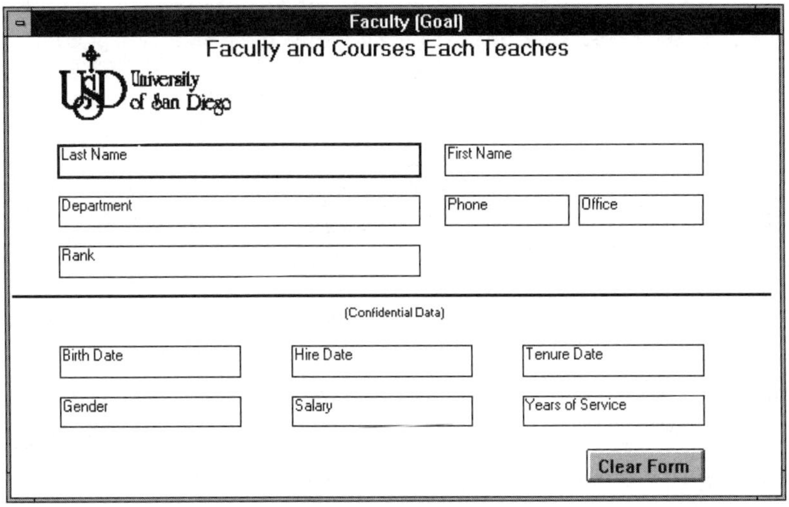

FIGURE 3.31
Faculty form with button

That's it! The Clear Form button is complete. Try it out to make sure it works. Return to goal mode by clicking the Return icon and then fill in some of the fields beginning with Last Name. Click the Clear Form button. All the fields clear, and the cursor returns to the Last Name field. Figure 3.31 shows the completed Faculty form, so far.

SUMMARY

This chapter describes how to design an attractive, easy-to-use form. We have stressed the importance of placing fields and other objects on an application's form to enhance its utility. It is best to place more important information in the upper left corner of a form, whereas less significant fields can be placed in lower positions.

We have built the first form of the Faculty application from the ground up. A new, blank form was created and sized. Field, text, graphics, line, and button objects were added incrementally to the form. We learned how to alter the attributes of individual fields as well as set the default attributes of each object class. Finally, we built both a value tree and an event tree. The value tree was incorporated in a field so that its value would be automatically calculated and displayed. An event tree comprising two built-in ObjectVision functions was attached to the Clear Form button. We end with a fully functioning, single-form application that accepts input data and provides a convenient form in which one college faculty member's information may be displayed. Subsequent chapters build on this foundation to add more forms and features to create a feature-laden, complete faculty information gathering and display application.

KEY TERMS

Complete mode The status of a form when all needed data has been entered. The mode is indicated in parentheses on the form title bar.

Edit mode The status of a form when a developer has executed the Form command of the Tools menu and is using one of them. Frequently called *design mode*.

File name The name under which the entire ObjectVision is stored or saved. The name conforms to standard DOS file-naming conventions. A file name can differ from the form name.

Form event tree An event tree, associated with a form, that is executed whenever a form event occurs (such as opening or closing a form).

Function, built-in Functions recognized by ObjectVision resemble those of spreadsheet functions like Quattro Pro for Windows. Functions can be used in expressions, and two types exist: value and event.

Goal mode The status of a form when it is incomplete: some fields still require data. It is indicated in parentheses in the form title bar.

Grid An invisible grid causes objects to rest on grid coordinates, not between them. Movement is constrained to that of a coarse, medium, or fine grid mesh.

Override (value tree) A value tree calculation can be overridden by entering a value into the associated field. Overridden fields are recognized by their shading.

Prompt mode The form status when a referenced field is not present in any of the application's forms. A temporary form, Scratchpad, is displayed to prompt for the required field value.

Properties The characteristics displayed by objects on a form. The number of characteristics varies by object type; fields have the largest number of alterable properties.

Selection list It displays a list of values that can be entered for the selected field. Only one of the displayed values can be chosen. A user cannot type in a value.

Stack event tree An event that is associated with an entire application. A stack event can occur when an application is opened or closed.

REVIEW QUESTIONS

True or False Questions

1. **T F** It is not necessary to involve users actively in the initial design specifications of an application.

2. **T F** Aesthetics is a subjective way of measuring a form's overall visual appeal.

3. **T F** An application's file name must be the same as its form name.

4. **T F** A ruler can be displayed on a form both in edit mode and in goal mode.

5. **T F** Fields and tables are the only objects that can accept input data.

6. **T F** You can check the information flow path while in edit mode. Simply move to the first field and then repeatedly press Tab or Enter to move to successive fields.

7. **T F** A field label can be placed in one of four places within a field: top, bottom, left, or right.

8. **T F** When you save an application with the File|Save or File|Save As commands, the form and any filled-in fields are saved on disk.

9. **T F** You can specify text sizes from 4 to 127 points for most typefaces by typing the desired point size in the Label Font dialog box.

10. **T F**   Value trees can be defined for both graphic objects and fields.

11. **T F**   When creating an ObjectVision application, the form is the most important component.

12. **T F**   Users should not have a say in the design or look of a form.

13. **T F**   An object's default properties can be changed according to your needs.

14. **T F**   All properties of an object can be set to their original default values in a single operation.

15. **T F**   A button with *no* event tree does nothing.

Multiple Choice Questions

1. A field object's values can be restricted to those whose contents are displayed on a drop-down list whenever the field is entered. What is that selection method called?
   a. selection list
   b. combo box
   c. check box
   d. radio button
   e. true/false

2. All properties *except* which one of the following can be altered for a graph object?
   a. color
   b. borders
   c. name/text
   d. line width

3. Which object class of those listed has the fewest properties that can be either set or inspected?
   a. line
   b. field
   c. text
   d. graphic

4. Object default properties are established with which command?
   a. Properties|Object
   b. Edit|Properties
   c. Form|Select|Defaults
   d. Objects|Defaults

5. Value trees can contain branches, conditions, and _____.
   a. results
   b. formulas
   c. conclusions
   d. functions
   e. none of the preceding

EXERCISE

1. In Chapter 2 we examined an Educational Allowance application and form used annually by human resources personnel to review employee benefits. Construct a limited version of that form that includes the graphic, form title text, and line objects. Create the four buttons (label them *Store, Previous, Delete,* and *Next*) but omit their event trees. Place only these fields on your form: Name, Employee No., Hire Date, Last Year's Performance, and Years of Service. Develop, with Paintbrush, a graphic of your own choosing. Position the objects, as closely as possible, to match Figure 2.1.

BUILDING A MULTIFORM APPLICATION

O B J E C T I V E S

This chapter discusses several important ObjectVision application development tools. Through the use of examples, we introduce how to do the following:

- *Create additional forms for an application*

- *Incorporate buttons, which cause prescribed actions to occur*

- *Use some of the several ObjectVision built-in functions*

- *Build a variety of value and event trees and attach them to objects*

- *Create multicolumn and row objects called tables*

When you finish this chapter, you will have nearly doubled your knowledge of ObjectVision and its utility in creating Windows applications. This chapter is chock full of application development information and examples.

4.1 INTRODUCTION

We continue to develop the Faculty application from Chapter 3 in this chapter. First we divide the information on the form into two forms. Then we add buttons to the forms to facilitate moving from one to another. A value tree is developed to calculate automatically one of the field values, and several ObjectVision functions are introduced. These functions, similar to those found in spreadsheets, provide convenient alternatives to writing complex mathematical expressions. While always keeping the end user in mind, we examine how to incorporate help into various objects of the Faculty application.

After a few key end users have examined and used your Faculty form, they collectively decide that a few fundamental changes are in order. Foremost among the observations coming from the user committee is that some information fields are more sensitive than others. They feel strongly that the fields Birth Date, Hire Date, Tenure Date, Gender, Salary, and Years of Service should appear on a separate form. They suggest that the current form be split into two forms. The first form encountered by a user should contain the fields shown in the top half of the form (see Figure 3.31), whereas a second form should hold the remaining fields—those considered confidential. The user committee also suggests that the application eventually incorporate safeguards to allow only selected people access to the second form. In addition, the committee requests that users be able to save completed forms in a simple, straightforward way.

We begin by modifying our original design to incorporate the suggested changes. Along the way, we will use other facilities to implement and augment the application.

4.2 ADDING FORMS TO AN APPLICATION

Many of the applications you create will have more than one form. Part of the great versatility of ObjectVision applications is the virtually unlimited number of different forms that can be part of a single application. Imagine, for a moment, creating a tax application. You might duplicate the 1040 tax form as several ObjectVision forms and the various tax schedules (itemized deductions) as their own forms. All of the forms created comprise one application. Then you can easily script the order in which the user sees each of the forms by using various ObjectVision built-in functions that open, close, and clear forms.

We will create a second form for the Faculty application. On that form we will place the six confidential fields mentioned previously. Then we will create a few buttons on each of the two forms that will allow the user to move smoothly between them.

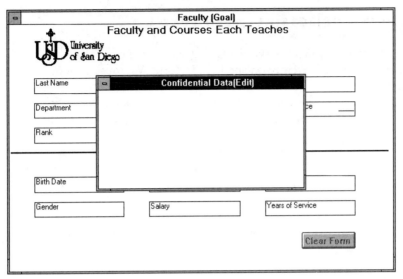

CREATING A NEW FORM

Start by creating a new form by following these steps:

1. Make sure that you are in edit mode, then choose Form|New (the New command in the Form menu).

2. Enter the form's new name in the Form Name text box: type `Confidential Data` and press Enter or click OK. A new (albeit small) form appears (see Figure 4.1).

Next enlarge the form to an appealing size. Make it 6.5 by 2.5 inches.

1. Recall that the ruler is displayed when you execute the command View|Ruler.

2. Move the arrow pointer to a corner or side of the form until it changes to a double-headed arrow.

3. Click and drag a side or corner of the window until the form is the right size. If you run into the edge or corner of the ObjectVision application, simply move to the form title bar, click it, and drag it to open up more space.

The next task is to move the six confidential fields from the main Faculty form to the new Confidential Data form.

MOVING OBJECTS BETWEEN FORMS

We have already created the fields that are to reside on the Confidential Data form—they are currently on the Faculty form. We must now move (not copy) them to the new form. First make the Faculty form the selected form by executing the Form|Select command. When the Form Name dialog box appears, the names of all the forms in the current application are displayed. Click the Faculty form and select OK (or double click the name). The Faculty form is brought to the foreground, and the Confidential Data form disappears. (It is still available, merely hidden.) We will move the six fields to the new form by using a simple cut-and-paste operation. Follow these steps to select the six fields to be cut:

1. Click on the Birth Date field.
2. Press and hold the Shift key and click on the lowest, rightmost field, Years of Service.

The Shift key trick allows you to select multiple, contiguous fields. All fields encompassed between the first and last fields clicked are included in the group. Selected fields are shown with dashed lines instead of solid ones, and the entire group is enclosed in rectangle with a handle at each corner. Using a related shortcut, you can select particular objects by pressing and holding the Ctrl key as you click various objects. Only specific objects, not contiguous objects between them, are selected. They exhibit dashed lines instead of solid ones.

Next we **cut** the selected objects. When they are cut, the group of objects is placed on the Windows Clipboard. They can then be copied into the new form. Cut the selected objects by executing the Edit|Cut command. Figure 4.2 shows the selected objects prior to executing the Cut command.

The cut fields are to be placed on the Confidential Data form, so move back to that form by executing the Form|Select command. Choose Confidential Data and click OK. Then **paste** the objects from the Clipboard onto the form:

1. Execute Edit|Paste to bring the objects from the Clipboard to the form.
2. Position the dashed line representing the group so that the top edge of the dashed line is about three-quarters of an inch from the top of the form. You can move the group by moving the pointer arrow.
3. When you are satisfied with the position, click the arrow to drop the group onto the form.

A dashed line and handles still surround the objects, and you can adjust their group location again, as the individual objects now appear within the dashed rectangle (see Figure 4.3).

Most of this new form is complete and only a few details are missing. We will add a title and spiff it up with a rounded rectangle.

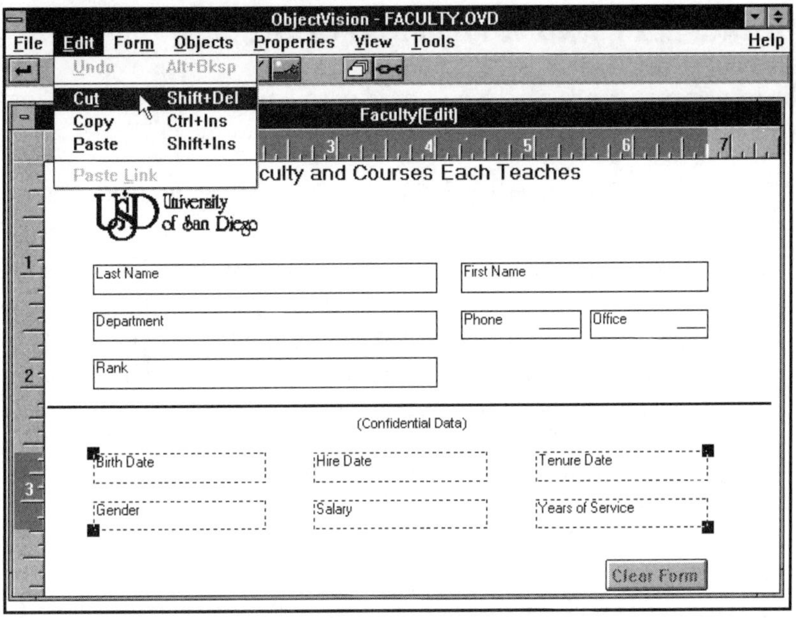

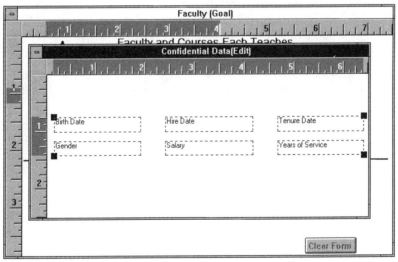

FIGURE 4.2
Cutting selected objects to the Clipboard

FIGURE 4.3
Confidential Data form after pasting objects

ADDING TEXT AND A FILLED RECTANGLE

The form's appearance can be enhanced with a title and a filled rectangle that outlines the title. First add a title to the top of the form:

1. Select the Text icon from the object bar, or execute the Objects|Text command.

2. Enter the string `Confidential Data` in the Text Value dialog box and press Enter.

3. Move the object to the top of the form and expand the text box to the full width of the form. (Click and drag one of the text box handles to the nearest edge. Repeat this process for the other side.)

Next enlarge the text and center it within the form.

1. Click the property inspector (right mouse button) for the text and select Label Font.

2. Using the scroll bar, find and select the MS Sans Serif type font. Click on the 24 point size and check the Bold box. Click OK to confirm your choices.

3. Center the text on the form by clicking the property inspector and selecting Alignment. The Field Value Alignment dialog box appears.

4. Click the Center check box and click OK. The text appears centered in its box.

5. Remove the border (the "box") that surrounds the text by selecting the Borders property of the property inspector. Deselect Outline by clicking it (the check mark will disappear). Click OK.

The form label "Confidential Data" is large, bold, and centered at the top of the form. Next we add a rounded rectangle as background to emphasize the text:

1. Select the Rounded Rectangle icon from the object bar or execute Objects|Rounded Rectangle.

2. Move the Rounded Rectangle crosshair cursor just above and to the left of the text and click.

3. Using the rectangle handles, size the rectangle so that it completely surrounds the text and extends beyond each end of the text.

Click the Return icon in the object bar to see the form so far. Your form should look similar to Figure 4.4.

You have probably observed that when you click on a pair of overlapping objects, first one is selected and then the other. When dealing with layered objects like the text and the rounded rectangle, be careful not to shift the position

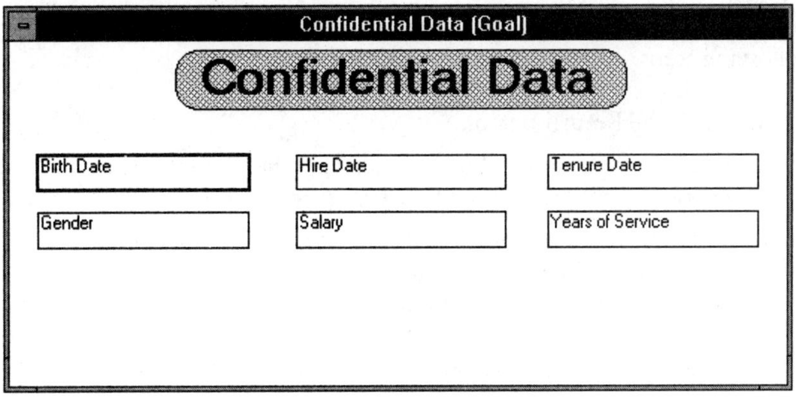

FIGURE 4.4
Confidential Data form with text and rectangle

of either one inadvertently. Unfortunately, there is no way to group objects in ObjectVision.

We must provide users with a way to move back and forth between the two Faculty forms. That facility is built next!

4.3 CREATING BUTTONS

As you recall from Chapter 3, buttons can be added to forms to initiate one or more actions. The action-initiating component of a button is inherent in its attached event tree. Several buttons will be added to both forms.

ADDING BUTTONS TO THE CONFIDENTIAL DATA FORM

Two buttons will enhance the Confidential Data form and help the user jump between the two forms. One button transfers the user to the main Faculty form and pushes the Confidential Data form into the background. The other button, when pressed, clears all the fields in the Confidential Data form.

First we will create a button that displays the Faculty form. While in edit mode, select the Button icon from the object bar. Type Return to name the button when the Button Name dialog box appears. Click OK. Then position the button crosshair so that the button is centered in the bottom of the Confidential Data form. Click to drop it onto the form and use a handle to stretch the button so that it is about 1.5 inches long. Note that the default label font for all buttons is always 10 point System. A button's label font cannot be changed.

Next we add the action part of the button, its event tree. This event tree will cause the Faculty form to be displayed whenever the Return button is clicked. That is equivalent to using the Form Select command, but it is much easier to operate for those users not familiar with ObjectVision. Create the event with the following steps:

1. Click the Return button.

2. Click the right mouse button to display the property inspector menu and choose Event Tree. The empty event tree for the Return button appears.

3. Click the Maximize button on the right of the title bar and then click the Conclusion icon on the Event Tree menu bar. After the Event Name dialog box appears, click the Combo Box icon located to the right of the Event Name box. This displays the available events to which the button can respond. Only Click, Select, and Unselect are available.

4. Choose Click from the selection list. Click is placed in the Event Name dialog box. Thus, the button will take an action only when it is *clicked.*

5. Click OK to close the Event Name dialog box (as shown in Figure 3.28). The Action for Return dialog box displays. The action you want to perform is one that selects the Faculty form when the button is clicked.

6. The function @FORMSELECT is what you want. You can type it directly or select it from the list of functions (as was shown in Figure 3.29). If you click the Function button in the Paste into Conclusion box, you can scroll to the @FORMSELECT function and click it. In either case, enter the function

   ```
   @FORMSELECT("Faculty")
   ```

   in the Action dialog box and click OK. (Be sure to enclose the form name in double quotes).

7. Press the Enter icon to close the dialog box and return to the form.

The form now has the Return button event tree. In short, when a user clicks the Return button, the function @FORMSELECT("Faculty") is executed. That function transfers the user's cursor to the Faculty form in the application stack.

The second button required for the Confidential Data form is one to clear all the fields. It is similar but not identical to the Clear button developed earlier for the Faculty form. Briefly, create another button called Clear_Form (that is an underscore between the two words, not a blank). Though it would be nice to label it "Clear," there already is a button by that name and all objects in an application must have a unique name. Follow the previous steps to create the event tree for this button. "Click" is the event name that triggers this button into action. However, enter these two lines in the Action for Clear_Form dialog box:

```
@FORMCLEAR(@SELECTEDFORM)
@FIELDFIND(Birth Date)
```

Notice the second event tree function is different from the one found in the Return button. The @FIELDFIND function locates the enclosed field and places

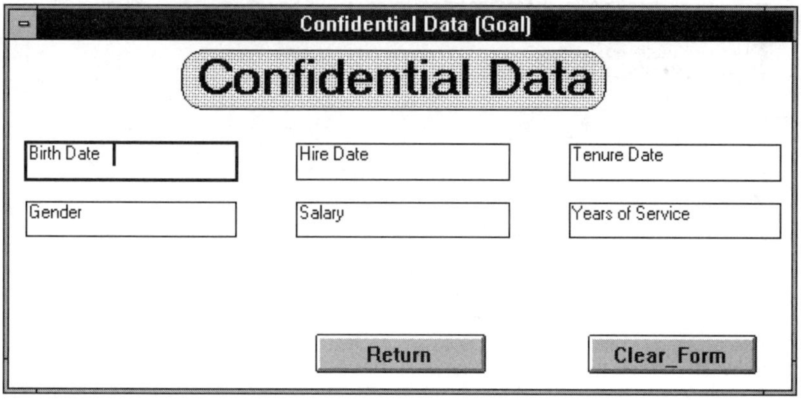

FIGURE 4.5
Confidential Data form with buttons

the cursor there. The field name must be spelled exactly the same as the corresponding field. It is not enclosed in quotation marks. Why not use the @RESUME function as we did before? Here's why.

@RESUME restores guided completion. That does not guarantee that the cursor will stay on the Confidential Data form. In fact, if any of the fields in the Faculty form are empty, then the cursor is placed in the first of those fields. We do not want to switch forms until the user explicitly presses the Return button. Thus, the Clear_Form button should clear the form and then keep the cursor on the Confidential Data form in the Birth Date field. Figure 4.5 shows the completed form.

We now will add buttons to the Faculty form. This is a good excuse to try out the newly minted Return button. First press the Return icon to switch back to goal mode. Then click the Return button at the bottom of your form. Voila! The Faculty form displays.

Before adding buttons to the Faculty form, we will remove the unnecessary text string, (Confidential Data), now that sensitive data has been moved to another form. Remove the string by clicking it and then executing the command Edit|Cut or using the shortcut keys Shift-Del. The text disappears. While still in edit mode, move the line object farther down the form so that it is positioned about one-quarter of an inch above the Clear Form button. Simply click and drag it. Be sure to keep the line centered on the form. Now we are ready to add two important buttons to the main Faculty form.

ADDING BUTTONS TO THE FACULTY FORM

Two buttons are added to the Faculty form to provide easy ways to save the form and its data and to move from the Faculty form to the Confidential Data form. The mechanism for creating buttons and developing their individual event trees is identical to the steps for the other buttons created. New to the description that follows are the functions that make up the event trees.

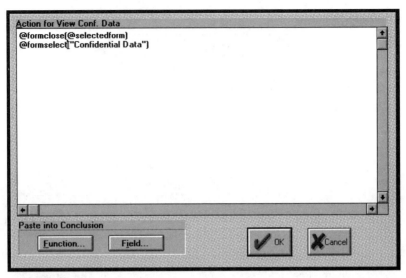

FIGURE 4.6
Event tree functions to switch forms

Implementing a Form Switch Button

A user could move between the two forms by executing Form|Select and then clicking on the form name. But that does not have a polished, end-user feel to it. It is much better to provide a button that displays the Confidential Data form. Create a button labeled "View Conf. Data" following the same initial steps given for the Return button on the Confidential Data form. The code for the event tree consists of two functions, not just one. Enter the two lines:

```
@FORMCLOSE(@SELECTEDFORM)
@FORMSELECT("Confidential Data")
```

Figure 4.6 shows the dialog box just after the preceding have been entered prior to pressing Enter.

Observe that functions can be spelled either with or without uppercase letters. They are translated to uppercase after you save the event tree by clicking OK. Remember to include the at sign (@) prefix when typing an ObjectVision function name.

Place the View Conf. Data button in the bottom center of the form. Using its handles, stretch the button to about 1.5 inches long so that the entire button name is visible.

If you recall the logic of the Clear_Form button, you notice that we have introduced a new function, @FORMCLOSE. Why did we include that function in the event tree? @FORMCLOSE provides a way of clearing the current form from the screen before the @FORMSELECT function displays another form. The @FORMCLOSE function could have been omitted without any true change in form-switching functionality. It is largely a matter of style. For this applica-

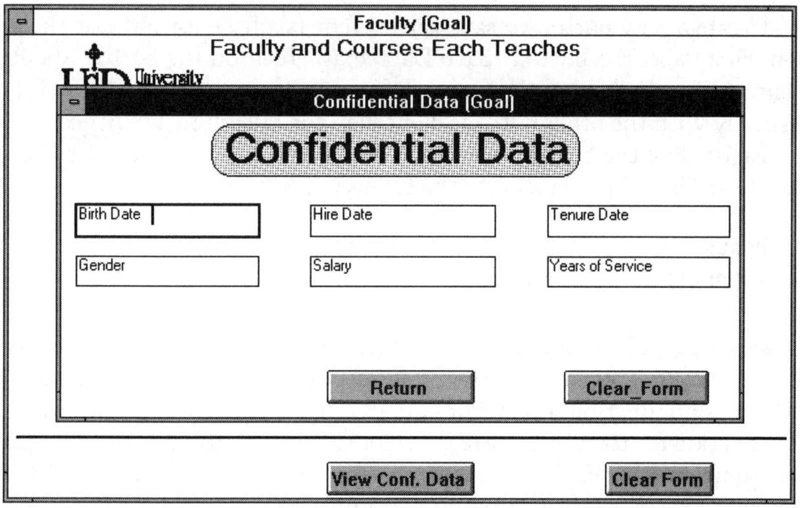

FIGURE 4.7
FIGURE 4.7
Omitting @FORMCLOSE to display two forms

tion, we prefer having the Confidential Data form displayed without any distracting background form. On the other hand, if you omit the @FORMCLOSE function, the outer edges of the Faculty form appear behind the Confidential Data form. That can have the advantage of imitating layers of papers stacked on a desk. Figure 4.7 shows the screen "desktop" when we omit the @FORMCLOSE function from the View Conf. Data button.

Test the newly created button by returning to goal mode and then clicking View Conf. Data. The Faculty form is removed and the View Confidential Data form is displayed if the button has been correctly constructed. Press the Return button to redisplay the Faculty form.

Implementing a Save Information Button

Users will want to save information they have entered into the Faculty fields. After all, the application would be little better than its paper-form counterpart if it were not, in part, for the Windows application's ability to save and retrieve data. For now, we will limit the user's ability to save information. Users can save the current form's contents on disk by clicking a button. After the data is saved, ObjectVision is exited and control returns to Windows.

Whenever the application is retrieved, the previously saved information will be redisplayed within the various Faculty application forms. Obviously, if a user wants information on more than one faculty member, more copies of the form must be made, each with a different file name. That works but it has obvious limitations: Many files must be saved, wasting disk space, and retrieving a particular faculty file is difficult. In Chapter 5, we expand the capabilities of the application by allowing unlimited data to be stored in a database, releasing the user from the time-consuming process of saving multiple application files.

Create a new button to save the current faculty data and exit the application. First, label the button "Save Data/Exit." Position the button about three-quarters of an inch from the form's left side and near the bottom so it lines up vertically with the other buttons. Lengthen the button to 1.5 inches.

Right click the button, select the Event Tree choice, and in the Action for Save Data/Exit dialog box enter the following two functions:

```
@SAVE
@APPEXIT
```

These are part of a group of functions known as miscellaneous event functions (see the Appendix for a list of them). If you are unsure of the exact syntax of any ObjectVision function (for example, does it have arguments or not), then choose the Function button of the Paste into Conclusion box to scroll through the available functions. When you click on the @FORMSELECT function (one of the miscellaneous event functions), for example, the function and example arguments are pasted into the Event Tree dialog box:

```
@FORMSELECT("FormName")
```

The argument FormName and the double quotation marks are highlighted. When you enter the actual form name, it replaces the highlighted FormName. It is a good idea to use this method until you become thoroughly familiar with the ObjectVision functions. Pasting functions from a function scroll list ensures that you include the proper function arguments and spell the function name correctly. It is always a good idea to test the latest form enhancement. But first save the form manually by executing the command File|Save. If your button causes you to exit the application *without* saving the form, then all the modifications you have made since your last save operation will be lost! Suppose you discover an event tree has somehow malfunctioned. How do you change it?

Editing an incorrectly entered event tree is simple. Suppose, for example, that you test the new button and discover it does not behave as you expected. On closer examination of the event tree, you discover that an incorrect function was used or one was omitted. Edit the event tree by performing the following:

1. Right click the button whose actions you wish to modify (for example, Save Data/Exit). The object's properties are displayed.

2. Click the Event Tree choice in the property inspector. The triggering event (click, usually) and its conclusion statements are shown surrounded by dashed lines.

3. Right click the mouse. A box is displayed with two choices: Condition and Conclusion. You can change either the trigger condition for the event or its conclusion (see Figure 4.8).

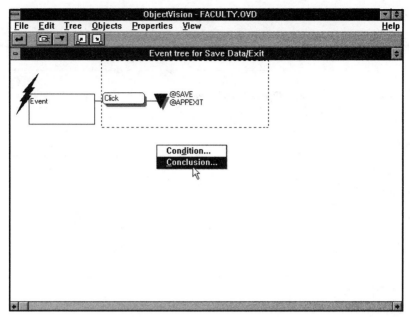

FIGURE 4.8
Editing an event tree conclusion

4. Choose Conclusion. The Action for Save Data/Exit dialog box reappears.

5. Now you can delete lines, insert functions or other statements, and press OK.

Double click the Event Tree dialog Control-menu box to complete the process.

4.4 CREATING FORM AND APPLICATION EVENT TREES

Event trees can be assigned to a number of ObjectVision objects: stack, form, button, field, table column, text, and graphic. Button event trees are associated with buttons, as explained previously, and the event tree takes action only when a few events are recognized. For buttons, these events are click, select, unselect, and a special function, @EVENT. A form can have an event tree of its own, distinct from objects on its surface containing their own event trees. A *stack*, the ObjectVision synonym for an entire application (comprising its forms), can also have an event tree. Stack and form event trees can react only to selected events. Table 4.1 shows a listing of objects and the events they may receive and process. Notice that four objects—table, rectangle, rounded rectangle, and line—cannot receive any events whatsoever.

TABLE 4.1
Objects and the events they may receive and process

Object	Click	Open	Close	Select	Unselect	Change	@EVENT	Ctrl Keys (A–Z)
Stack		✓	✓				✓	✓
Form		✓	✓	✓	✓	✓	✓	
Button	✓			✓	✓		✓	
Field or Column				✓	✓	✓	✓	
Text	✓							
Graphic	✓							
Table								
Rectangle								
Rounded Rectangle								
Line								

EVENTS RECOGNIZED BY OBJECTS, FORMS, AND STACKS

The click condition has been used in the buttons on the Faculty and Confidential Data forms. A **click condition** is an event that occurs when the mouse cursor is on an object and the left mouse button is clicked. Besides buttons, text and graphic objects can process a click event, provided they have event trees specifying that condition.

An open event occurs when an application is opened in ObjectVision using File|Open or another form is opened using a command or function (such as @FORMSELECT). A close event is received when a form is closed (such as @FORMCLOSE) or another application is opened. In the latter case, the *stack* receives the close event.

A form is *selected* when its title bar is highlighted. When a user changes the focus so the form title bar is unhighlighted, it is *unselected*. Multiple forms may appear layered upon each other. Only the foremost form has the selected event.

A **change condition** occurs when a value has been entered in a field or column (thus changing the field or column) or when a form has been completed. The event occurs after a user selects another object by pressing Enter or Tab or by clicking the left mouse button. The change triggers when a calculated or linked (database) value appears in a field or column. You can use this opportunity to check the validity of a newly entered value, for example.

@EVENT is a special function that allows you to generate your own, custom events having specially defined names. Any object that has a name can receive a user-defined event created by @EVENT. Examples of this function are shown in subsequent chapters.

Finally, 26 special key combinations, Ctrl-A through Ctrl-Z, can be recognized by the stack event tree. Used as shortcut keys to cause application-wide events, these prove to be a convenient way to customize end-user menus. These will be illustrated later in this chapter.

Next we discover how to add event trees to both forms and the entire application. Form and application events, contained at a higher level than ordinary object events, affect the form or application they contain.

ADDING A FORM EVENT TREE

The Faculty application does not yet have a form event tree. A form event tree can initiate actions when a form is closed or open or when a form is selected or unselected (see Table 4.1). For example, we can create a form event tree that has Open as a condition and @FINDFIELD(Last Name) as the conclusion of the Faculty form event tree. Each time the Faculty form is opened, the cursor (or focus) moves to the Last Name field—even if it has a value already. You add the form event tree to the Faculty form by following these steps:

1. In edit mode, right click the Faculty form and select Event Tree (or choose Properties|Form|Event Tree).

2. Build the form event tree in the same way as an event tree for any object. In particular, choose the event name Open when prompted, and enter the function @FIELDFIND(Last Name) as the conclusion.

You can test the form event tree. Enter goal mode and then enter anything in the Last Name field. Next push the View Conf. Data button and then the Return button. The focus should return to the Last Name field. The cursor normally would be on the field where it was before the form switch, First Name.

ADDING AN APPLICATION EVENT TREE

Application, or stack, event trees can receive a limited number of events, no matter which form is active. The application event tree, positioned at the highest level, is the appropriate place for application-wide events to be acted upon. We will explore this feature by creating a stack event that will act on two events, each one having two separate conclusions.

First, we want the application title to contain something more specific than a file name. Notice in Figure 4.8, for example, that "ObjectVision–FACULTY.OVD" appears in the application title bar. We will change it to "Faculty Information."

Second, we can create a shortcut key that is recognized throughout the application. When a user presses Ctrl and then the C key (noted as Ctrl+C henceforth), it signals the application to clear all fields and tables of forms and go to the main Faculty form. The cursor is placed on the Last Name field. Recall that the Clear Form button on the Faculty form does that same thing. However, placing those functions in the application event tree makes them available throughout the application, no matter which form is being completed.

Both of these events can be placed in a single stack event tree. You can assign an event tree property to a stack in the Form Tool by choosing Properties|Stack| Event Tree. Alternately, you can click the right mouse button while it is on the application title bar and then select Event Tree. From this point on, the process is like any other event tree. The only difference is that there will be two events and their corresponding conclusions rather than one. When the Event tree for Application dialog box displays showing its empty event tree, do the following:

1. Click the Conclusion icon on the object bar.

2. Begin by setting the title when the application opens: Enter Open in the Event Name text box and click OK.

3. The title establishing function is @SETTITLE. Enter @SETTITLE("Faculty Information") and then click OK.

4. Repeat steps 1 and 2: Click the Conclusion icon and enter Ctrl+C (type C, t, r, l, +, C) and click OK. We choose "C" because it Clears the form. The Ctrl+C condition is in a branch below the Open condition and conclusion.

5. Enter the two functions @CLEARALL and @RESUME on two lines in the conclusion node for this branch of the Action for Application dialog box. Click OK. Figure 4.9 shows the application (stack) event tree with the two events and their associated actions.

6. Press the Return icon on the object bar to close the event tree.

Test the stack event tree. First switch to goal mode. Then save the application so that you can see what happens when you open the new Faculty application (execute File|Save). Now open Faculty and observe the application title bar. It now displays Faculty Information instead of the application file name. Test out the Ctrl+C function: Enter anything in some fields then hold down the Control (Ctrl) key and tap the letter C. The form clears.

PRINTING DECISION TREES

It is important to document the applications you create, and part of that documentation is a listing of all the event trees and the value trees. Hard copies of these trees are useful for recalling the logic behind forms, buttons, and the stack.

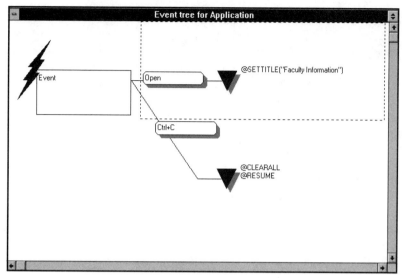

FIGURE 4.9
Application (stack) event tree with two conditions

You can print a decision tree whenever you are editing it. To print it, adjust the size of the tree by clicking the Reduce or Expand icons on the object bar. Then choose File|Print Tree to print the displayed decision tree. You can print *all* value or event trees in an application by executing File|Print All. Note that Print All prints trees of the type you are editing (value or event) in the application. You can print either form or stack trees while editing them by using File|Print Tree. Print All prints only object value or event trees. End users are precluded from printing decision trees because runtime ObjectVision omits the Tools menu. Executing Print All while in goal mode, for example, will print the forms of an application—not its decision trees.

4.5 BUILDING MORE COMPLEX DECISION TREES

Event trees illustrated in this text have been rather simple. They frequently have one simple condition (click, for example) and an associated event. Value trees shown in our application are the essence of simplicity. Now we want to show the versatility of decision trees by building one that is slightly more complex. After studying the example value tree and understanding the types of branches available, you will be able to construct value and event trees of arbitrary complexity—trees containing many condition/conclusion branches. It just takes a little practice to become proficient and confident.

TYPES OF DECISION TREE BRANCHES

As we have seen, decision trees comprise branches, conditions, and conclusions. There are two types of branches, restricted and unrestricted, that can be used to build value trees. A **restricted branch** is simply a branch that is associated with (tests values in) a particular field. An **unrestricted branch** is not limited to testing values of a single field. It can consist of branches whose conditions are arbitrarily complex and contain references to various objects. Restricted branches are simpler to build but have limited utility. Unrestricted branches are slightly more difficult to build but are far more versatile than restricted branch forms. You can have unrestricted branches in both value and event trees. Each type of branch has its place in ObjectVision application development. First we will build and discuss a restricted branch value tree attached to the field Years of Service.

CREATING A RESTRICTED BRANCH DECISION TREE

A restricted branch is useful if the value tree is based on values in other fields. For example, suppose you create a field labeled "Vesting" that indicates what percentage of an employee's pension rights can be retained. Typically, an employee's vesting percentage increases from zero to one hundred over a period of a few years. The percentage represents how much of the company-contributed retirement money an employee can receive if he or she leaves the company before full vesting occurs. A vesting plan might be as follows: zero percent the first year, 33 percent after the first year, 66 percent after the second year, and 100 percent ("full vesting") after the third full year of service. A value tree with four branches is built to represent the vesting logic. Each branch's condition is based on the Years of Service field. The sample value tree is shown in Figure 4.10.

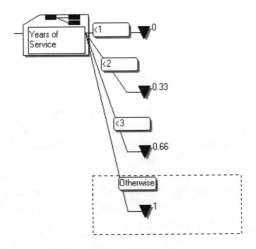

FIGURE 4.10
Restricted branch value tree

Rather than implement the new field, Vesting, we can build a simpler restricted branch value tree for a field that already exists. The Years of Service field located on the Confidential Data form can be spruced up a bit. Instead of displaying the calculated years that have elapsed between the hire date and the current date, we will enhance the existing value tree. The tree will contain two branches: one that displays question marks if the Hire Date field is empty (it was not filled in for some reason) and one that calculates the years of service in the standard way as we have in the original tree.

Move to the Confidential Data form in preparation for altering the Years of Service value tree. Execute Tools|Form to enter edit mode and right click the Years of Service field. Select the Value Tree property. Remove the current value tree: With the Value tree for Years of Service dialog box displayed, execute the command Edit|Cut. The value tree becomes empty. Follow these steps to create a restricted branch value tree:

1. Maximize the value tree, then click the Branch icon on the object bar. The Field Name dialog box appears. Select the name of an existing field that will be tested by various tree branches.

2. Scroll the list, if necessary, and click Hire Date. The field name becomes a branch upon which we build the tree.

3. Click the Conclusion icon. The Condition dialog box is displayed. If a user omits entering the Hire Date, then Years of Service will be undefined. Avoiding this case is simple: Merely test for a hire date that is zero (the value if a date is omitted) and display something suitable in Years of Service. Otherwise, display the elapsed number of years as usual.

4. Enter 0 (zero) in the Condition dialog box and click OK. The Conclusion for Years of Service dialog box appears. It is here that you enter whatever is to be displayed for the employee's tenure if his or her hire date has not been entered.

5. Enter three question marks (???) in the conclusion and click OK.

6. Click the Conclusion icon again to specify the next branch of the tree. The Condition dialog box again indicates the default condition, Otherwise. As this is the only other condition to be processed for Years of Service—because the field either is or is not filled in—Otherwise serves as a good catchall condition. Click OK to install the Otherwise branch condition.

7. The conclusion expression for this branch is the expression:

   `@INT((@TODAY-Hire Date)/365.25)`

   Enter that expression.

Steps 6 and 7 can be combined in this case because we have cut the expression shown in step 7. It still resides on the Windows Clipboard. Therefore, you can add another branch by executing Edit|Paste after step 5 above. Click OK and the cut branch with the default Otherwise condition is pasted below the existing

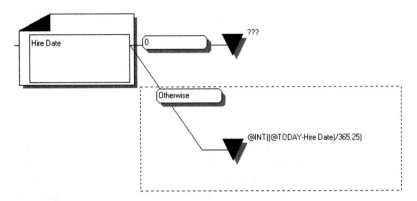

FIGURE 4.11
Revised restricted branch value tree for Years of Service

branch. Figure 4.11 shows the completed Years of Service value tree. It is a re-stricted branch value tree because the two branch conditions are compared to the single field, Hire Date.

Value trees are evaluated from the top condition down. When a condition is found that is true, then the evaluation halts. Otherwise, the evaluation is con-tinued against each branch in turn. If no condition proves true and the last branch is reached, then NA is displayed. Using Otherwise as the *last* condition (branch) in a value tree guards against the possibility of undefined results (NA).

CREATING AN UNRESTRICTED BRANCH DECISION TREE

An unrestricted branch is a special type of branch that can evaluate expressions and the values of any number of different fields. Both value trees and event trees can have unrestricted branches.

A *condition* in an unrestricted branch can be any valid ObjectVision expres-sion containing references to fields and functions as long as the expression re-turns the value of "Yes" or "No." An unrestricted branch *conclusion* for a value tree can be any valid value tree conclusion.

Event tree unrestricted branches are identical to those of value trees. How-ever, an unrestricted branch conclusion can be any event conclusion. That is, event trees must result in event conclusions, and value trees must contain con-clusions that result in values (not events).

Building an unrestricted branch value tree is a great way to understand this valuable ObjectVision structure. We will create a new field in the Confidential Data form that will display one of three messages. If the employee is 65 years old or greater, the Message field displays (Suggest Retirement). If the employee has not reached 65 years of age but has reached one of the important anniversary dates, then the Message field displays a reminder such as:

Time for the 10th year anniversary pin!

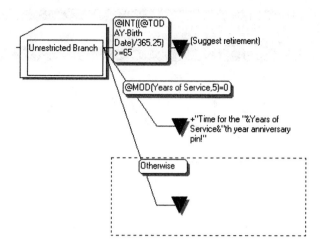

FIGURE 4.12
Unrestricted branch value tree

(The university likes to recognize employees with a pin every five years of service.) The third possible message is really no message at all. In other words, if the employee is not of retirement age and is between anniversary dates evenly divisible by five, then nothing is displayed in the Message field. Figure 4.12 shows the completed Message value tree containing three branches. This unrestricted branch tree employs functions, field names, and character strings in both its condition expressions and its conclusion nodes. Some of the expressions are not fully displayed in the figure, so each condition and conclusion is presented next.

Create a new field labeled "Message" that spans the length of the form and is placed just above the Confidential Data form buttons. Enter an unrestricted branch value tree in edit mode by displaying the object's property inspector and selecting Value Tree. The following steps get you started in creating the first of the three branches:

1. Click the Branch icon on the object bar.

2. Select the choice <Add Unrestricted Branch> displayed in the Name Field dialog box. The unrestricted branch is added to the Value tree for Message (see Figure 4.13).

3. Click the Conclusion icon. The Condition dialog box is displayed. Into this box type the first expression, the one to determine if an employee has reached 65 years of age.

4. Enter the following expression (be very careful about parentheses):

   `@INT((@TODAY-Birth Date)/365.25)>=65`

   Press Enter. The Conclusion for Message box appears.

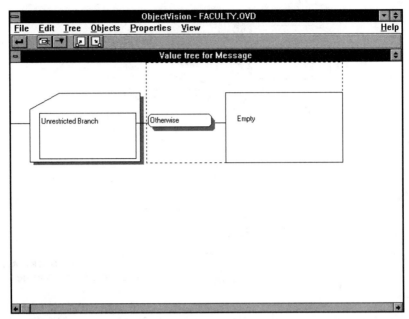

FIGURE 4.13
Unrestricted branch being added to value tree

5. Enter the conclusion (be sure to include the initial apostrophe or the expression will be invalid):

   '(Suggest retirement)

   Press Enter.

   Two more branches are needed in the value tree for the Message field. One displays an anniversary message if the Years of Service is one of the five-year milestones. The other message is an empty string that occupies the Message field when neither of the preceding conditions holds (when the employee is both younger than 65 and not in an anniversary year). Figure 4.14 shows the completed value tree we are building.

   Repeat steps 3 through 5 to add the anniversary test. Enter the following expression for the second branch condition:

   @MOD(Years of Service,5)=0

Enter the following conclusion node for the second branch condition:

   +"Time for the "&Years of Service&"th year anniversary pin!"

Its important to note that the expression begins with a plus sign. Between the double-quoted strings is the value of the anniversary. The ampersand (&) is the

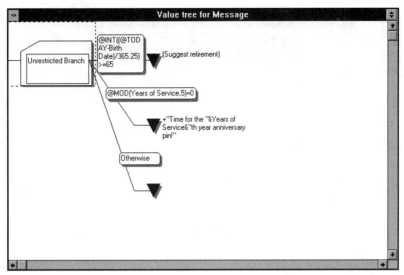

FIGURE 4.14
Value tree for Message field

concatenation (linking) operator and forms the complete phrase. For example, if an employee is having her or his fifteenth work anniversary, then the Message field displays:

```
Time for the 15th year anniversary pin!
```

Add the third branch by repeating steps 3 through 5 once more. The condition for the third branch is the default, catchall branch condition Otherwise (see Figure 4.14). This prevents "NA" from being displayed, should none of the other branch conditions be true. Click OK and then press Enter again when the Conclusion for Message dialog box is displayed. If you do not enter a conclusion, then an empty string is the result. Thus, nothing is displayed in the Message field unless retirement is approaching or another fifth-year anniversary has arrived. Figure 4.15 shows an example of the Message field for a senior employee.

Keep in mind a few crucial rules regarding field names and character strings used in expressions. When beginning an expression with a field name, precede the field name with a plus sign in any expression. Otherwise, the field name is treated as a literal character string. That is, the expression

Hire Date-Birth Date

is not the same as the correct expression

+Hire Date-Birth Date

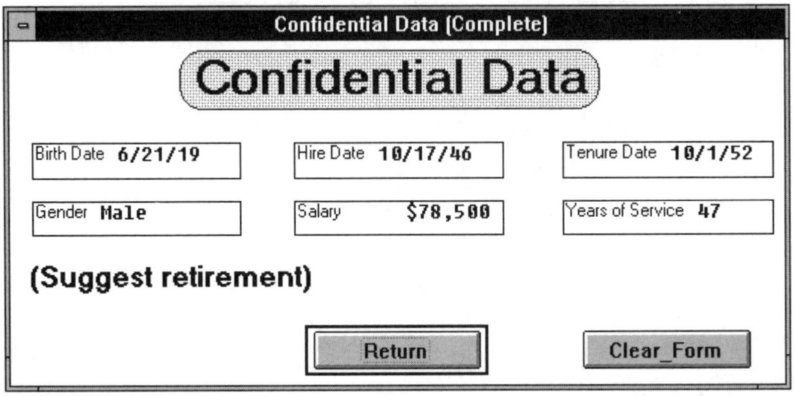

FIGURE 4.15
Example message for retirement-age employee

Similarly, the expression

(Help is available)

is not the same as the identical message *without* the parentheses. Begin a character string with an apostrophe whenever the string starts with a parenthesis. Doing so indicates it is a literal character string, not the beginning of a mathematical expression. Generally, the rules about expressions are the same as those for spreadsheet formulas. Remember that and you can write semantically correct condition and conclusion expressions for all value and event trees.

4.6 ADDING TABLE OBJECTS

The Faculty application we are building has the title "Faculty and Courses Each Teaches" (see Figure 4.1). The Faculty form actually consists of two forms and can hold information about individual faculty members, but there is no field or other structure to display which courses he or she is currently teaching. Useful information about courses might include:

1. Course name (such as Business or BUS)
2. Course number (such as 101 or 210)
3. Course section number (to identify individual sections of Accounting 101, for example)
4. Course title (such as International Management)

Each faculty member at the university used in this example teaches a maximum of four courses per semester. One way to display the preceding course

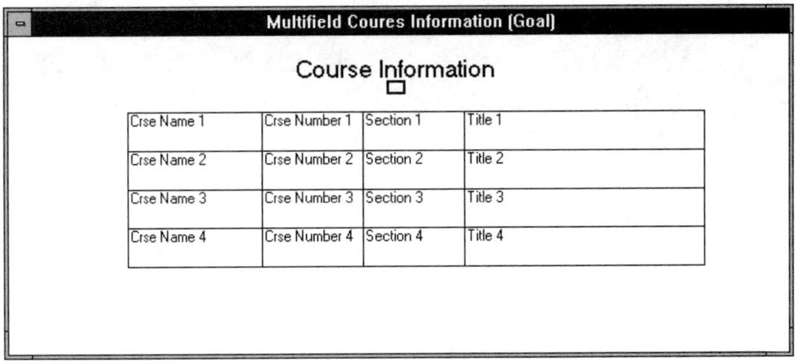

Multifield Coures Information (Goal)

Course Information

Crse Name 1	Crse Number 1	Section 1	Title 1
Crse Name 2	Crse Number 2	Section 2	Title 2
Crse Name 3	Crse Number 3	Section 3	Title 3
Crse Name 4	Crse Number 4	Section 4	Title 4

FIGURE 4.16
Multiple fields displaying course information

details for up to four courses is to create sixteen fields: four fields for each of the four courses. Figure 4.16 shows what that portion of the form might look like.

Several things are wrong with that approach. It is time-consuming to select, size, and position 16 fields to form a grid. Names must be unique across an entire application, so you must think of 16 unique names (it would not be too difficult to think of only 4 names like Crse Name and Crse Number). Finally, the 16 cells are visually confusing (it looks a lot like the television game "Jeopardy"). What we need is a matrix-type object. ObjectVision provides such an object, called a *table*.

A table is a uniquely named object having one or more uniquely named **columns**. Each column can be widened or narrowed independently, similar to a spreadsheet. There is no limit to the number of **rows** in a table, and they are inseparable. Tables can be used to display invoice rows (columns may contain item description, quantity ordered, price, extended price) team rosters with names and numbers, and so on.

In short, a table is just the object we need to display course information for each professor. When the Faculty application is completed—including the course table—it can be used to post office hours.

CREATING A TABLE

Creating a table is a relatively simple task. A faculty member can teach up to four courses, and each course (a row) will contain four pieces of information. Thus, we will create a four-row by four-column course information table that we will call "Courses Taught." Open the Faculty application (if not already displayed), invoke edit mode if necessary by executing Tools | Form, and display both a horizontal and vertical ruler showing *characters* as the metric (execute View | Ruler and check Characters in the Ruler Preferences dialog box). Continue creating the table by following these steps:

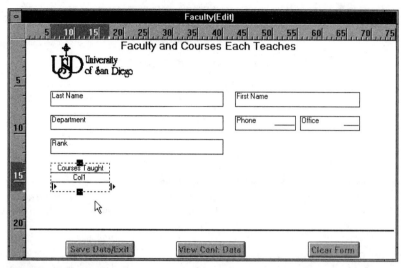

FIGURE 4.17
Positioning the Courses Taught table

1. Click the Table icon on the object bar. The default object name, Table1, appears in the Table Name dialog box.

2. Change the suggested name to "Courses Taught." Click OK to finalize the new name. The table crosshair pointer appears.

3. Position the crosshair below the Rank field so that the upper left corner is at approximately character position 5 on the top ruler and character position 13 on the left ruler. Click the left button to drop the one-column table on the form (see Figure 4.17).

CREATING AND DELETING ROWS

One row and one column is the default table structure in ObjectVision. That is not sufficient for our purpose here, and we must first increase the number of rows in the table. Proceeding from step 3 above, we can create four rows by doing the following:

4. Position the pointer over the handle at the bottom of the table. Click and drag it down to create four rows. A number appears in the upper left corner of the table as you drag the handle. It indicates the current number of rows. Continue dragging it down until 04 is displayed. Figure 4.18 shows the table object as the fourth row is being created.

You can easily delete any extra rows if you have created too many. To delete one or more rows, select the handle at the bottom of the table and then drag it up. Release the mouse when you have completed the delete row operation.

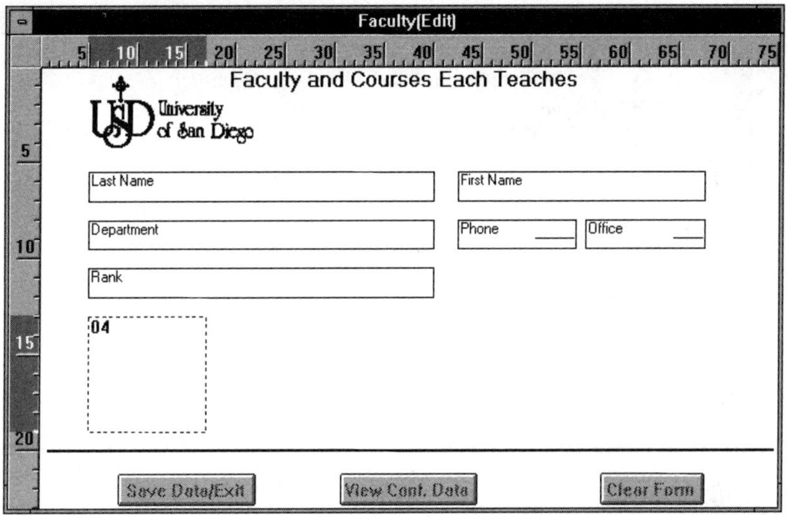

FIGURE 4.18
Dragging a table handle to create four rows

There are now enough rows to list up to four courses, but we must increase the number of columns to contain the four pieces of information for a given course.

CREATING AND DELETING COLUMNS

Follow the steps below to create additional columns in the Courses Taught table.

1. Move the pointer to the right side of the table. The pointer changes to a triangular handle. Click the handle. The table changes to a dotted outline.

2. Drag the triangular handle to the right to create a new column. The new column is named Col2.

3. Repeat steps 1 and 2 to create the third and fourth columns.

The four-column table, with its handles displayed, is shown in Figure 4.19. Observe that the table has two square handles that are used to add rows, whereas the triangular handles are "pulled" to create new columns.

If you create more columns than are needed, they can be deleted easily. First select the *column* to be deleted. Currently the entire table object is selected, so you must move the pointer to the column name. Click the column name to select the column to be deleted. Then use one of the selected column handles and drag the selected side to the opposite side. You are effectively reducing the column width to zero. After you release the mouse button, you are prompted whether or not you wish to delete the column. Answering "yes" deletes the column. Be

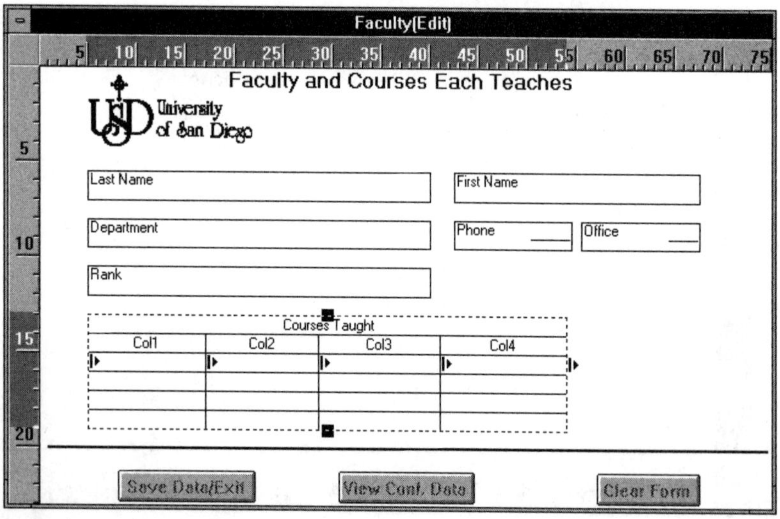

FIGURE 4.19
A four-column table

careful when responding to the prompt. The Edit|Undo command will *not* restore a deleted column.

RENAMING A TABLE OR COLUMN

The column names (Col1, Col2, and so on) are generic and should be renamed. Left to right, the columns are destined to hold the following course information: (1) course name, (2) course number, (3) section number, and (4) course title. Begin with the left column and rename it.

1. Click the column title ("Col1"—be careful to not click the table title) to select the column to be renamed.

2. Click the right mouse button to display that column's property inspector.

3. Choose the Name/Text property. The Field Name dialog box appears with Col1 shown in reverse video.

4. Replace it by typing **Name**, then click OK. After the Field Name dialog box closes, the new column name is displayed.

Repeat the above steps to replace Col2 with **Number**, Col3 with **Section**, and Col4 with **Title**. You can rename the table in a similar way: Select the table title bar, right click, select Name/Text, and enter the new table name.

We could rename the table by selecting the table title bar and then invoking the property inspector. Next, click the Name/Text property and type the new table name. As the table name Courses Taught is fine, we do not change it.

ALTERING COLUMN WIDTHS

Though you cannot always predict how wide table columns must be to accommodate data, an intelligent guess can be made based on what is known about course names, numbers, and so on. First display the top ruler (execute View|Ruler to display the Ruler Preferences dialog box) and select the Characters ruler preference. It is much easier to make columns identical widths or to determine their needed width if the rule displays character positions rather than inches or centimeters.

We will widen the Name column to 13 characters, the Number and Section columns to 10 characters, and the Title column to 30 characters. First widen the Name column:

1. Deselect the table, if necessary, and select the Name column. Object-Vision shows you have selected a column by framing it with a dashed line, and square handles are placed at each corner of the column.

2. Click and drag either of the handles on the right side of the column. Watch the shaded area on the ruler, and stop dragging when the shaded area is 13 characters wide. Release the mouse.

Repeat the preceding steps to change the widths of the remaining three columns. Remember to watch the shaded portion of the top ruler as you drag the column handle. Figure 4.20 shows the last column being sized. Note the shaded area on the top ruler line indicates the current width of the selected column.

The font and bold attributes of both the table name and any of its column names can be changed if you want to enhance the table. In fact, we can bold

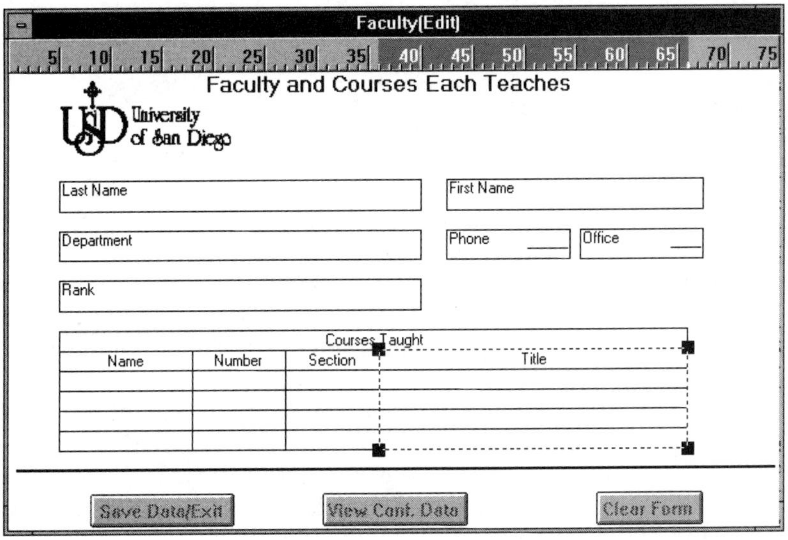

FIGURE 4.20
Sizing a column

(darken) both the table name and the four column names. Select the whole table and right click to select Label Font. Check the Bold check box. Click OK. Using the same steps, make the column titles bold. We now have a table that can contain up to four courses for any given faculty member.

REMOVING TABLE OR COLUMN TITLES

Occasionally you may wish to suppress table title displays or table and column title displays. For example, you might wish to create a simple, matrix table object in which each column's title is insignificant. Both table titles and their columns can be suppressed and restored.

Removing a Table Title

You can change the size of a table's title bar easily. You can either increase its height or make it disappear entirely. Render the title invisible by selecting the table title. When the dotted lines appear, select the square handle on the top of the table. (The pointer changes to a square when it is near the table handle.) Click and drag the handle toward the column titles until the title is removed. When the dashed line on top of the title bar meets the solid column title bar, the table title is eliminated. What remains is the table, with all its column titles, but without the table title.

Restoring a table title is equally simple. There is no table title that you click to select a table. To select a table—not simply one of the columns—double click in any cell in the table. (Double click a *cell,* not a column title.) That selects the table and places the handles in the center of the top and bottom sides. You can now move the pointer to the top handle. Click and drag that handle up to display the table title. You can enlarge the vertical size of the table title by dragging the handle up farther.

Removing a Column Title

You can remove column titles, but you must first remove the table title. Removing column titles follows the same steps as those for eliminating a table title. Select the table. Select a column, any column, by clicking its column title. The entire column is surrounded by dashed lines, and two column handles appear. With the pointer, select the top column handle. Click and drag the handle to reduce the size of the column title to a line. That eliminates all titles at once, of course, for it is not possible to eliminate some column titles and not others in a given table.

You can restore a hidden column title by double clicking any cell. When the handles appear, click and drag the *top* one up to display the column titles. You can then restore the table title once the column titles are restored. Figure 4.21 shows what the Courses Taught table looks like after both its table title and column titles have been hidden.

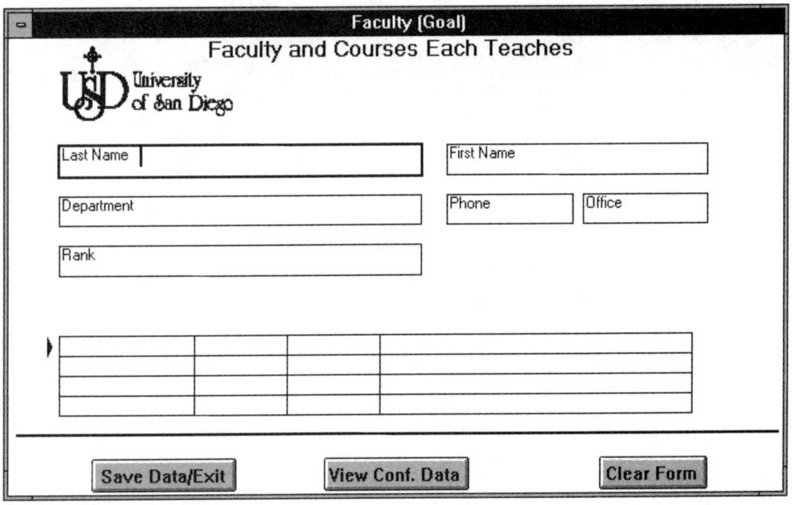

FIGURE 4.21
Table without table or column titles

In our table, we will leave both table and column titles in place, as they provide needed labels for the information that is to be filled in. Without column titles, a user would have no clue about what data should be entered in each column.

4.7 PROVIDING OBJECT HELP

ObjectVision provides help to the application developer through the Help menu on the menu bar. In addition, you can press the function key, F1, to obtain general help on all facets of ObjectVision. However, the type of help provided to application developers is not appropriate for application *users*. For that audience, ObjectVision help is confusing and, at best, only minimally helpful. Providing help for individual fields, buttons, and table columns falls on the shoulders of the developer.

We will add customized help messages to some of the Faculty fields and buttons. Specifically, we can attach a help message to the Last Name field so that the user may press F1 to see if there are any spelling or capitalization restrictions. You can let your user know there is help available for a field, button, or column by placing a graphic symbol next to the object. We will illustrate that notion later in this chapter.

To enter a help message for the Last Name field:

1. Choose Tools|Form to go to edit mode, and then select the Last Name field.

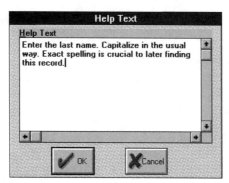

FIGURE 4.22
Providing customized object help

2. Choose Properties|Object or right click the mouse to display the field's property inspector. Select Help. The Help Text dialog box displays the Last Name field name in the text box.

3. In the text box, type the message that is desired. Enter a message such as:

   Enter the last name. Capitalize in the usual way. Exact spelling is crucial to later finding this record.

   Click OK to store the message. Remember to press Ctrl-Enter if you want to move to a new line. If the text extends beyond the right border of the text box, the user will have to scroll the message box to see the entire message.

Figure 4.22 shows the Help Text dialog box for the Last Name field. Return to goal mode to test help. Select the Last Name field and press F1 to see your newly minted Last Name field help. You can add help to the other fields and buttons in the Faculty application. We leave that as an exercise at the end of this chapter.

We hinted earlier that a graphic could be used to indicate that help is available for selected objects on your forms. One example is a circled question mark. The question mark, created in Paintbrush, is an imported graphic and is positioned next to those Faculty form fields that have additional help information. This graphic may provide users with a sense of security or it may clutter the form. It may be preferred to omit the symbols and provide help (albeit, tacit) for all fields, buttons, and table columns. Figure 4.23 shows how to indicate help is available through the use of the question mark graphic.

4.8 SOLICITING USER FEEDBACK

Figure 4.24 shows the completed first page of the Faculty application, including faculty and course information. The application has reached a critical milestone. Its initial design is complete, and its two major forms have been developed.

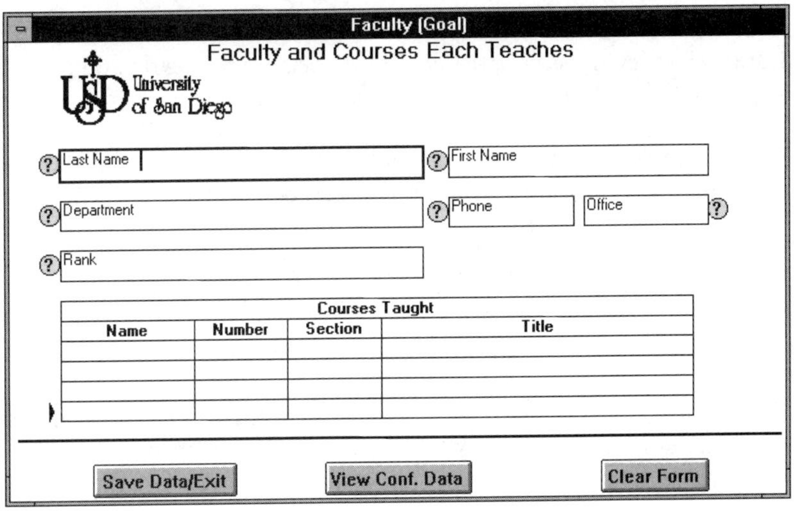

FIGURE 4.23
Using a graphic to indicate object help is available

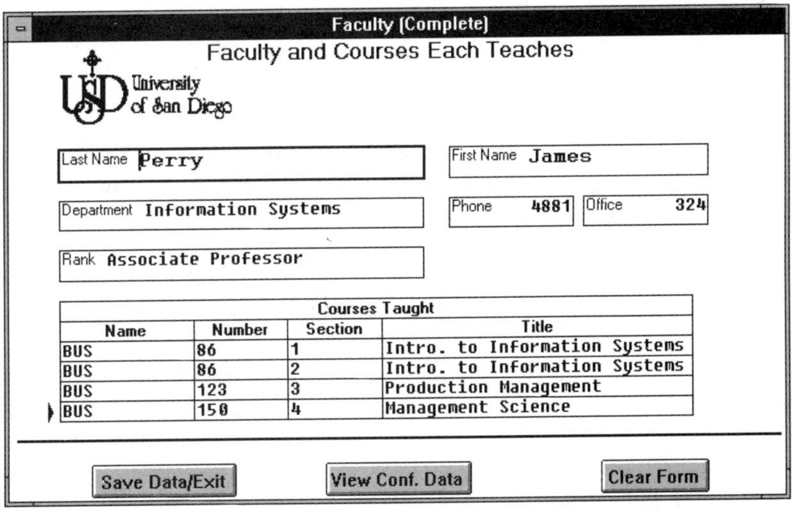

FIGURE 4.24
Completed faculty form

You may need to make changes here and there after the users have examined it, but the fundamental "look" of the application is nearly complete.

At this stage in the development, the Faculty application can benefit from close end-user scrutiny. Users should be given the prototype application to examine and try out. User prototype evaluation is an essential part of application development. The details of how to conduct a user evaluation of the prototype system is beyond the scope of this text, but below are some brief suggestions.

Remember, the users *are* the customers—the reason you are developing the application. So they must be satisfied. Enlist their support early and frequently as you proceed. You might do some or all of the following:

- Let the users play with the application for a short period and then conduct a user-satisfaction survey. Several books and published articles have a wealth of information on what the survey should ask.
- Survey the utility of online and offline documentation.
- Conduct personal or telephone interviews of users.
- Create trouble reports or implement a suggestion box mechanism.

In short, get lots of user feedback. Listen to them and implement their suggested changes. They will quickly become allies rather than resisters when you solicit their help and listen to their recommendations.

SUMMARY

This chapter introduced how to create a multiform application. You learned how to create a new form and move objects from one form to another. We discussed how to add buttons and their associated event trees. Both unrestricted and restricted decision tree branches were illustrated. A restricted branch was used to compare one field against a variety of values. An unrestricted branch was constructed to test several logical conditions and generate results that depended on associated branch conditions.

Some of the ObjectVision built-in functions were used to clear a form, go to the last unfilled field, establish an application title, locate a particular object on a form, save the application to disk, exit ObjectVision, and close and select forms. We illustrated how to combine character strings and numeric results into a single message string. And we examined how to provide object help to users.

The table object was also introduced. Each column of a table can contain a separate fact. The collection of columns for any row contains related information. We showed how to create a table, how to name, add, and remove columns, how to add and remove rows, and how to hide and restore both a table name and column names.

Having completed this chapter, you can now create one or more forms and place on them all of the ObjectVision objects. In addition, you can write rather elaborate decision trees for both buttons and fields that cause actions to occur or that generate values based on arbitrarily complex expressions. These expressions may contain arithmetic operators as well as ObjectVision built-in functions and references to other form objects.

KEY TERMS

Application event tree An event associated with the entire application. It is created by clicking the application title bar.

Change condition A condition in which a field or table column value has changed. It is detected after the focus moves to another object.

Click condition Detected when the left mouse button is clicked. An event tree can trigger its event action when the object is clicked.

Column An object similar to a field, but it contains multiple values. A column is not an independent object; it is part of a table.

Cut When a selected object is deleted from a form. (It is placed on the Clipboard.)

Help, object An attribute of several object types, a customized help message is displayed when F1 is pressed.

Paste The act of transferring data from the Clipboard to the active window.

Restricted branch A decision tree branch that is associated with a field.

Row An element similar to a field, it is not an independent object. It is part of a table, and contains multiple values spanning columns.

Select condition Detected when the focus moves to the object. When you press Enter, the next object is selected. Likewise, clicking an object with a mouse causes both the select and click conditions to occur.

Unrestricted branch A decision tree branch whose logic is not restricted to values in a single field. Its expression can reference functions and several fields simultaneously.

Unselect condition The opposite of the select condition; this condition occurs when the focus leaves the current object. Pressing Tab or Enter, for example, moves the focus from the current object.

REVIEW QUESTIONS

True or False Questions

1. **T F** You can print both event and value trees simultaneously with the Print|All command.

2. **T F** All objects can have event trees.

3. **T F** An application can consist of more than one form.

4. **T F** In edit mode, you can select more than one object to be copied to the Clipboard by pressing the Shift key as you click several objects in turn.

5. **T F** Once you have cut an object, it can be pasted onto another form of the same application.

6. **T F** If you copy a field (Edit|Copy) and paste it back into the same form, both fields will have the same name. Further, if you change the name of one field, both names are changed.

7. **T F** ObjectVision built-in functions all have at least one argument. The list of one or more arguments follows the function name and is enclosed in parentheses.

8. **T F** Two date fields in a form may be subtracted from one another. The difference is expressed in *years*.

9. **T F** For a single application, all button names must be unique, regardless of the number of forms the application has.

10. **T F** Every value tree must contain the otherwise condition. If it does not, then an error is indicated.

Multiple Choice Questions

1. The function that returns the remainder when two values are divided is
    a. @REM
    b. @MOD
    c. @INT
    d. @DIV
    e. @ROUND

2. Decision trees can comprise
    a. one simple condition
    b. branches, conditions, and conclusions
    c. only restricted branches
    d. none of the preceding

3. Printing a decision tree
    a. is useful to recall the logic stored behind forms, buttons, and stacks
    b. is not possible when editing it
    c. can be done by executing Print All in goal mode
    d. none of the preceding

4. Restricted branches
   a. are found in value and event trees
   b. can reference only one field
   c. are identical to unrestricted branches but are more difficult to build
   d. cannot be associated with value trees

5. An event tree can be assigned to
   a. buttons, stacks, and forms
   b. fields, table columns, text, and graphics
   c. buttons, fields, text, forms, and graphics
   d. both a and b are correct
   e. none of the preceding

6. A table
   a. is similar to a matrix, having rows and columns
   b. comprises sizable rows and columns
   c. has a permanent title
   d. both a and b are correct
   e. none of the preceding

EXERCISES

1. Create a one-form student information application. It should have a title, a graphic of your own design (use Paintbrush), and the following fields: First Name, Last Name, Student Identification Number, Major, Phone, and Birth Date. Set the field type appropriately for each field, and restrict the Major field to this list: management, information systems, marketing, economics, and accounting.

2. Modify exercise 1 by adding a Clear Form button. In addition, add a field labeled Age that calculates and displays a student's age.

3. Create a button that saves the application and exits ObjectVision.

CONNECTING FORMS TO DATABASES

OBJECTIVES

This chapter describes how to connect ObjectVision forms to databases so that large quantities of information can be stored. Although the Faculty application was enhanced in Chapter 4, it still lacks the ability to store more than one form's worth of information—it has no "memory." In this chapter we add the facility for the application to store and retrieve information from a database. The following key points are discussed:

■ *How to link ObjectVision fields to corresponding database tables*

■ *How to create a database table from ObjectVision without the use of a separate database product*

■ *How to return database values to ObjectVision fields automatically when a key field value is entered*

■ *How to link an ObjectVision table to more than one database table*

■ *How to establish relations between related database tables and retrieve their values into Object-Vision fields and table columns*

After you finish this chapter, you will have learned about linking form objects to external database files. The Faculty application is functionally whole when you reach the end of the chapter. All that remains is to develop printed reports used by various administrative units, a topic developed in Chapter 6.

CASE: FACULTY INFORMATION FORM (Continued)

After using the prototype Faculty information system, the administrators decide that they like the general layout of the two forms and are satisfied with the available "fit and finish" of the buttons, logo, and titles. They realize that this form is the prototype. However, they make it clear they want to be able to store and retrieve data about their faculty and the courses they teach. Wanting the system to be easy to use, the administrators indicate they would like to be able to update faculty and course information as well as delete irrelevant information when necessary.

With these requirements firmly in mind, we will design and implement the enhancements. In particular, we can see that the faculty database system will likely comprise three external files: one for faculty data (name, hire date, and so on), one holding current course offerings (for example, three sections of Economics 101) and their assigned instructors, and a file containing *all* course titles. The latter contains names of courses that can be matched to course numbers and is a comprehensive list of all courses that are available but not necessarily offered during the current semester.

5.1 INTRODUCTION

Though the Faculty application contains the requisite forms to satisfy the information needs of the university administrators using it, one important capability is missing: information storage and retrieval. An administrator can easily enter the information for each faculty member, but she or he must save each form under a separate name for each faculty member. This is an inadequate, time-consuming, and confusing way to save faculty records on a disk. The problem is, in short, that the "database" is limited to information found on one form. What is needed is a general purpose data store that uses the Faculty forms as windows through which the information is entered or reviewed. The exact form of the data store is not important as it can be reliably connected to the ObjectVision form.

ObjectVision provides the ability to link ObjectVision fields and tables to database storage facilities. This linkage can be thought of as a collection of electronic wires connecting each field in a form to a corresponding database field. Because the links are bidirectional, information can flow from the form to storage (save) or from the database fields to the form (retrieve). In addition to the two methods of entering information—manually or via a value tree—these links provide another way to fill ObjectVision fields and table columns.

Details of exactly how individual field values are stored into or retrieved from a particular database file system are handled by the database system and are transparent to an ObjectVision user. Database storage methods, access techniques, and database table theory are important topics, but they are beyond the scope of this text and unnecessary for the ObjectVision developer. ObjectVision currently supports these database and nondatabase storage systems: ASCII, Btrieve, dBase, DDE, and Paradox. What that means is ObjectVision understands the *format* of each of the preceding storage structures and can construct that format and save or retrieve records stored therein. We need not have any of the database software products themselves (such as, dBase or Paradox) to store and retrieve information in those formats. From an ObjectVision application such as Faculty, you can create the links to a database format that ObjectVision can construct. Subsequently, you can store records into the database and retrieve, delete, or edit them. There are three types of individual links connecting Object-Vision fields to a database: read, write, or both. Read links deliver data from the database fields to ObjectVision fields and table entries. Write links do the opposite; they write the value of ObjectVision fields and table entries into the database on disk.

The next section illustrates how links work. We create a new form that is used to enter information about classes offered during the current semester. Links that can both read and write are established between the form and a database that is created by the ObjectVision application.

5.2 LINKING A FORM TO A DATABASE

Our first task is to create a database containing information about currently offered courses. This material is often found in a registration packet, which lists all courses by department, their section numbers, what time each section meets, and the class location (building and room number). For simplicity's sake, we will omit some of the course offering details because they do not enhance our understanding of linkage. Of course, although the omitted information is important in the finished application, we simply leave it out to create a simpler form while learning about database linkage.

We need a simple form that can be used to enter the following course offering information: the last name of the professor who teaches the course, the course name, number, and section. A form with four fields and an identifying title will suffice. Figure 5.1 shows an example of a Class Offerings data entry form.

Here are the important features of this form to help you create your own. The form, which is labeled "Class Offerings This Semester," is approximately 5 by 3 inches. At the top of the form is the text "Add Courses for Current Semester," which is bold and in a MS Sans Serif, 14 point font. It is centered. Four fields receive the data that is stored in a database. A field labeled Professor holds the

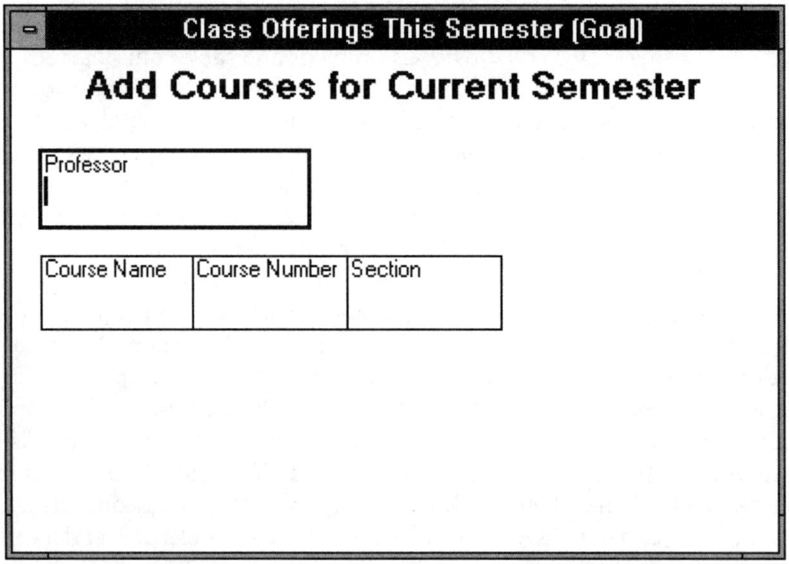

FIGURE 5.1
Class Offerings data entry form

instructor's last name and is about 2 inches long. The remaining fields—Course Name, Course Number, and Section—are each 1.5 inches long. The four field types are all alphabetic. Course names, numbers, and sections can contain letters as well as numbers. Choosing alphabetic field types provides maximum versatility for a wide variety of course labeling schemes. Finally, none of the fields has an associated value tree.

It is useful in this type of application to constrain the possible values that can be entered for Course Name. You will find several instances where that is the case. In our example, we want the entered course name to be consistently spelled and abbreviated. Being a short list of possible course names, we choose the *selection list* data type. The list will have only four entries: BUS, GBA, ACCT, and ECON. A selection list works well when the number of choices is small and you want to control the allowed value input. On the other hand, selection lists are not a good idea for large numbers of choices—say a list of over 15 or so values. Users find long, scrolling lists of values cumbersome. Choices in the preceding list of four values are ranked in order of frequency, with the most likely choice first in the list and the least likely at the end. After looking at the current semester's offered courses, it is determined that the BUS course name is clearly in the majority. Economics courses are the smallest number of offerings this semester.

ESTABLISHING THE DATABASE ENGINE

Before beginning make sure you have the Class Offerings This Semester form displayed. (If you do not wish to create it yourself, the application can be found

Links icon

FIGURE 5.2
Links icon on the Object bar

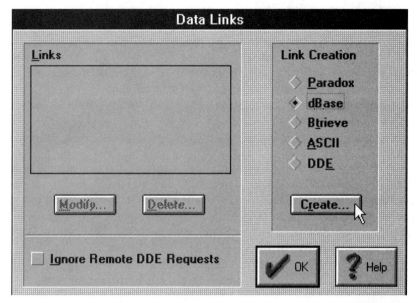

FIGURE 5.3
Data Links dialog box

on the disk accompanying this text. It is called FIG05-01.OVD.) Be sure to enter edit mode so you can use the full set of developer tools.

When a linkage is established between ObjectVision fields and a database system, the information entered on a form can then be saved to the database and later retrieved. The first step in establishing links between ObjectVision fields and table columns is to select the Tools|Links command to specify information about the links. Alternately, you can click the Links icon found on the object bar. Figure 5.2 shows the location of that icon. Starting with this step, you begin defining the relationships between the Class Offerings form and a yet to be created database where the currently offered business course information will be stored.

After you click Links, the Data Links dialog box is displayed (see Figure 5.3). Notice the Link Creation radio buttons on the right side of the dialog box. The five format choices for accessing stored data are listed: Paradox, dBase, Btrieve, ASCII, and DDE. ObjectVision can create database files in any of the listed formats. Of the five choices, Paradox and dBase are quite popular, as they correspond to a large volume of widely distributed database products. Btrieve is the storage format used on the Novell network, and ASCII files are simple, text-based files created by any text editor such as Windows Notepad or MS-DOS edit program.

By default, Paradox is the selected database type. Click dBase, as we want to save and retrieve our course information in this example using the dBase storage format. Note that once data is stored in either dBase or Paradox format, you also can access those files directly from the dBase or Paradox database programs, respectively. Because currently there are no links from the Class Offerings form to any database, the Links text box is empty. After one or more links exist, the Links box displays their names. The Modify and Delete buttons are dimmed indicating they are inappropriate choices because no links exist to be either modified or deleted. We can *create* a link, however, by clicking the Create button located just below the five database format choices. Click Create to continue the process of establishing a linkage between the form and a dBase database.

NAMING THE LINK

The Link Creation dialog box, shown in Figure 5.4, is displayed after you click the Create button. The title bar displays "dBase Link Creation" because we have chosen the dBase engine. Fill in the Link Name text box with a symbolic name that identifies the link. A link name can use any ANSI characters and can be up to 63 characters long. A link name identifies a link between a file and your ObjectVision application. Choose a name that will help you remember the purpose of the link. We have chosen the short but descriptive name "class" (see the Link Name text box in Figure 5.4).

You do not need to enter the dBase file or index names at this point. They will be filled in automatically when you select a name later in the link creation process. Complete this step by clicking the button labeled Create Database (the mouse pointer arrow is poised over the button in Figure 5.4). If you were establishing links to an *existing* database, then you *would not* click the Create Database button.

DESCRIBING THE DATABASE FIELDS

ObjectVision displays the Database Table Creation dialog box, which is used to define each database field prior to creating the database structure (schema). Figure 5.5 shows the dialog box, with suggested database field names listed in the Table Definition text box. Database field names are generated from the field objects already on our form. Notice, however, that the blank character spaces are eliminated in the database field names. Also, they are truncated to ten characters in accordance with dBase field-naming rules. If the Paradox engine had been selected, then Paradox's field-naming rules would permit both spaces in names and longer names.

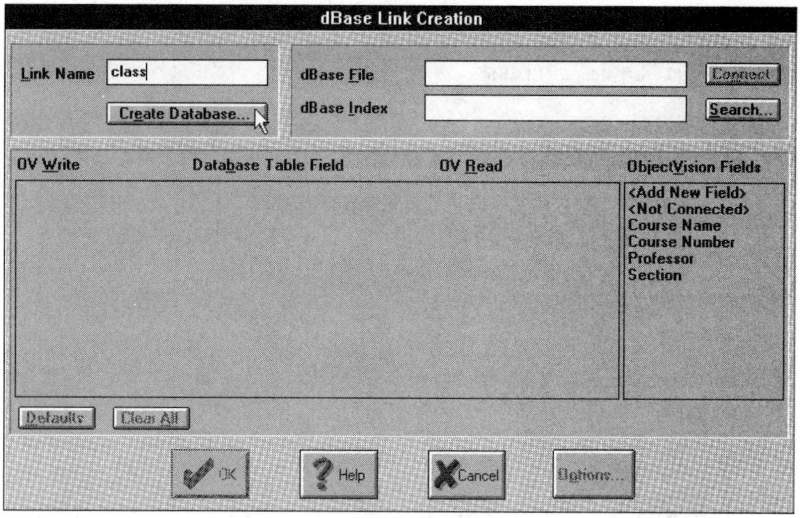

FIGURE 5.4
dBase Link Creation dialog box

The asterisk appearing next to the Professor field indicates which field will be used to organize (index) the database. When creating a database from an ObjectVision form, it is the upper, leftmost field on the form by default. This default works well because we want the list of courses to be sorted by professors' last names. The reasons for this sort order will become clear later. It obviously is not an optimal order for a printed schedule.

Located at the top of the dialog box is the dBase Table text box. Enter into that box a database file name up to eight characters long. We have entered CLASS identifying the database. The link name and database table name are not related and need not be the same.

Field definitions can be added, modified, deleted, or cleared by the like-named buttons shown in Figure 5.5. Additionally, the check box labeled "Index" indicates whether or not a field is part of the **index** of the database. Notice, for example, that the Index box is checked. That means Professor is the organizing field upon which the database is indexed (sorted). Other fields can be included in the index as well.

The current data types for each field are shown in the Table Definition text box. We will modify, slightly, each of the definitions. The highlighted field is also displayed in the Field Definition text boxes above the Table Definition box. When you want to change a field, select it in the Table Definition box. It also appears in the Name and Field Type text boxes, which can be modified. With Professor already highlighted, modify its length to 13 characters. Click the Field Type text box which contains CHAR(17) and type, in its place, CHAR(13). Click the Modify button to validate the change. Then follow these steps to change the remaining fields:

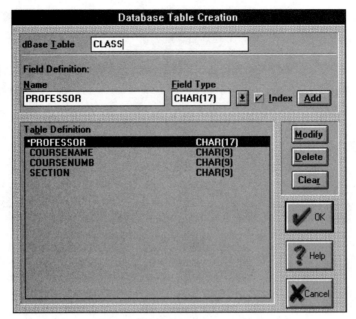

FIGURE 5.5
Database Table Creation dialog box

1. Highlight COURSENAME in the Table Definition text box.
2. Click on Field Type and type CHAR(4).
3. Click the Modify button.
4. Highlight COURSENUMB in the Table Definition text box.
5. Click on Field Type and type CHAR(4).
6. Click the Modify button.
7. Highlight SECTION in the Table Definition text box.
8. Click on the Combo box (the down arrow) found to the right of Field Type. It displays a list of acceptable field types in a drop-down list. Select NUM(nn,nn). Type NUM(2,0). This defines a numeric entry with two digits and zero (0) decimal places.
9. Click the Modify button.

Figure 5.6 shows the Database Table Creation box after changes have been made.

Click OK to establish the fields as modified. The dBase Link Creation dialog box is displayed again with the Link Name and dBase Table names entered automatically from the dBase Table name we entered in previous dialog box. Now that the database field names have been defined and the database definition has been saved on disk, we can establish the relationship between ObjectVision application fields and external database fields.

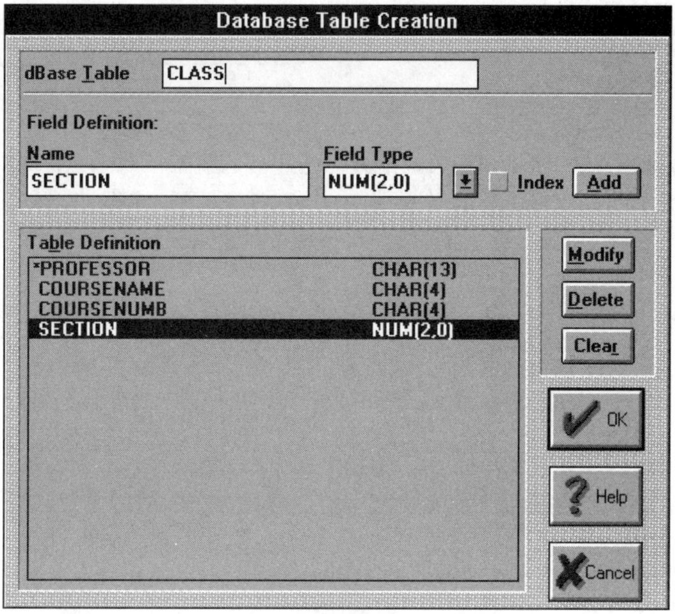

FIGURE 5.6
Modified field definitions

CONNECTING OBJECTVISION FIELDS TO DATABASE FIELDS

To establish the relationships between the newly created database fields and our ObjectVision application fields, click the Connect button found in the upper right corner of the Link Creation dialog box (see Figure 5.4). ObjectVision inserts the database field names in the center column. At this point, there are no connections to the database. In particular, there are no write connections—the type of connections that permit ObjectVision fields to be written to the database. Nor are there any connections to read from the database into the ObjectVision form fields. That is because the columns OV Write and OV Read on either side of the Database Table Field column are empty.

A database field is *connected* to an ObjectVision field when the ObjectVision field name appears in either the OV Write or the OV Read column (or both). Not all database fields need be connected. Start with the highlighted database field PROFESSOR. To connect it to the corresponding ObjectVision field by the same name, click the Defaults button located in the lower left corner of the Link Creation box. Both read and write connections are established for database field names that exactly match the ObjectVision field names. The latter are found in the ObjectVision Fields list box (see Figure 5.4). Both database fields called PROFESSOR and SECTION are read and write connected to their ObjectVision counterparts. However, the database fields COURSENAME and COURSENUMB must be connected manually. Because they are spelled differently than the ObjectVision fields, the Defaults button did not connect them. (Note: any existing connections are not affected by using the Defaults button).

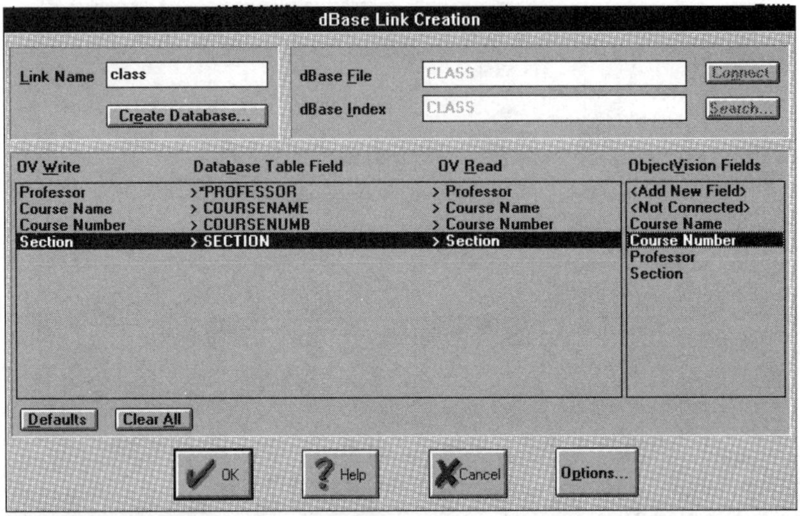

FIGURE 5.7
Connecting database and ObjectVision fields

Highlight the database name COURSENAME by clicking it once. Then, make the connection—both read and write at once—by double clicking Course Name found in the ObjectVision Fields list box. Similarly, connect the database field COURSENUMB: Click it and then double click Course Number in the list of ObjectVision fields. Now all the database field names are connected to ObjectVision fields (see Figure 5.7).

You can remove both read and write connections by selecting the row whose connection is to be removed. Then double click on the <Not Connected> field found in the ObjectVision Fields list box. Both connections are erased. Individual read or write connections can be removed by reversing the procedure: Select the <Not Connected> field. Then double click under the OV Read or OV Write column corresponding to the row whose connection is to be removed. For instance, if you double click on the Professor field under OV Read, its read connection is removed. However, the write connection remains. That means you can write that field to a database, but you cannot retrieve it from the database into an ObjectVision field. Click OK to preserve the settings as shown in Figure 5.7.

SELECTING DEFAULT DATABASE LINK AUTOMATIC BUTTONS

Once you have connected ObjectVision and database fields and click OK to complete that work, the Link Automatic Buttons dialog box appears (see Figure 5.8). By checking the **Link Automatic buttons** you want and then clicking OK, ObjectVision creates database (link) navigation buttons complete with event trees. Each button choice in the list has a corresponding @function. The Top button, for instance, moves to the first row of the database. The Previous button

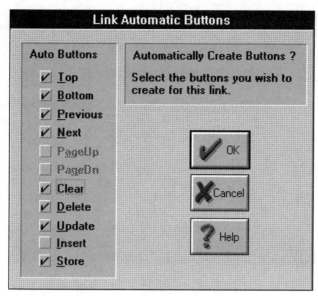

FIGURE 5.8
Link Automatic Buttons dialog box

moves back one record, whereas Next moves forward one record. Buttons that you check are placed on the form and remove the need for you to create database navigation buttons. Besides these navigation buttons, there are several data manipulation and update buttons. Among these are Store, Update, Delete, and Insert. Notice in Figure 5.8 that a subset of the buttons have been checked. Insert, PageUp, and PageDn havae not been checked. Click OK to complete the button selection process.

The Data Links dialog box is displayed again (Figure 5.9). Notice that the link name *class* appears in the Links list box. Most of the work is done. Simply click OK once more to close the Data Links dialog box and return to the application.

ObjectVision automatically inserts into the Class Offerings form all the buttons that we checked in the Link Automatic Buttons dialog box. We have rearranged those buttons slightly so that they are grouped more conveniently. Figure 5.10 shows the new arrangement.

FINE-TUNING THE BUTTON EVENT TREES

The buttons have been rearranged into two groupings: those that nondestructively move around the database (navigation buttons) and those that alter the contents of the database (data store/alter buttons). Above each grouping, we have placed labels identifying the two groups. All buttons are shown at their original size.

Each button has an event tree associated with it, and the triggering event for each button is *click*. Event tree conclusions contain functions, which are collectively

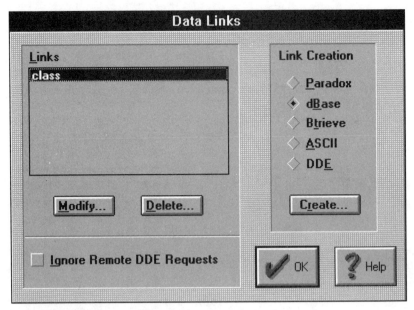

FIGURE 5.9
Data Links showing the Class link

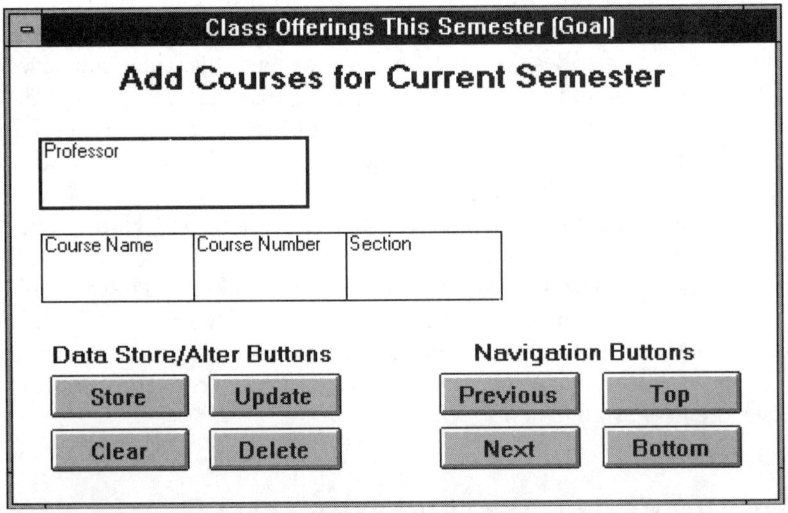

FIGURE 5.10
Finished Class Offerings data entry form

called *linking functions*. (All of the linking functions are listed in the Appendix.) Except for the Store button event tree, all conclusions consist of a single linking function.

The Update button contains the function @UPDATE("class"), which replaces the current database record with the contents of a form's fields for each form field connected to a database field. Like the other linking functions in the event trees for these buttons, the argument inside the parentheses names the link. That name is not the actual database name; rather, it is the link name entered in the Link Name text box of the Link Creation dialog box (Figure 5.4). By design, each button contains a linking function whose name is identical to the button name. The Clear button contains the function @CLEAR("class"), which erases the information on the form (but not in the database) in preparation for writing a new record. The remaining buttons and their event tree conclusion node functions are listed in Table 5.1.

TABLE 5.1
Database Buttons and their event functions

Button	Event Tree Function
Bottom	@BOTTOM ("class")
Clear	@CLEAR ("class")
Delete	@DELETE ("class")
Next	@NEXT ("class")
Previous	@PREVIOUS ("class")
Store	@STORE ("class") @CLEAR ("class") @RESUME
Top	@TOP ("class")
Update	@UPDATE ("class")

Briefly, the functions operate as follows. @UPDATE updates the current database record with the information in the form. @DELETE deletes the current record from the database. @PREVIOUS and @NEXT move to the previous and next record, respectively. @TOP moves to the first record in the database and displays its fields in the form. Similarly, @BOTTOM moves to the last record in the database and displays its contents in the form's fields. Attempting to move above the first record or past the last record results in an Error dialog box being displayed. The messages indicate an attempt to move into an undefined position in the database.

We have altered the behavior of two of the buttons. The conclusion node of the Store button event tree has been changed to behave slightly differently. When a user has filled in the four form fields, he or she presses the Store button to save the form data in the associated database, CLASS. Besides simply storing the information, we want the form to clear and the focus to move back to the Professor field in preparation for the next information to be entered. By default, the Store button stores the data in the database but does not clear the form. We prefer that the form be cleared as just described. We alter the event tree's only conclusion node so that it contains the following lines:

```
@STORE("class")
@CLEAR("class")
@RESUME
```

The Store button is strategically placed so that it is the first button selected after the last field, Section, has been filled in. Most of the time, a user will simply want to store the form's contents in the CLASS database. Conveniently, the Store button receives the focus. The user can simply press the Spacebar or click the button to store the form data.

The Delete button's event tree has also been changed slightly. Normally, the conclusion node responding to the click event contains the @DELETE function. In particular, ObjectVision automatically placed the function @DELETE("class") in the Delete button event tree. By clicking that button, a user deletes the current record. We feel that the user should be warned before taking such a drastic action. Accordingly, we alter the function to the following form:

```
@DELETE("class",1)
```

Notice the second, optional argument we added—the digit 1. When present, that second argument causes a Warning dialog box to be displayed with the message **Delete the current record?** along with the OK and Cancel buttons. This is simply good planning. It gives the user a chance to back out in case the Delete button was clicked accidentally.

STORING CLASS OFFERINGS DATA IN A DATABASE

Entering data into the Class Offerings form and preserving it are both simple tasks now that the form is linked to an associated database. Simply enter professor and course information about the semester's offerings and click on the Store button. Immediately, the data is stored in the dBase-style database on disk. After pressing Store, the form clears and you continue with the enter data and store scenario. Though not an exciting chore, that is the way data is entered into the database. However, we have eliminated the data entry process by providing the database CLASS.DBF (and its associated index file, CLASS.NDX) complete with several example classes and professors. You can use the supplied database, or you can try your hand at entering some or all of the information yourself.

REVIEWING THE CLASS OFFERINGS
DATABASE INFORMATION

Perhaps the easiest part of using the Class Offerings form is reviewing the information that has been placed in the database. First clear the form by pressing the Clear button. Next go to the first row of the database by clicking Top and review what you see. You see the record for Professor Ambrose (teaching Business 123, section 1). Continue reviewing the other class offerings: Click the Next button repeatedly to display row after row of class information. Notice that the data is displayed in alphabetical order by professor's name because the link field has been designated as the organizing (index) field during the link definition process (see Figure 5.6). Clicking Bottom goes to the last row (record) in the database (one of Professor Zoller's classes). Mistakes can be corrected by first displaying the errant record and then moving directly to the field. Simply enter the correct information into the field and make any other changes. Then click Update to place the altered information back into the database. If you forget to click Update, then the changes are not posted to the database and are therefore lost. Entire records can be removed from the database by displaying them and then clicking the Delete button.

CREATING THE COURSE TITLES DATABASE

While the Class Offerings form and its associated database CLASS.DBF provide information about the current semester's course offerings, that database does not list *all* the courses that are generally available from one semester to the next. This encyclopedic list of courses—typically found in undergraduate and graduate catalog course listings—can be created via a form in the same way the Class Offerings data has been created. The database comprises four fields that are labeled with names such as CNAME, CNUMBER, CTITLE, and CCREDITS. A typical row representing Business 16, a three-credit course titled Quantitative Business Analysis, would contain these four values for the corresponding fields:

CNAME	CNUMBER	CTITLE	CCREDITS
BUS	016	Quantitative Bus. Analysis	3

The creation of this form has been left as an exercise. However, the database, in dBase format, is available on a disk supplied with this text. It consists of two files, a database and its index (whose names are CLASSNME.DBF and CLASSNME. NDX). The latter file is an index file, which keeps the database rows in order by course name and course number. You can use CLASSNME in the finished application instead of creating it from scratch. We encourage you to create a form, define a link, and populate a database before you begin reading the next chapter.

5.3 ESTABLISHING OTHER FIELD LINKS

We have learned how to create a database and populate it by using the Object-Vision link tool. Recall that we created a form and then defined the linkage between ObjectVision fields and database fields. This section describes link establishment from a slightly different perspective: We assume that a database containing faculty information already exists. That is, we connect the Faculty form fields to databases that have already been defined and filled with data by some other software product. Thus, we can concentrate on the process of coupling application fields to their corresponding databases and database fields and do not have to spend time on how to create a database with ObjectVision.

In this section, we will connect several of the Faculty fields to a dBase database. The featured database contains information about each faculty member, including last name, first name, department, phone number, office number, and rank. (Years of Service is a calculated field and therefore not stored in the database.) Additionally, the database contains five confidential fields: Birth Date, Hire Date, Tenure Date, Gender, and Salary. These correspond to the fields that are displayed on the second form (Confidential Data) of the Faculty application (see Figure 4.15). The database contains a total of eleven fields. The dBase-format database, FACULTY.DBF, and its associated index file, FACULTY.NDX, are available on disk. Table 5.2 names the three databases that are linked to the Faculty application and provides a brief explanation of the contents of each database.

TABLE 5.2
Databases linked to the Faculty form

Database Name	Database Format	Data Fields Stored in Database
CLASS.DBF	dBASE IV	Class name, number, section number, and assigned professor.
CLASSNME.DBF	dBASE IV	Class name, number, title, and credit hours.
FACULTY.DBF	dBASE IV	Faculty member's last and first names, department, rank, gender, office number, phone number, birth date, hire date, year tenured, and annual salary.

Linking a form to a database provides several advantages over having to create a copy of each form from the ones stored on disk. When a form is linked to a database, the form acts as a window into the database, and each row of the linked database can be displayed, in turn, in the form's fields. There are several advantages that accrue with forms linked to one or more databases:

- You can easily access the records in an external table without having any knowledge of a database or its access "language."

- You can see information from several different sources including different databases. That is, information can be assembled from various sources into a single form.

- Using ObjectVision, you can access information from other Windows applications.

- Maintaining, altering, or changing information is simpler with a form whose fields and tables are linked to a database.

Locating a particular piece of information in a database through a form interface is possible because each record in the underlying database is uniquely identifiable by a key field or fields. The key field or fields form the record's **primary key**. Database products permit the database records to be indexed on the primary key field, thus maintaining the rows in ascending order on the index field. Having this index field available reduces the time it takes to locate and display a record from the database.

CONNECTING OBJECTVISION FIELDS TO DATABASE FIELDS

The process of linking a form's fields to one or more databases is similar to the process described in Section 5.2. The main difference is that we are not *creating* the database with ObjectVision. Rather, we are merely establishing the connections between ObjectVision objects (fields in this case) and corresponding database fields. In this section we illustrate how to connect the eleven ObjectVision form fields to the FACULTY database. The next section describes how to connect an ObjectVision table to one or more databases, because that process differs significantly from field linkage steps.

Any ObjectVision field can have a connection to a database field. The connection can be a read connection, a write connection, or both. A **read connection** allows data to be transferred from a database entry to the ObjectVision form. A **write connection** allows data to be transferred from an ObjectVision field and written into the database. A field connection with both types of connections means that the ObjectVision field can both retrieve its value from the database and write an altered value back to the database.

Before establishing connections between the Faculty forms and the database FACULTY.DBF, be sure that the Faculty application—in its latest form (see Figure 4.24)—is open. Execute Tools|Form to enter edit mode. Now, we are ready to establish the connections between the eleven Faculty application fields and their corresponding database entries.

To link the Faculty form to a dBase database:

1. Choose Tools|Links (or click the Links icon). The Data Links dialog box is displayed (see Figure 5.3).

2. Be sure that dBase is selected as the Link type (the default is Paradox).

3. Click the Create button. The Data Links dialog box closes and the dBase Link Creation dialog box is displayed (see Figure 5.4). The I-beam insertion point is in the Link Name text box, ready for you to enter the symbolic link name.

4. Type any name you would like. For example, type the name faculty. Next, press Tab to move the insertion point to the dBase File text box.

5. If you cannot remember the name of the file to enter, click the Search button (see Figure 5.7). A list of database files and index files is displayed.

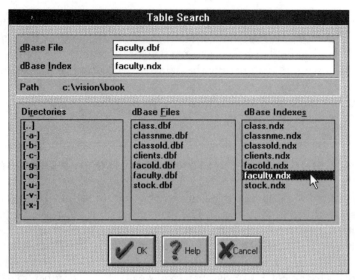

FIGURE 5.11
Table Search dialog box

Figure 5.11 shows an example of the Table Search dialog box that is presented.

6. With the file and index names displayed, you can easily locate the Faculty database and index file names. Select the FACULTY database file by clicking the file name FACULTY.DBF in the dBase Files. Similarly, select the associated index file FACULTY.NDX from the dBase Indexes column. After each file name is clicked, its name appears in the corresponding text box at the top of the dialog box. Click OK to close the Table Search dialog box. The Link Creation dialog box is redisplayed.

7. Finally, click the Connect button to complete this first phase.

The Connect button, displayed in a bold typeface signifying it can be activated, retrieves all the database column names (also known as field or attribute names) and places them in the Database Field Column so they can be subsequently associated with form fields. Figure 5.12 shows the dialog box with FACULTY database field names listed in the Database Table Field column.

SELECTING DEFAULTS FOR EASY CONNECTIONS

At this point there are no connections to write from the ObjectVision fields in the form to the database. Likewise, there are no read connections to permit the transfer of information from the database to fields in the form. Click the **Defaults button** found in the lower left of the Link Creation dialog box. The ObjectVision fields found in the form (also listed in the dialog box) whose names

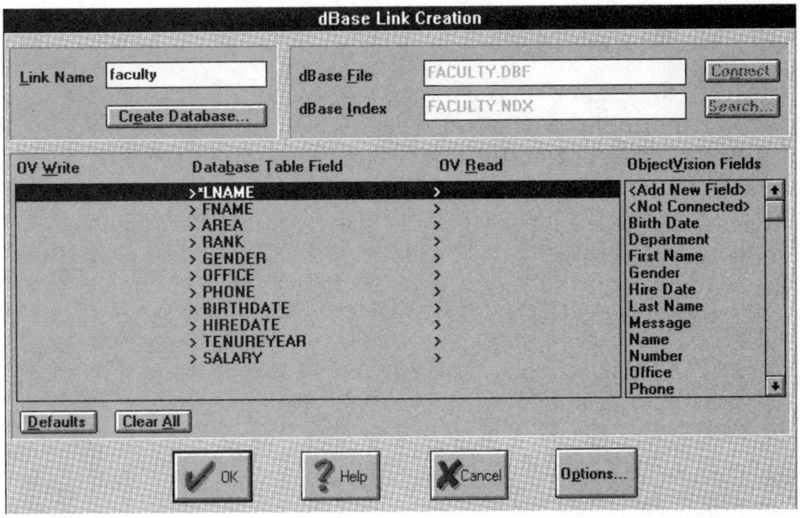

FIGURE 5.12
dBase Link Creation dialog box for FACULTY

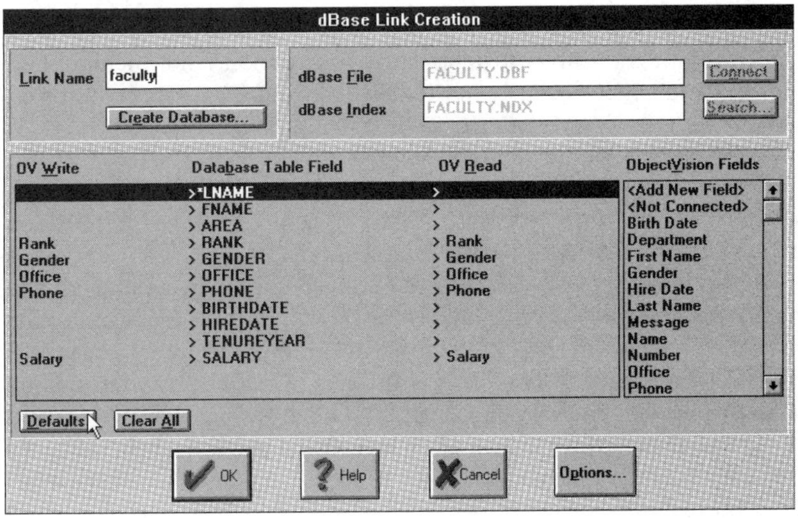

FIGURE 5.13
Connecting fields with the Defaults button

match the listed database fields are automatically entered into the OV Write and OV Read columns. Fields in the form that are not spelled the same as the database fields (for example, the form field First Name) must be entered manually. Using the Defaults button is the fastest way to connect matching fields with both read and write connections. Figure 5.13 shows the Faculty form fields that are associated with the database fields they flank.

LINKING THE REMAINING FIELDS

Notice that the column on the right is labeled OV Read. Fields in that column can read data from the database. The OV Write column on the left contains columns that can write information from the application to the database. Examine Figure 5.13 again for a moment. The form field Rank is found in both the OV Write list and the OV Read list. Thus, a value in the form's Rank field can be written to the database field (also called RANK). Because Rank is in the OV Read list, an empty form can receive the value of the Rank field *from* the database.

The ObjectVision Fields box on the right side of the Link Creation dialog box contains a list of all fields in the ObjectVision application (file). These entries can be used to change the link connections manually. There are two convenient ways to connect any remaining ObjectVision application form fields to a database. The OV Read and OV Write connections can be made one at a time or together. We will connect the highlighted database field, LNAME (see Figure 5.13), to the corresponding application field, Last Name, so that both the read and write connections are established simultaneously.

1. Click the database field (LNAME in this case) you want to connect.

2. Double click the ObjectVision field you want to couple to the selected field in the Database Table Field. The ObjectVision field Last Name is placed simultaneously in the OV Read and OV Write columns on either side of the LNAME database field.

Notice that the highlighted bar moves down to the next database field, FNAME. You can double click the associated ObjectVision field in the ObjectVision Fields list to connect it to the highlighted database field.

The other, more versatile way to establish links is to set individually either the OV Read or the OV Write link. For instance, suppose you want to be able to fill in the Gender field from its database field but not allow it to be written back to the database (a read-only form field). The OV Read field corresponding to the database field GENDER would contain "Gender," whereas the OV Write column for GENDER would remain empty—precluding writing GENDER to the database. We will manually connect both the OV Read and the OV Write links for the AREA database field.

AREA is the database field name that corresponds to the Faculty form field we title Department. To link the OV Read and OV Write columns individually, do the following:

1. Click on the ObjectVision Department field found in the ObjectVision Fields list.

2. Double click the column (OV Read or OV Write) to which you want the connection made. Finish the job by double clicking the other column for the same database field.

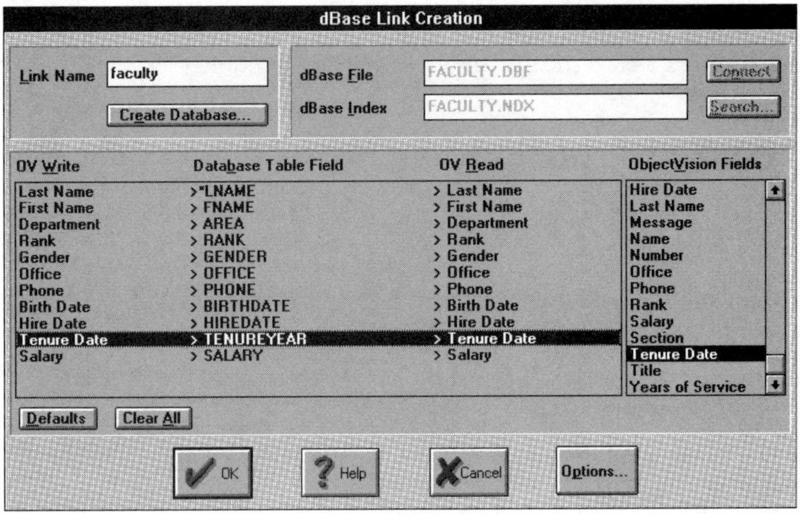

FIGURE 5.14
Completing the OV Read and OV Write connections

You can see that by clicking either the OV Read or the OV Write column, you control which of the links (read or write) is established for a chosen ObjectVision field. Connect the remaining database fields to their corresponding Faculty application fields. Figure 5.14 shows the completed links. Notice that there are ObjectVision fields listed that are not connected to, or associated with, any database fields. That is okay. For example, the Message field (see Figure 5.14) is not linked to the database because its value is wholly generated from a value tree and need not receive a value from the database.

DISCONNECTING LINKS

There are two ways to disconnect existing OV Read and OV Write connections: simultaneously or individually. You can disconnect both connections simultaneously by executing these two simple steps:

1. Click the row containing the connection you want to "break."

2. Double click <Not Connected> found in the ObjectVision Fields box located on the right side of the Link Creation dialog box (see Figure 5.13). Both the read and write connections are erased.

To remove either the OV Read or the OV Write connection:

1. Click <Not Connected>.

2. Double click (careful here) either the OV Read column or the OV Write column corresponding to the database field you want to disconnect. Be

careful not to double click over the database field name, as that will disconnect both the read and the write connection.

SETTING THE LINK OPTIONS

Several different link options are available with ObjectVision. The link options can provide several automatic features, including updating the database, locating a record based on a user-supplied key and delivering the remaining fields to a form, and inserting new records into the linked database. Select from the link options choice by clicking the button labeled Options found in the lower right area of the Link Creation dialog box (Figure 5.14).

Click the Options button, and the Optional Link Capabilities dialog box is displayed (see Figure 5.15). On the left side are the Link Options check boxes. If Auto Insert is checked, then the information from a form is automatically inserted into the database when you type values in a blank form and then move off the record (with database navigation buttons). Auto Update automatically updates database records that are both read and write connected. The database row is updated whenever you change one or more values in a form and then move to a different database record. The updates occur automatically, before a new database row is displayed in a form.

The options labeled Cascade Deletes and Cascade Updates cause secondary database rows associated with the primary database links to be deleted or updated, respectively, at the same time as the primary records. Our Faculty application does not make use of any of these four options because the functions are handled explicitly by buttons placed on the form itself.

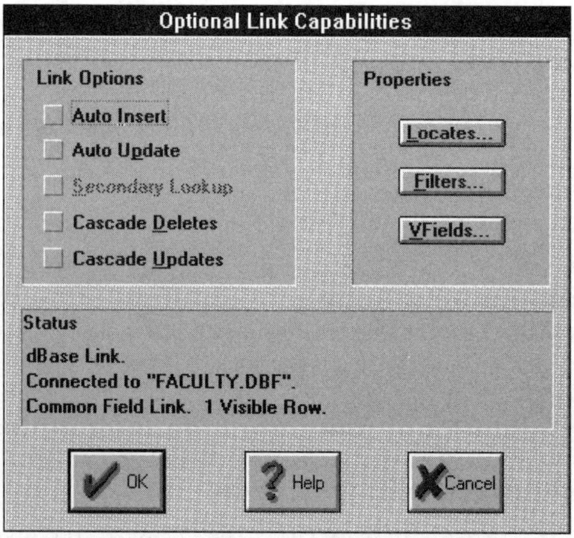

FIGURE 5.15
Setting optional link capabilities

UNDERSTANDING THE LINK STATUS

The link Status box displays information about the current link. It shows what type of table is linked (dBase in our example), the table name (FACULTY.DBF), and what type of ObjectVision object is connected (Common Field Link). A **common link** is the name given when form fields are linked to a database. You will learn later in this section that the two other types of links, primary and secondary, are links between a form table and a database. Because a common link is used in our example, the number of visible rows is limited to one (only one database row shows on the form at once). Table objects can display more than one row, of course.

ESTABLISHING A LOCATE FIELD

Three "properties" are shown in the Optional Link Capabilities dialog box: locates, filters, and VFields (see Figure 5.15). Briefly, the locates property specifies a special field that ObjectVision monitors. Whenever the contents of that field change, ObjectVision attempts to find a corresponding record in the database containing that value. If an index field in the database corresponds to the value in the locate field, then the remaining database field values are read and placed in the form. This is perhaps the most important of the optional capabilities provided by ObjectVision. In the Faculty form, for example, we can designate Last Name as a locates field. Then, whenever we enter a last name in a blank form, the entire record for a faculty member with that last name, if found, is automatically delivered to the form. All the fields are filled in automatically. Locates is the most important link property.

The filters option allows you to enter a logical expression that is evaluated before a database record is passed through the link to the form. For example, you could enter a filter expression that limits retrieved faculty records to members of the finance department.

VFields stands for **Virtual Fields** and represents a field that does not exist in the database but that can be determined from it. Only the expression used to calculate the virtual field exists.

Of the three properties, we implement the most important one—locates. Click the Locates button to begin the easy process of establishing a locates field. Figure 5.16 shows the Locate Indexes dialog box displayed when you click the Locates button. Notice that the dBase index field LNAME appears in the Table Index Field column. The ObjectVision field Last Name appears in the Locate Field column.

Recall that a **Locate field** is an ObjectVision field that triggers a database search whenever the field value changes. If the search is successful, then that record's fields are written into connected ObjectVision fields on the form. It is important to understand that locate fields can only operate with databases that have been indexed. Furthermore, they can locate database rows only on the fields used to index the database table.

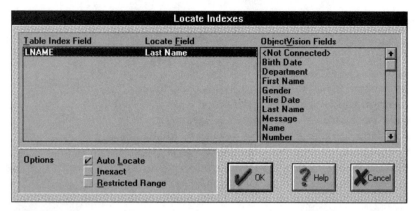

FIGURE 5.16
Establishing record search options

At the bottom of the Locate Indexes dialog box are three locate options: Auto Locate, Inexact, and Restricted Range. The option used most often, Auto Locate, is checked by default. It causes the link to position itself on the record in the database table that matches the value entered into the ObjectVision field. This occurs automatically every time the locate field value in the ObjectVision form changes. For example, the locate field in our Faculty form is Last Name. Its corresponding database field is called LNAME. When you fill in the Last Name field of a blank form with, for example, Perry, and press Tab to move to a new field, dBase searches the database looking for the record whose LNAME field is Perry. After finding the record in the database, the remaining ten fields are delivered to the form and placed into their respective fields. Thus, Auto Locate makes it easy to retrieve a previously stored record knowing a key value—the locate field. The other two options, Inexact and Restricted range, are mutually exclusive. That is, they cannot be used together.

Inexact, another Locate Indexes Options check box, allows you to specify incomplete locate values used to search for database records. For example, if you entered the partial last name Mo in the Last Name field, the link would search for a partial match and return the first database record whose LNAME field begins with Mo. This option is particularly handy if users do not always know the correct spelling of names, part numbers, or other primary access keys.

Restricted Range allows only database records that *exactly* match the value entered in the locate field to be retrieved. You could restrict the range of last names to just "Moore." The link then delivers all database records that match, but you will never be able to create or update any other records. They are masked from your view. You cannot move to any other record in the linked database that does not exactly match the locate value. For our application, we leave the Auto Locate box checked but not the other two Locate Indexes Options.

Click OK to close the Locate Indexes dialog box. The Optional Link Capabilities dialog box reappears (Figure 5.15). Click OK once more to close the dialog box. After the Link Creation dialog box appears, click OK again. The Link Automatic Buttons dialog box appears (Figure 5.8). As before, we select some of the buttons by clicking their check boxes. Select only the following buttons: Top, Bottom, Previous, Next, Store, Update, and Delete. Click OK to return to the first link dialog box displayed, Data Links. Click OK to complete the process. We have now established a common link connecting each of the eleven Faculty fields to a database called FACULTY.DBF. One field found on the Confidential Data form, Years of Service, is not stored in the database. Its value is calculated by a value tree defined for the field. It should not be saved to or retrieved from the database because the value changes with the current date.

When you complete the link definition process, the database positioning and alteration buttons are placed on the surface of the ObjectVision form. Next we will briefly rearrange the buttons into more logical groupings.

PLACING AND MODIFYING LINK AUTOMATIC BUTTONS

The Link Automatic buttons are selected as one of the last steps in defining a common link. They are placed on a form's surface in a somewhat random way. Before moving on, you may want to examine the buttons' event trees, move and group buttons, and even resize some buttons. We will regroup the buttons into related groups and rename the Save/Exit button as "Exit." We have kept the original three buttons that appear on Faculty form: View Conf. Data, Clear Form, and Save Data/Exit (see Figure 4.24).

Select View|Ruler and select the Characters option to show rulers on both the top and the left sides of the form. Then rearrange the buttons into groups similar to Figure 5.17. The buttons are organized into related groups. Left to right, these groups are form manipulation buttons, database alteration buttons, database navigation buttons, and application exit. The space between button groups is three characters, and the top row of buttons is at character position 21 (the top edge of the top row). If you are careful in placing the buttons, you can squeeze them all onto one screen and avoid using the scroll bar. Notice that the Exit button—which is renamed from Save/Exit—is in the lower, rightmost position. That is a good location because the lower right is usually the final place a user's eyes rest after completing or viewing a form. Exit is twice the vertical size of other buttons.

Before you continue reading, be sure your application looks approximately like the one in Figure 5.17. Try out the new link to make sure it works correctly. If you want to see the application, as it stands, in action, then use the version of the Faculty application that corresponds to its development at this point. It is the file FIG05-17.OVD on the disk included with the text. Take a moment to try the application. Test the link to ensure that data is delivered to all the fields. First enter goal mode. Then do the following:

1. Clear the form: Click the Clear Form button or press Ctrl+C.

2. Next, enter Lounsbury into the form's Last Name field.

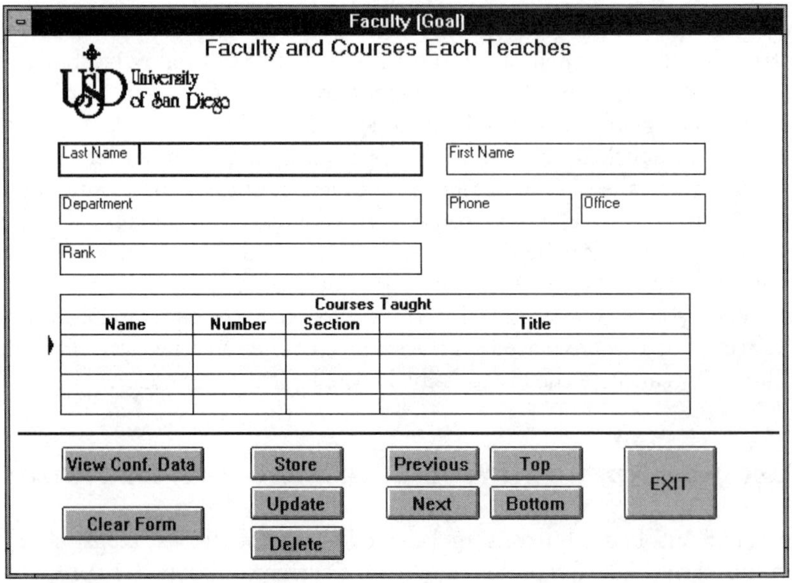

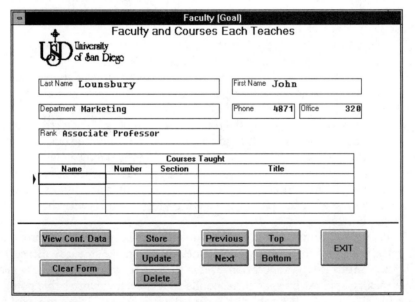

FIGURE 5.17
Faculty form with buttons rearranged

FIGURE 5.18
Test of the common link to the database

The link between the form (Faculty) and its database (FACULTY.DBF) is correctly working if the remaining form fields are all filled in automatically. Figure 5.18 shows the first page of the Faculty form with information filled in by the link.

The next section describes how to link a table to one or more databases. The process is similar to linking fields, but there are some significant differences.

5.4 LINKING TABLE OBJECTS TO DATABASES

The connections we have created between the fields of the Faculty form and those of the databases are called *common links*. Recall that common links exist whenever one or more ObjectVision (application) fields are connected to external files or databases. Table objects, such as the ObjectVision table Courses Taught (in Figure 5.17), can also be linked to databases. Because tables can display several database rows at once, slightly different linkage mechanisms are employed.

Two types of links can be used to connect ObjectVision table objects to databases: primary and secondary. If there is more than one link between a table object and a database, then the first link established is called the **primary link**. That link must be the one that fetches the multiple database records to fill in the table rows. All other links may be created in any order, and they are called **secondary links**. They usually fill in additional table column information *after* the primary link delivers table rows. In this section we show how to link a table to two databases. The primary link created retrieves the first three table columns—Name, Number, and Section—from a database. A secondary link uses the course name and number to look up the course title from another database and deliver it to the last table column, called Title. First, we will create the primary link between Courses Taught and a dBase database.

The purpose of the table Courses Taught is to display all courses that are scheduled to be taught by the professor whose name appears in the Last Name field. A user can type in a professor's last name to retrieve information about where her or his office is as well as the time-sensitive information about courses she or he is teaching this semester.

A table comprises one or more columns containing one or more rows. Similar to a field, a table *column* can display values from several records instead of merely one. For multirow tables, there is only one *current* row. That row is marked with a small, right-pointing triangle. The current row of the table shown in Figure 5.18 is the first one. The columns of the table display up to four courses (an artificial limit, but one we hope few professors exceed). Beginning with the leftmost column, each row displays the name of the course (such as BUS or ACCT), its number, the section number, and the course title (such as Contract Pricing). When we finish, each of these columns will be linked to a database that delivers, row by row, up to four rows associated with a professor. The Last Name field is the key that tells the table linkage which fields to deliver to the application form and which to skip. The table receives values in two parts: the first three columns are associated with one database and the last column (Title) receives its information from a separate database. The reasons for placing information in two databases is to follow good database design rules (normalization). The details of these rules are important but beyond the scope of this book.

We build the database links in two steps. First, the primary link is established between the Name, Number, and Section columns. Then, a secondary link is created to deliver the title once the course name and number have been determined. You specify the primary link by creating it *first*.

CREATING A PRIMARY LINK

The process of establishing the first link between a table and a database is essentially the same as discussed previously for fields and databases. Briefly, you link the Name, Number, and Section columns of the Courses Taught table to a database labeled CLASS.DBF (supplied on disk for your convenience). First execute the command Forms|Tool to move into development (edit) mode. Then follow these steps:

1. Click the Link icon or execute Tools|Links. The Data Links dialog box displays.

2. Select dBase from the Link Creation check boxes and then click the Create button to begin describing the new table link to the dBase style database.

3. As before, enter a new link name in the Link Name text box. Link names can be up to 63 characters long and comprise any ANSI character (including blanks). For convenience, enter the link name ClassesTaughtPrimary (without spaces).

4. Click the Search button to locate the database and index files for the database file holding the preliminary class information for each professor. They are called CLASS.DBF and CLASS.NDX, respectively. Select each of those from their respective lists and click OK.

5. Click the Connect button in the Link Creation dialog box.

6. Establish the OV Write and OV Read connections so that they match those shown in Figure 5.19. Notice, in particular, that the database field PROFESSOR is write connected to the ObjectVision field Last Name but is *not* read connected. That allows the link to update or add a new professor's name and classes to the CLASS database if needed. The OV Read connection for the database field PROFESSOR is not needed because it is already being delivered to the application through a previously created link. Having two sources deliver the same information to an application is unnecessary and confusing.

7. Next, click the Options button.

8. Click the Locates button in the Properties list. Then double click the field Last Name. This associates the ObjectVision field Last Name with the database index field PROFESSOR, permitting the Last Name field to be monitored for changes. When you change this ObjectVision field, the database is searched for a matching value in the PROFESSOR field.

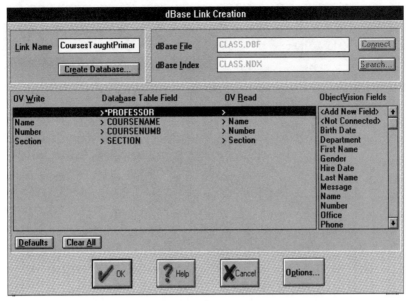

FIGURE 5.19
Establishing a primary link

9. Click the Restricted Range check box to restrict retrieved database rows; click OK to leave the Locate Indexes dialog box.

10. Check the Link Options selections labeled Auto Insert and Auto Update. This allows ObjectVision to write any changed rows in Classes Taught to the CLASS database. It is important, as we will not add any more database Link Automatic buttons to the application (such as a Store button). If a new entry is created, then the Auto Insert will automatically add the new class assigned to a professor to the database. This is easier than requiring a user to press a Store or Update button. The correctly configured Optional Link Capabilities box is shown in Figure 5.20.

11. We do not need any more Link Automatic buttons, so merely click OK. The Link Creation dialog box is displayed.

12. Click OK twice: once to close the Link Creation dialog box and a second time to close the Data Links dialog box.

The creation of the primary link between the CLASS database and the Courses Taught table object is completed.

Before trying out the new primary link, make a small change to the Number column of the Courses Taught table. Use the property inspector to change that column's data type to alphanumeric. This change will facilitate displaying course numbers whose leading digit(s) are zero. If the data type were left at the general default, then some of the course titles would not be delivered (later) to the Title column. Remember, right click the column name to change the type for a column (do not click an individual cell).

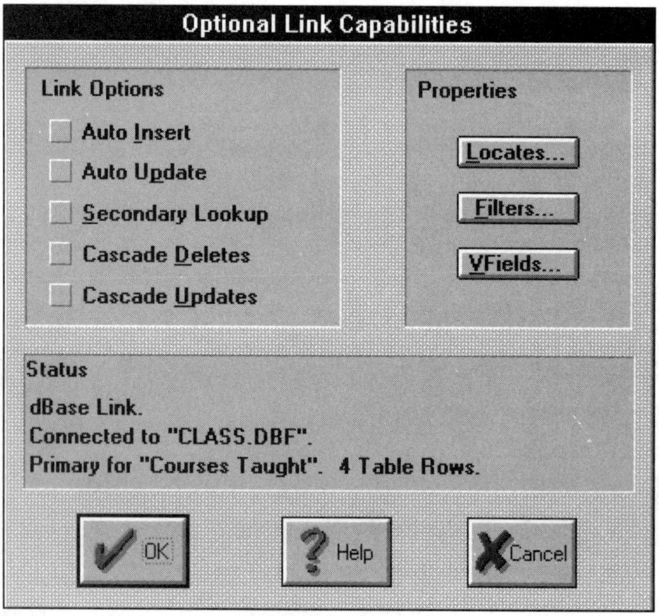

FIGURE 5.20
A primary link status display

Try out the new linkage. First click the Return icon to enter goal mode. Then clear the form by clicking the Clear Form button. Then enter into the Last Name field the name Helmsley (be careful to spell it exactly as shown—including capitalization). If you created the links correctly, then the table will display the four courses that Helmsley teaches. If you choose not to follow all the preceding steps, open the file called FIG05-20.OVD supplied on the disk packaged with this book (the work has been done for you).

In the next section, we create a secondary link to fill in the title of each course. Each step of the process is described.

ESTABLISHING A SECONDARY LINK

The ClassesTaughtPrimary link delivers the Name, Number, and Section columns to the Courses Taught table whenever the Last Name field changes. Those three table column values are stored in one database called CLASS. Stored separately, the Title column values are permanently stored in the CLASSNME database. Though we could save a bit of work by storing all four table columns in one database, doing so could lead to inconsistent database values. We could store a course title with each occurrence of its course name and number in the CLASS database. Then, the courses taught by Baker this semester would be these database rows:

PROFESSOR	COURSENAME	COURSENUMB	SECTION	TITLE
Baker	BUS	190	1	Business Policy
Baker	BUS	190	2	Bus. Pol.
Baker	BUS	190	8	business policy

Notice, in particular, that there are three variants on the course's title—it is spelled three different ways. Of course, you might spell these consistently if they were entered as a group, but they could be spelled differently if the courses were input into the database in time-of-day order. This example illustrates the problem with combining two distinct "facts" into one database table. The course title consistency problem disappears if a course title occurs only *once* in a distinct table. So, a separate database, called CLASSNME.DBF, is created to hold course names, numbers, and titles. One database row corresponds to one course, regardless of the number of sections offered for that course.

A separate database must be searched to locate each course title and deliver it to the ObjectVision Title column. This secondary link is created after the original, primary link is established. The primary link must first deliver the name and number values before those ObjectVision column values can be used to search the class titles database (CLASSNME) for its corresponding title. The steps to create this secondary link are nearly the same as for a primary link. Some steps are abbreviated because they replicate those shown earlier. The process is as follows:

1. Click the Link icon. Click the dBase selection in the Link Creation dialog box, as the database is in dBase format. Then click the Create button to begin the process of defining the link.

2. Enter CoursesTaughtSecondary in the Link Name text box. Click the Search button, and select the database CLASSNME.DBF and the index file name CLASSNME.NDX for the database and index files, respectively. Click OK.

3. Click the Connect button. Connect the CTITLE field, both OV Read and OV Write, to the ObjectVision column name, Title. (You may have to scroll the ObjectVision Fields display to locate Title. Choices are arranged in alphabetical order.) Click the Options button. The Optional Link Capabilities dialog box is displayed. Notice, particularly, the Status information (see Figure 5.21). It indicates a secondary link is being defined and one record per row is retrieved.

4. Click the Locates button. Double click the ObjectVision Fields entry, Name, to associate it with the dBase index, CNAME. Click the Table Index Field entry, CNUMBER (that selects it). Then double click the ObjectVision Field entry, Number. The latter two operations define the ObjectVision table columns in Courses Taught that are used to look up a course title in the course titles database, CLASSNME. Figure 5.22 shows the Locate Indexes dialog box immediately after selecting the two search columns. Click OK to close the Locate Indexes dialog box.

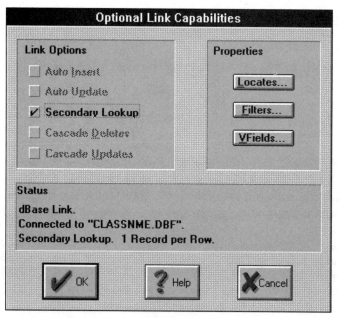

FIGURE 5.21
Optional link capabilities for a secondary link

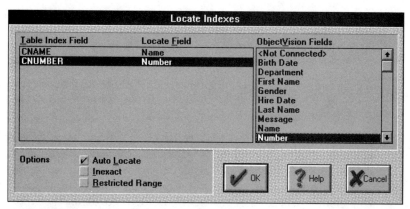

FIGURE 5.22
Defining database search columns

5. Click OK to close the Optional Link Capabilities dialog box. Click OK once more to close the Link Creation dialog box.

6. Finally, click OK to close the Data Links dialog box.

The secondary link called "CoursesTaughtSecondary" has been defined. It delivers the course titles to various rows in the Courses Taught table using the Name and Number columns as search criteria. The CLASSNME database is searched, and when a match is found, the corresponding database field CTITLE is delivered to the Title column for the given ObjectVision row.

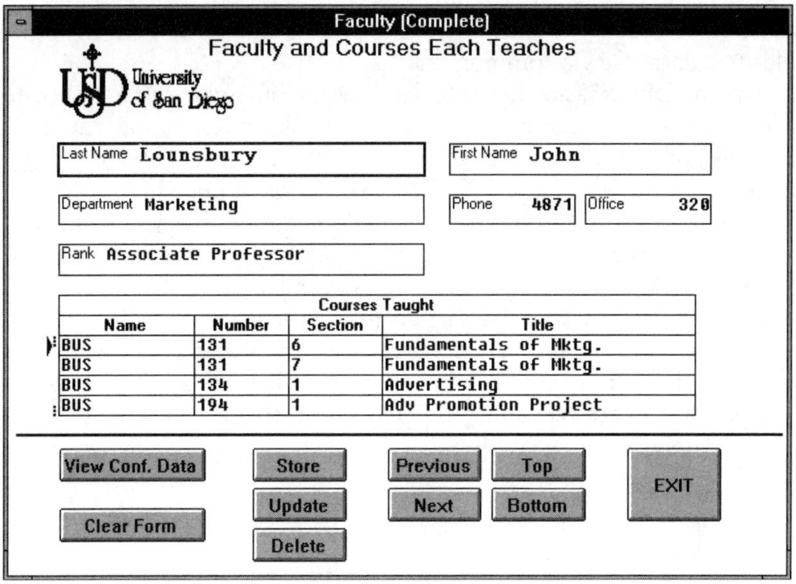

⊟	Faculty (Complete)	

Faculty and Courses Each Teaches

University
of San Diego

Last Name **Lounsbury**   First Name **John**

Department **Marketing**   Phone **4871** Office **320**

Rank **Associate Professor**

Courses Taught			
Name	Number	Section	Title
BUS	131	6	Fundamentals of Mktg.
BUS	131	7	Fundamentals of Mktg.
BUS	134	1	Advertising
BUS	194	1	Adv Promotion Project

View Conf. Data	Store	Previous	Top	
	Update	Next	Bottom	EXIT
Clear Form	Delete			

FIGURE 5.23
Completed Courses Taught table links

We can test our completed table links to see if they deliver a professor's name, department, and so on as well as information about courses taught. Return the form to goal mode and clear it. Enter into the Last Name field the value Lounsbury. Notice that course titles are now displayed for each course listed in the Courses Taught table. Figure 5.23 shows an example display.

We have completed the Faculty application. If you have been creating this application along with the text explanation of it, then now is a good time to save your application. For your convenience, we have stored the finished Faculty application in the file called FIG05-23.OVD. You can save the application by merely clicking the Exit button. The Exit button event tree contains the @SAVE function, which saves the application. A subsequent instruction, @APPEXIT, exits ObjectVision.

SUMMARY

This chapter described how to create and use links to databases. The links can provide a convenient way of storing information manually entered into a form. In addition, links can deliver information to a form's fields and tables by accessing associated databases. Databases supported include ASCII, Btrieve, dBase, DDE, and Paradox. Links can be used to join information simultaneously from disparate external data sources, as long as each source has one or more fields whose value uniquely identifies each row. This chapter has shown how to link fields to a database via common links.

Linking ObjectVision tables to databases is somewhat different because multiple database rows can be delivered to the ObjectVision application. Primary table links provide the chief mechanism for moving rows between ObjectVision and a database. Secondary links use information supplied by primary links to locate additional, related information in databases. Primary link values are used to search the databases identified by the secondary link. Using database indexes, the primary keys must match index keys in order for related information to be retrieved. In relational database language, this is usually called a *join operation*.

You learned how to create links, connect and disconnect specific link fields, and create database navigation and alteration buttons. Several link options (for example, the locates capability) were also described that facilitate precise or "fuzzy" database retrieval.

KEY TERMS

Common link A common link is the type of connection established between field objects and databases.

Defaults buttons (link) The Defaults button makes read and write connections between database fields and ObjectVision objects (table columns or fields) by searching for application names that exactly match database field names, thus saving time.

Index A database index is created based on one or more database fields and allows the program to locate database records quickly.

Link Automatic buttons One or more buttons that contain link-specific event trees and that facilitate navigating, searching, or altering a database. Any of 11 buttons may be selected and automatically placed on a form.

Locate field A locate field is the ObjectVision field that triggers a link. When a new value is entered into a locate field, it is used to search the linked database, and the remaining database fields are read and delivered to the application.

Primary key A primary key is a database field or fields that uniquely identifies each row. The combination of course name and course number, for example, form a primary key for the CLASS database.

Primary link The first link established between a table object and a database. Only tables can have primary links, not fields.

Read connection Values for read-connected ObjectVision objects are read from a database and placed into a form's fields and columns.

Secondary link Links to tables created subsequently to the primary link are called secondary links. They fill in additional information based on values delivered by the primary link.

Virtual field A field whose value is determined from an ObjectVision expression. The field does not exist in any database but is calculated from database values delivered by a link.

Write connection ObjectVision fields can write information into database fields when they are write connected. Write connections allow new database records to be inserted and existing database records to be updated.

REVIEW QUESTIONS

True or False Questions

1. **T F** An ObjectVision field is the only object that can be linked to a database field.

2. **T F** Both Paradox and dBase databases can be linked to a given Object-Vision application.

3. **T F** ObjectVision fields can obtain their values from a database field, but the database field cannot be updated or written to from the application.

4. **T F** Every ObjectVision application must have at least one database to which it is linked.

5. **T F** Link names may be up to 65 characters in length.

6. **T F** An application's locate field is monitored for a change. When it changes, that triggers a search of the associated database to locate a record matching the locate field value.

7. **T F** You can *create* a Paradox database from ObjectVision without a copy of the Paradox database system software.

8. **T F** When creating a dBase link, you must connect *all* database fields to ObjectVision fields with an OV Read or an OV Write connection.

9. **T F** Link Automatic buttons are optional. You can create your own database navigation buttons if you wish.

10. **T F** Secondary links are used exclusively with ObjectVision fields. They cannot be defined for ObjectVision tables.

Multiple Choice Questions

1. ObjectVision can create database files in which of the following formats?
   a. dBase
   b. ASCII
   c. Btrieve
   d. all of the preceding

2. The links converting ObjectVision fields to a database can be of what type(s)?
   a. read only
   b. write only
   c. read and write
   d. all of the preceding

3. What is the default database type displayed in the Data Links dialog box whenever you create a link?
   a. DDE
   b. Paradox
   c. dBase
   d. none of the preceding

4. What symbol indicates that a particular database field is used to organize (index) a database?
   a. *
   b. ^
   c. @
   d. none of the preceding

5. A primary link is the first link established for what structure?
   a. table
   b. field and a form
   c. table and a field
   d. form and a table

6. Which of the following is true about a VField?
   a. does not exist in a database
   b. can be determined from a database
   c. is virtual
   d. all of the preceding

7. What type of field, found in an ObjectVision form, triggers a database search whenever that field changes?
   a. search
   b. connect
   c. locate
   d. link

8. Pressing the Defaults button is the fastest way to connect matching fields with what type of connections?
   a. read only
   b. write only
   c. read and write
   d. all of the preceding

9. Which are the three properties of the Optional Link Capabilities dialog box?
   a. locates, filters, and VFields
   b. common link, primary link, and secondary link
   c. store, clear, and resume
   d. none of the preceding

10. Navigation buttons do what?
    a. move around the database without altering it
    b. store information in a database
    c. alter information in a database
    d. cannot have an event tree conclusion

EXERCISES

1. Create an ObjectVision form containing information that is stored in a dBase database. The database contains information about previously owned automobiles that are for sale. The table, which you should name AUTOS, should contain five information fields. The ObjectVision form should, of course, contain the same number of fields. The fields on both the form and database are these:

   Brand (text field)
   Model (text field)
   Year (date field)
   Mileage (numerical field)
   A unique reference number (numeric)

   Be sure to include an appropriate title of your own choosing across the top of the ObjectVision form.

2. Create a database table from an ObjectVision form. The table should store information in a Paradox database. The table contains information about people who are offering used automobiles for sale. Name the table OWNERS. The ObjectVision form and the database both should contain the following fields:

Owner's last name (text field)
Owner's first name (text field)
Owner's telephone number (text field)
A unique advertising reference number (numeric)

Note that the unique advertising reference numbers should be the same numbers you entered for exercise 1.

3. Relate both the databases AUTO and OWNERS. Build a database link and corresponding ObjectVision application that combines the data from both databases on one form. Join the two tables by selecting records whose reference number fields match. The reference number field is the "glue" that relates the two databases. Print out at least two ObjectVision form examples of owners and automobiles for sale.

DESIGNING AND PRINTING REPORTS WITH CRYSTAL REPORTS

OBJECTIVES

This chapter describes the report generator that is bundled with ObjectVision and ObjectVision Pro, Crystal Reports. You will learn how to create a report that prints the information found in the Faculty database. In particular, you will learn:

- *How to use the Crystal Reports menus*
- *The basic anatomy of a report*
- *How to insert fields into the report*
- *How to link report columns to databases*
- *How to change field and text fonts and their other display characteristics*
- *How to sort records and entire groups before printing them*
- *What functions and operators can be used in expressions*
- *How to hide repeating fields and selected report sections*

Crystal Reports provides a comprehensive reporting facility that complements ObjectVision functions. It is a full-featured, easily learned, report-generating system that enhances ObjectVision applications by providing a means to produce hard copy output or linked databases. This section leads you through several of its features. A complete discussion of all Crystal Reports features is beyond the scope of this one chapter. You can find full discussion in the comprehensive manual titled *Crystal Reports 2.0 for Windows* that is packaged with the product. The manual and software are produced by Crystal Services.

6.1 OVERVIEW OF CRYSTAL REPORTS

Crystal Reports is more than a report writer. With Crystal Reports you can create lists and reports, label items, form letters, preprinted forms, legal documents, invoices, and more. Within a report, Crystal Reports gives you the ability to perform complex statistical, financial, or scientific calculations on your data. You can compare one data field value to another, or you can compare a calculated value of one expression to another. Because Crystal Reports provides the facility to test whether or not a group of conditions is met, you can create complex, multifaceted conditions that pinpoint data to be included or excluded from your report. Data from a database can be combined with free-form text to create sentences that can be included in letters or other business documents.

DATABASES THAT CRYSTAL REPORTS RECOGNIZES

Crystal Reports works with databases to produce simple or complex reports. You can use Crystal Reports in conjunction with any ObjectVision application that is linked to one or more databases. Databases that can be read by Crystal Reports are dBase (III, III+, and IV), Paradox, Foxpro, Clipper, and Btrieve. Because many products, including spreadsheets, can export information in dBASE (.DBF) format, you will find that most any information can be read by Crystal Reports. ObjectVision provides a facility for printing forms from within an application. This facility is the appropriate method for your applications that are not linked to one or more databases, as you can create a report only in conjunction with one of the database types listed above.

THE CRYSTAL REPORTS WINDOW

Crystal Reports is a Windows compliant product. Its familiar interface has many of the same menu selections as ObjectVision and other Windows products. Figure 6.1 shows the Crystal Reports window displayed when the product is first launched. Many of the general features of Crystal Reports look familiar. The Minimize and Maximize buttons are in the usual place, the upper right corner

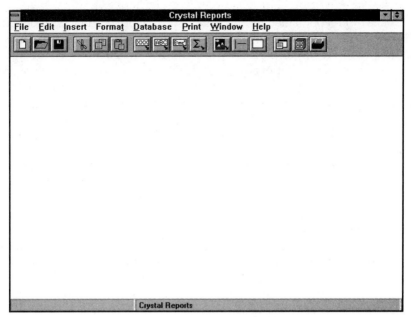

FIGURE 6.1
Crystal Reports window

of the window. The title bar appears at the top of the window. The menu bar is situated just below the title bar; below the menu bar is the Button bar. Each one is briefly described next.

The title bar displays the name of the program running in the window (Crystal Reports). Like other Windows products, you can click on a title bar to activate a given window whenever several document windows are displayed in the Crystal Reports window. They can be moved in the usual way—by dragging the title bar.

THE CRYSTAL REPORTS MENU

The Crystal Reports menu bar contains all of the Crystal Reports commands, which are displayed in a drop-down menu. The commands are, for the most part, familiar ones.

The File menu contains commands to open, close, and save report files. Like other Windows compliant products, the File menu contains the Print and Exit commands. A special Compile Report command creates an executable version of a report that can be printed on demand by simply clicking an icon without the need to open Crystal Reports first.

The Edit menu allows you to modify selected aspects of your report. You can cut, copy, and paste objects as well as remove report elements. You can edit formulas, edit and delete group sections, and change summary operations from the Edit menu. Field names can also be toggled on or off from Edit.

The Insert commands are quite different from other Windows products. The Insert menu is the central menu you use for creating reports. It contains commands to insert **database fields**, **text fields**, and **formula fields** into your developing report. Additionally, Insert is selected to introduce subtotals, grand totals, and summary fields into report group sections. Report embellishment fields, including the current date, page number, record number, and group number, can be inserted into your report using an Insert menu command.

The Format menu contains commands that dress up the appearance of a report. It contains commands to change fonts, format fields, and report sections, to introduce graphics, to draw lines, and to outline boxes. From Format, you can add field borders, alter the background color, and add drop shadows to fields.

The Database menu allows you to select and delete databases. Selected databases are used in your reports. One Database menu command helps designate new disk directories to search for database files to link to your report definitions.

The Print menu contains several print and print-associated commands. You can choose from the Print menu to print a report from the printer, on screen, or to a file. In addition, you can print out the report definition used to create a report. Print provides commands to filter records, including only those you want to see. Similarly, you can exclude selected groups. You can also specify whether or not to sort records or groups before printing the report.

In the Window menu are commands to rearrange icons and windows. It lists the report windows that are open and contains a command to close all open report windows at once.

Help is the standard Windows help with its familiar interface. Context-sensitive help is available, explaining every aspect of Crystal Reports.

THE CRYSTAL REPORTS BUTTON BAR

Crystal Reports places several frequently used commands on a Button bar that remains on screen unless you choose to turn it off. A command is represented by an individual button, and the graphic of each button suggests its use. Like the ObjectVision object bar, you activate a command by clicking the appropriate button once. Using the Button bar minimizes some of the steps necessary to perform commands, thereby increasing your efficiency. Figure 6.2 shows the Crystal Reports Button bar. Below each of the icons is a letter that references the icon as each is identified.

The following are the names of the icons, beginning from the left side of the Button bar: (a) New Report, (b) Open Report, (c) Save, (d) Cut, (e) Copy, (f) Paste, (g) Insert Database Field, (h) Insert Text Field, (i) Insert Formula Field, (j) Insert Summary Field, (k) Insert Graphic, (l) Insert Line, and (m) Insert Box. The last three icons are (n) Print to Window, (o) Print to File, and (p) Print to Printer. We will use each of these or their menu equivalents throughout the text. They will be explained further as they are used.

At the bottom of the window is the **status bar**, which displays valuable information to help you use Crystal Reports efficiently. Whenever the cursor is

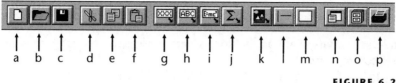

FIGURE 6.2
Crystal Reports Button bar

over an icon in the Button bar, the status bar displays a short description of the button's function. When you select a drop-down menu, the status bar displays a brief explanation of the currently selected command in the menu. Highlight a name by moving the highlight bar with the arrow keys or clicking it with the left mouse button. If you have selected a graphic, field, text field, or graphic line or box, the status bar displays the name of the selected item. In addition, the status bar displays a file name for a graphic, the field name for a field, the text in a text field, the word *Line* for a line or *box* for a box, the field type for special fields, or the formula name for a formula.

Using the right mouse button will speed your work. It serves almost the same function as it does when using ObjectVision. A pop-up menu is displayed that allows you to select a subset of formatting options for the selected object. The pop-up menus are context sensitive and object specific in that they contain only those commands from Crystal Report primary menus that are available for use with the selected element. We will make frequent use of the right mouse button in lieu of traversing menus.

Crystal Reports has more than eight different types of cursors. Each cursor is tailored to the context of the situation. An I-beam cursor, for example, indicates when text can be entered. A pencil cursor appears whenever you insert a line or box object. The pencil is your drawing implement.

GETTING HELP

Comprehensive help is available through the Help menu, which has a format similar to other Windows help screens. It is a good idea to select Help whenever you are stuck. Context-sensitive help is given for any selected element. Alternately, you can select Search, enter any string, and help concerning that element will appear.

6.2 CREATING A REPORT

One of the best ways to understand how to use Crystal Reports is to design and create a report. After that task is complete, we can explore how to invoke various reports from ObjectVision. Designing and creating a report is a developer's activity—one which you will want to master. Further, you will want to understand how to port your completed report specifications to ObjectVision so that users can run your report designs and produce printed reports. The latter is an end-user activity that you should test before releasing your report designs to the user community.

In the following sections, we design, build, and test a report that displays information used in conjunction with the Faculty application illustrated throughout this book. The report will display information from the same three databases that the Faculty ObjectVision application accesses. Those databases are FACULTY (containing faculty member specific information), CLASS (containing courses assigned to each instructor that semester), and CLASSNME. The latter database holds the names for each course number offered by the business school. Figure 6.3 shows a facsimile of the report we will produce in this chapter.

Information from the three databases is brought together in one, comprehensive report showing, from left to right, the instructor's name, course number, section number, and course title. Notice an italic typeface has been used to enhance the course titles, and the report column headers are in a typeface that is different from the class teaching assignments listed below it. Data are pulled together from the three tables (files) that make up the Faculty database by joining pairs of databases (FACULTY to CLASS and CLASS to CLASSNME) on a common key. The instructor's name is drawn from FACULTY, whereas the course name and section are retrieved from CLASS, using the instructor's name as a common link field. Similarly, the course title is selected from the database CLASSNME. A course name from CLASS is used to match a class name in CLASSNME to retrieve a course's title.

Before creating a report with Crystal Reports, ask your users what reports they want and what information each report should display. After you have assimilated that information, prototype one or more reports and rapidly develop a typical result. Show an example output to your end user to make sure you are on the right track.

SELECTING A DATABASE

To begin a new report, invoke the Crystal Reports icon in the Program Manager. Then execute File | New Report or click the New Report icon on the Button bar. A list of database files is shown. Because every Crystal Report is based on one or more databases, you must select at least one. Figure 6.4 shows a typical display. Select the first of several databases used in the Teaching Assignments report, FACULTY.DBF, by highlighting its name and clicking OK.

Once you select the first database, Crystal Reports displays the Report Editor screen. Use this screen to insert and format data and to watch your report take shape. Figure 6.5 shows the Report Editor screen along with the Insert Database Field dialog box. The latter is displayed immediately after selecting a database. It reveals the names of all database fields found in the selected database, FACULTY. As is evident from the buttons in the dialog box, you can select fields to be inserted into the report by highlighting the field names and pressing the Insert button.

Faculty and the Courses They Teach

Instructor	Course Name, Section, Title		
Ambrose, James	BUS 123	1	*Production Management*
	BUS 150	5	*Mangement Science*
	BUS 150	6	*Mangement Science*
Armsworth, Andy	BUS 016	4	*Quantitative Bus. Anal.*
	BUS 016	5	*Quantitative Bus. Anal.*
	ECON 194	1	*Law and Economics*
Baker, Kelly	BUS 190	1	*Business Policy*
	BUS 190	2	*Business Policy*
	BUS 190	8	*Business Policy*
Brickman, Dennis	BUS 100	2	*Mgmt. People in Org.*
	BUS 100	3	*Mgmt. People in Org.*
	GBA 350	1	*Human Res. Mgmt.*
Buchanen, Jessica	ACCT 108	1	*Auditing*
	ACCT 108	2	*Auditing*
	ACCT 108	3	*Auditing*
Carroll, Nancy	ACCT 002	1	*Prin. of Acctg. II*
	ACCT 002	2	*Prin. of Acctg. II*
	ACCT 100	1	*Interm. Acctg. II*
	ACCT 100	2	*Interm. Acctg. II*
•	•	•	
•	•	•	
•	•	•	
Zoller, Dennis	BUS 112	1	*Investments*
	BUS 112	2	*Investments*
	GBA 402	1	*New Venture Fin. Mgmt.*

FIGURE 6.3
Class Teaching Assignments report

When you open a new report, Crystal Reports automatically creates three sections in the Report Editor: a Page header section, a Details section, and a Page footer section. Their names appear in the gray area on the left. On the right is a white area that represents the mock-up of a page. The **Page header** section is

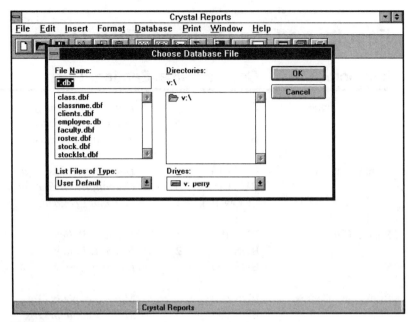

FIGURE 6.4
Selecting a database

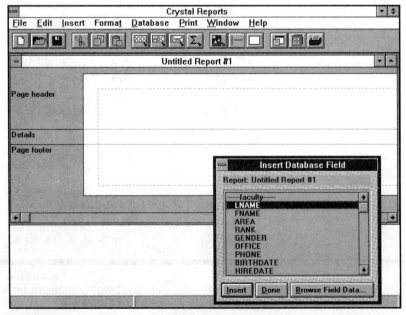

FIGURE 6.5
Report Editor screen and Insert Database Field dialog box

used for the report title, field headings, and other information that will appear at the top of each page. The **Page footer** section contains the page number and any other information that will appear at the bottom of every page. The Details section is the body of the report, and the majority of your report data appears here. You build a report by inserting data fields, formulas, and other report elements into the Details section.

Subtotals and grand totals represent aggregate information collected on some subset of the detail information. Aggregate or summary information is placed in a different type of "group" section that you can create. The Class Teaching Assignments report contains groups (see Figure 6.3) that are identified by each instructor's name. Later we describe how to establish groups in your report.

For now, we concentrate on placing information fields from the databases into the Details section. Then we refine the page header information that is to appear on each page. Before placing information in the Details section, we inform Crystal Reports about the remaining databases used to create the final Class Teaching Assignments report.

SELECTING AND LINKING ADDITIONAL DATABASES

Basic teaching assignment information is gathered from three databases. The first database selected previously, FACULTY, supplies but one field—the instructor's name—to the report in Figure 6.3. Remaining fields are found in related tables. We add these databases to the general mix of those available to the Crystal Reports system.

One of the most powerful features of Crystal Reports is its ability to include data from a variety of different databases and combine that data into a unified report. In order to include another database in a report, a relationship must exist between the proposed database and one that is already part of the report. Otherwise, it would not make sense to combine the two databases in one report. For instance, it would be foolish to include a database of new automobiles in the Class Teaching Assignments report, as there is no association between those two databases: faculty and automobiles. (Instructors probably drive cars, but which cars they drive has not been captured in any database.) However, it makes sense to include a database such as CLASS in the report. There *is* a relationship between FACULTY and CLASS. Each faculty member in the FACULTY database has been assigned one or more courses to teach. Therefore, their names also appear in the CLASS database. We add the CLASS database to our pool of available database fields.

Databases are added to a report by executing the Add File to Report command found in the Database menu. First click Database and then click the Add File command. A list of database file names is displayed in a dialog box. Select (double click) CLASS.DBF. The Define File Link dialog box appears (see Figure 6.6).

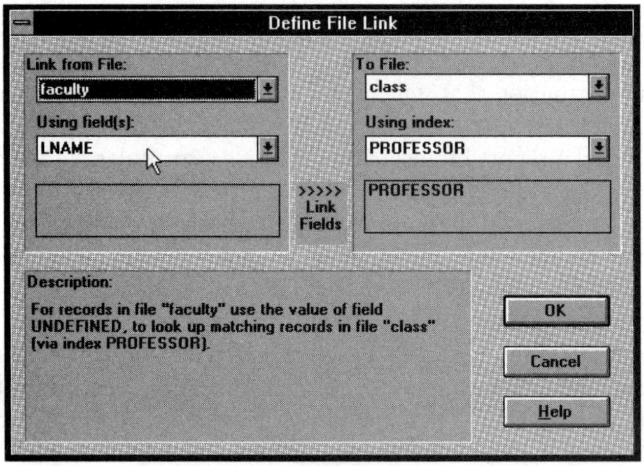

FIGURE 6.6
Linking one database to another

The arrow in Figure 6.6 is on the Using field(s) combo box. Click it and a list of field names from the FACULTY database appears. These are candidate fields that link the FACULTY and CLASS databases. Select LNAME—the common field found in both databases—because that column relates one database row to its match in the other database. Double click LNAME (or simply highlight LNAME and click the OK button). The File Links dialog box appears, which summarizes the linkage just established between the two databases (see Figure 6.7).

Notice the text found in the Description box. It indicates that the LNAME field is used to look up matching records in the CLASS database. Click OK to finalize this relationship between the two databases. The Define File Link dialog box closes. Click OK once more to close the File Links dialog box.

You have just related two databases by associating one field in FACULTY, called a **foreign key** in formal database jargon, to a **primary key** in a related CLASS database. We repeat this series of steps one more time to link in a third database, CLASSNME, that is required to complete the report. Repeat the process described above to add the final database, CLASSNME, to the list of databases associated with the report. The steps that follow will establish the connection or linkage (foreign key to primary key) between the CLASS database and the CLASSNME database. The database CLASS contains the columns COURSENAME and COURSENUMB that are used to find a matching row in the CLASSNME database. CLASSNME contains corresponding fields: CNAME and CNUMBER. The following steps tell Crystal Reports which keys in CLASS to use to match against selected columns in CLASSNME—that is, the linkage columns.

1. Execute the Add File to Report command of the Database menu. The Define File Link dialog box is displayed (see Figure 6.6).

2. Connect the CLASS database ("from") to the CLASSNME database ("to"): click the combo box and select CLASS in the Link from File text box. Then click the combo box and select CLASSNME in the To File text box.

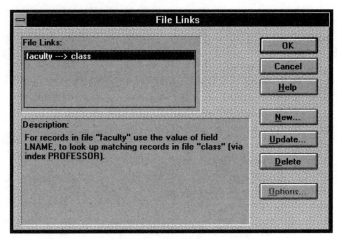

FIGURE 6.7
File Links dialog box

3. Click the combo box for Using Field(s) and select, in this order, COURSENAME and COURSENUMB. This action establishes the preceding fields as the foreign keys that are used to link CLASS to CLASSNME.

4. Click OK to close the Define File Links dialog box.

5. Click OK again to close the File Links dialog box.

You have completed the most difficult part of the process. The constituent databases have been identified, and the fields producing the pair-wise links have been established. FACULTY is connected to CLASS via the pair of fields LNAME (from FACULTY) and PROFESSOR (from CLASS). Likewise, database CLASS is connected to database CLASSNME by the four fields COURSENAME/COURSENUMB (from CLASS) and CNAME/CNUMBER (from CLASSNME).

A great deal of work has been completed. It is a good idea to save your in-process report periodically. Like other Windows compliant products, store the information by executing the File|Save command. The familiar File Save As dialog box appears. Enter the name Faculty and press Enter to save the report definition as a file named FACULTY.RPT (Crystal Reports automatically adds the file extension RPT to every report file).

INSERTING FIELDS INTO A REPORT DETAIL LINE

The body of a report contains information drawn from one or more databases. Report rows are usually sorted in some specific sequence so that it is easy to find a particular report item. Rows that display detailed database information are placed in the report band labeled "Details" (see Figure 6.5). In the Details section you may place any database fields or other expressions and text that you would

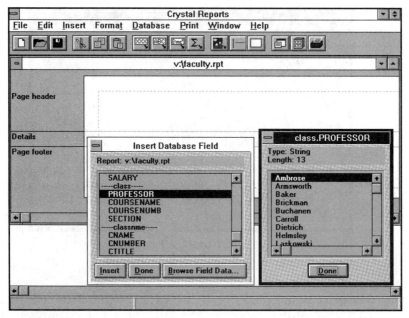

FIGURE 6.8
Browsing through a field's values

like displayed from the database. A field from a database is displayed whenever its name is placed on the report. The order in which information is placed into the report is not important at this point. Our goal is to simply arrange database fields so that the course information, drawn from the three databases, is arranged in the correct way across a given line.

To place selected database fields into the report, begin by executing the command Insert | Database Field. The Insert Database Field dialog box appears, containing the names of all databases linked to the report and fields each comprises. Familiarize yourself with the fields in these databases by scrolling down the list (see Figure 6.5). Notice that the **alias**—a name that can be used in Crystal Reports fields in place of a full path name and database name—serves as the header to the list of fields from that database. If you click any field name in any list, the Browse Field Data button becomes active. When you click that button a dialog box appears that lists field values for the selected field—a handy reminder of the values stored in various fields. Figure 6.8 shows an example listing the values for PROFESSOR stored in the CLASS database. When you are done scrolling through the field values, click the Done button. Control returns to the Insert Database Field dialog box. Now we are ready to begin building the heart of the report by inserting database fields.

Inserting database fields is straightforward. With the Insert Database Field dialog box displayed, do the following to place a database field into the report:

1. Scroll through the list of fields until the Instructor Name field, LNAME, is located. Select the field (click once).

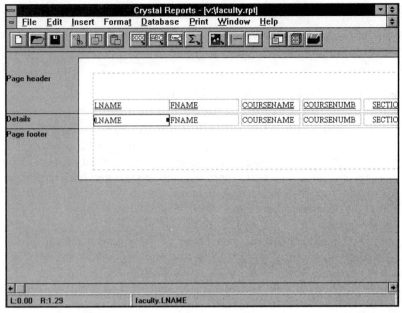

FIGURE 6.9
Draft report design with fields inserted

2. Press the Insert button located in the lower left corner of the Insert Database Field dialog box.

3. Move the mouse (do not drag it) until the rectangular cursor representing the selected field is along the left side of the Details band.

4. Click the left mouse button to "drop" the field onto the report work surface.

Repeat the preceding steps, placing the following fields from left to right in the Details section of the Report Editor:

- class.FNAME
- class.COURSENAME
- class.COURSENUMB
- class.SECTION
- classnme.CTITLE

Click the Done button on the Insert Database Field dialog box to close it. Figure 6.9 shows the Report Editor after the five database fields have been placed in the Details line. (The Title field and header are beyond the right margin of the report window but are inserted into the report properly.) Crystal Reports automatically places a field label in the Page header band above each field.

Whenever a field is selected, as LNAME is in Figure 6.9, handles appear on either end. You can drag these to enlarge or shrink any field or column header field. Left and right coordinates, shown in inches, appear in the lower left corner of the Report Editor. The database alias and field names of the selected field appear in the right panel at the bottom of the Report Editor.

PRINTING A REPORT TO A WINDOW

It is a good idea to produce a draft report periodically to see how the report will appear. Do not wait until you have applied all the finishing touches to the report. Review a report's output frequently during the development process. Incremental report review costs little and points out any mistakes early in the process. You can print a report on screen to review it and thus avoid wasting paper. We should see how our current report looks. Bear in mind that we have done little to enhance its appearance—it is a rough draft.

Printing a report in an on-screen window provides a quick check of its form and content before printing hard copy. To print on screen, select the Print menu from the Crystal Reports menu bar. Then click the command Print to Window. Alternatively, you can simply click the Print Report to Window icon located in the Button bar, third icon from the right. In either case, the report is built quickly and displays in its own window. The Print window overlays the report's design (see Figure 6.10).

It is evident that this report needs more work. All requisite fields are displayed, and each instructor's courses have been retrieved correctly. However, the rows are not listed in any discernable order. Furthermore, the column labels are not terrific looking. The Print to Window serves an important report preview function. (Moreover, the spacing between columns looks like a data processing report produced by a mainframe computer from the 1960s.) This report is merely run to demonstrate that our design correctly associates rows from disparate databases using the links we established previously. Later we will make the report more attractive through various techniques.

Look at the Print window for a moment as we describe some of its features. Crystal Reports displays the number of records read and selected as it is building the report. Of course, Figure 6.10 shows those numbers after the process is complete. The arrow buttons at the top of the Print window resemble those found on a VCR. The buttons in our figure are dimmed because all the report rows are contained on one page and the buttons are inapplicable. For multipage reports, the buttons are assigned the following actions. The left pointing arrow with the vertical line to its left moves you to the first page of the report. The left pointing arrow (without the vertical line) moves you to the previous page. Similarly, the right pointing arrow moves to the next page of the report, whereas the right pointing arrow with a vertical line moves to the last page of the report. The square box closes out the Print window. The magnifying glass allows you to see each page in its entirety by reducing the entire page so that it fits in the window. Report details vanish, but the overall page appearance is displayed. Finally, the Printer icon sends your report to the printer.

Like other windows, the Print window has Maximize, Minimize, and Restore buttons (when applicable). They operate in the usual way. The window

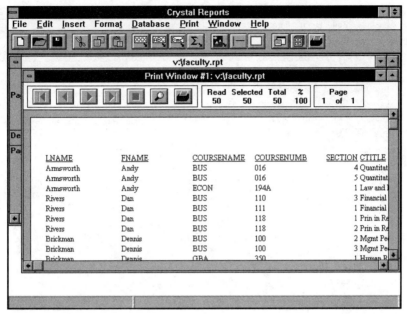

FIGURE 6.10
Window display of report

title bar shows the number of times the report has been printed to a window. Additionally, the report's disk file name is shown in the title bar. Scroll buttons on the bottom and side are used to move side to side and up and down in a given page, respectively. You can close the Print window by double clicking its Control-menu box. Close the report and we will continue to refine its design.

INSERTING A PAGE TITLE

Text page and column headings are added to enhance a report and clarify its meaning. We will first insert a heading into the report. Because the heading occurs at the top of each and every page, we insert it into the area in the Report Editor page layout labeled "Page header" (see Figure 6.9). Anytime you want to add a new element to a report, invoke the Insert command. Alternately, you may click one of the seven icons in the Button bar: Insert Database Field, Insert Text Field, Insert Formula Field, Insert Summary, Insert Graphic, Insert Line, or Insert Box. The page title to be included (see Figure 6.3) is "Faculty and the Courses They Teach." The steps to insert a page title follow:

1. Execute the command Insert|Text Field (click Insert and then click the Text Field command). The Edit Text Field dialog box appears.

2. Type the title: `Faculty and the Courses They Teach` and click the Accept button when finished.

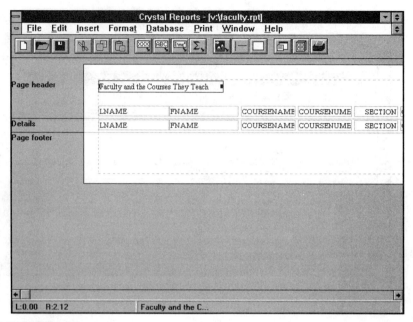

FIGURE 6.11
Report with page title

3. Position the field box in the top left corner of the Page header section and click the left mouse button to "drop" it onto the report.

The title looks too small for a page heading, but we defer altering its font and typeface until we alter all the field's characteristics. Figure 6.11 shows the report with its page title in place. Save the design by clicking the Floppy Disk icon or executing File|Save. (You can never be too cautious.)

6.3 CHANGING THE DATA WITH FORMULAS AND FUNCTIONS

The Class Assignments report would look better if it could shed that 1960s data processing look. Part of the problem is that the columns of instructors' first and last names are surrounded by a great deal of white space and thus are difficult to read. All columns suffer from the same visual problem: too much empty space between the course names, numbers, and sections. If there were just some way to bring these related elements closer together. Instructors' names would be more attractive if last names were followed by a comma, one blank, and then the first name. Similarly, course names could be more easily read if they had a form such as "BUS 190," where the name and number are separated by only one blank.

Crystal Reports built-in functions, along with the ability to write formulas, collectively provide the developer with powerful tools to build expressions of arbitrary complexity and elegance. Our needs for formulas and functions are simple. We need to **concatenate** each instructor's last name with his or her first name, separated by a comma and blank. (Concatenation simply means to join two or more character strings end to end with one another.) Correspondingly, we will use functions and an operator to concatenate each course name with its number. These composite instructor and course strings are formulas. Formulas are assigned unique names and are treated in exactly the same way as simple database fields. Formulas are a set of instructions that may be used to calculate information you cannot obtain directly from database data fields. We create two formulas to replace four fields currently in our report.

CREATING THE FACULTY NAME FORMULA

We will create a single formula that comprises each instructor's last name followed by first name. First, however, delete the current LNAME and FNAME fields from the report as they will be redundant. You can delete more than one field by holding down the shift key and clicking each field to be deleted. Include the column labels also:

1. Press Shift and click LNAME in the Page header section.
2. With Shift depressed, click FNAME in the Page header section followed by FNAME and LNAME from the Details section. As you select a text or database field, notice that two square handles appear at both ends of a field. These indicate a field has been selected.
3. Press the Del (delete) key to remove the selected fields. Alternately, you can execute the Clear command of the Edit menu. In either case, the four fields disappear from the report definition.

Next we build the relatively simple formulas to display the instructor's name and course names. Inserting a formula into a report resembles inserting a database field. First you select the Insert menu. In the Insert menu are several choices, shown in Figure 6.12 (some are bold and others are dimmed, indicating they are inapplicable). To begin building a formula, click the Formula Field choice. The Insert Formula dialog box appears. Choose a formula name, enter it, and click OK when you are finished. Enter the formula name Faculty Name and press Enter. The Crystal Reports Formula Editor is displayed.

The Formula Editor is a dialog box that contains a complete set of tools to create formulas and check their correctness. The editor allows you to assign a name to your formula for easy reference, enter the formula, check the formula's syntax to ensure it is correct, and accept the formula for use in your report. After the formula is placed in your report, Crystal Reports prints the results of the

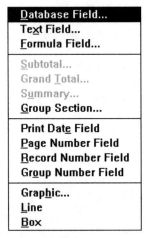

FIGURE 6.12
Insert menu

formula whenever you print a report. The output is analogous to spreadsheet output, whereas the formulas in a report are comparable to spreadsheet formulas. Figure 6.13 shows an example of the Formula Editor dialog box.

Enter formulas in the Formula text box in one of two ways: via the Fields box or manually. The Fields box displays all report fields and connected database fields. You can see all field names by scrolling through the list of them. To enter a field via the Fields scroll box, move the I-beam cursor to the place you want to insert the field and click the left mouse button to set the cursor. In the Fields scroll box list locate the field you wish to insert into the developing formula. Formula names already entered into your report appear at the top of the list preceded with the "@" sign. Select a field. The Formula Editor enters the field into the formula text at the insertion point. Alternately, you can simply type in the field name. It is best to use the scroll box method, because it ensures field names are spelled properly.

Besides field names, the Formula Editor displays two other important formula building blocks: functions and operators. Those are displayed in their own scroll boxes in the middle and the right side of the Formula Editor (see Figure 6.13). Form the composite faculty name formula by executing these steps:

1. Locate and select (double click) TrimRight(x) from the Functions scroll box. That function trims trailing blanks, if any, from the enclosed argument. It is entered into the Formula text box. The I-beam insertion point is between the parentheses of the function.

2. In the Fields scroll box, locate and insert the field name `faculty.LNAME`. It is entered into the Formula text box at the insertion point.

3. Move the formula insertion point I-beam outside the right parenthesis and enter `+", "+` (plus sign, double quotation mark, comma, blank, double quotation mark, and plus sign).

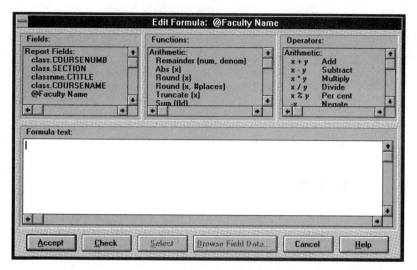

FIGURE 6.13
Formula Editor dialog box

4. Locate and select the TrimLeft function. (It removes blanks on the left of a string that signify the argument.)

5. Select the field name `faculty.FNAME` from the Fields scroll box. Click Accept to signal that the formula is complete.

6. Move the rectangle cursor representing the formula into the leftmost portion of the Details line.

7. Finally, shorten the faculty name rectangle by dragging either handle toward the other. Reduce it to about two inches total length (observe the rectangle's left and right positional coordinates in the bottom left of the Report Editor).

The completed formula you just created is this one:

```
TrimRight({faculty.LNAME})+", "+TrimLeft({faculty.FNAME})
```

An instructor's last and first names are read from the database, blanks are removed, and a comma is inserted between the last and the first names. Review what the formula yields by running the Print to Window command.

CREATING THE COURSE NAME FORMULA

Next, we will create a course name formula. To create the formula, first delete both the report fields COURSENAME and COURSENUMB. Then repeat the preceding process to create a formula called CNAMENUMB that combines a course name and a number. The finished formula for CNAMENUMB is the following one:

```
TrimRight({class.COURSENAME})+" "+TrimLeft({class.COURSENUMB})
```

Move it into place to the right of the faculty name formula.

There are over ninety functions and more than twenty-five operators available in Crystal Reports through the Formula Editor. Due to size limitations, we cannot discuss each of them. Most will be familiar if you use spreadsheet programs or most any programming language. For further details on built-in functions consult the Crystal Reports documentation provided with the product.

USING AND ALTERING TEXT FIELDS

Earlier we examined how to add a page title. Recall that we executed the Insert | Text Field command. Alternately, we could simply have positioned the I-beam cursor in the Page header section and created a title by typing it directly—not going to the effort of executing a command. Whether you use a text field or you type text directly may seem inconsequential, but it *does* make a difference. It is significant because text fields are superior to plain text in all ways. First, text column headers are somewhat difficult to align over columns. You must use the Tab key to place successive text entries correctly. Text fields do not suffer from this shortcoming. Second, a text field (versus ordinary text) can be manipulated (for example, shortened) easily by selecting the field and dragging its handles. Finally, it is easier to align text fields. Similar in nature to spreadsheet cells containing text, Crystal Reports text fields can be aligned left, right, or centered within their individual fields.

Whenever you insert a database or formula field into the Details section, Crystal Reports automatically places a text field just above the inserted field. That text field matches the name of the database field or formula name. Its size is that of the inserted detail line item. Sometimes these column labels are adequate; other times (as in our report) they are not. We will change each of existing text fields found in the Page header section. Because the text fields already exist, we can simply select and edit each one in turn:

1. Position the mouse over the column heading text field Faculty Name and right click it. A pop-up menu is displayed.
2. Select the Edit Text Field command (see Figure 6.14).
3. Enter the text **Instructor** in the Edit Text Field dialog box.
4. Press the Accept button to finalize the change.

Repeat the preceding steps for the next text field, CNAMENUMB. Replace it with the title **Course Name, Section, Title**. Stretch the text field with its handles so that it is as long as the Detail line database field items below it. You may need to use the horizontal scroll bar to see the right end of the Course Title field. Finally, delete the remaining two column text fields from the Page header (SECTION and CTITLE) as they are now redundant.

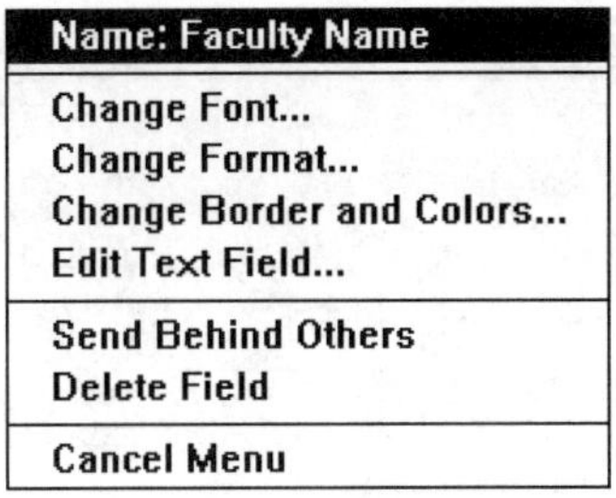

Name: Faculty Name
Change Font...
Change Format...
Change Border and Colors...
Edit Text Field...
Send Behind Others
Delete Field
Cancel Menu

FIGURE 6.14
Editing a text field

6.4 SORTING AND GROUPING

Crystal Reports provides the facility for sorting individual report rows. You may form groups (related records whose identity is specified by a key value defining a group) that also can be sorted.

SORTING RECORDS

Reports are frequently most useful when their rows are sorted into some particular order. Our report shown in Figure 6.10, for instance, is useful, but its rows are not in order. Far more effective would be that same report in which the rows were sorted by instructors' names and their course names. Crystal Reports allows you to sort your data by record and by group. Data is sorted using the Windows sort rules established in the International dialog box in the Windows Control Panel. Report rows can be sorted on one or more soft fields. In single field sorts all the data is sorted based on the values in a single field. For example, we could sort the Class Assignments report on the Course Title field. For multiple field sorts, Crystal Reports first sorts the entries by the first field selected. Then it sorts any entries in the second field without disturbing the sort order of entries in the first field (the traditional primary key/secondary key sort rules). The same pattern is followed for additional sorting fields.

The Class Teaching Assignments report would be better if its rows were sorted first by instructor's last name, next by course names for each instructor, and then by section numbers for matching courses. The three sort fields, in the order specified, are sufficient to deliver information in a highly useful order. This type is a multiple field sort because up to three fields are involved in defining the final order that report rows are displayed. For each sort field, Crystal Reports requires two things: the field you want your sort to be based on and the sort direction (ascending or descending).

To begin the process of designating the sort fields, select the Record Sort Order command found in the Print menu (an admittedly strange place for a sort command to be found). The Sort Order dialog box appears (see Figure 6.15). From

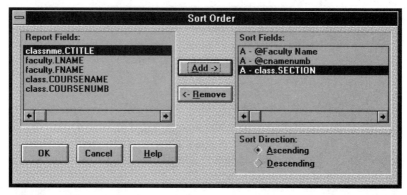

FIGURE 6.15
Specifying record sort fields

the Report Fields list, select the following fields and click the Add button (the order in which the fields are selected is pivotal—from most important to least):

1. @Faculty Name (a formula field)
2. @cnamenumb (a formula field)
3. class.SECTION

Click OK to accept these three sort keys. Notice that the sort order of all fields is ascending (indicated by the letter "A" preceding each sort field listed in the Sort Fields list). You can select either Ascending or Descending *before* adding a selected field to the Sort Fields list.

FORMING AND SORTING GROUPS

Crystal Reports allows you to group and summarize your data for maximum reporting results. As noted before, a **group** is a set of records that are related to each other in some way. In our teaching assignment list, for example, a group could be each instructor and his or her assigned classes. A group could instead be defined for each department in the university, where one group is the math department, another is the computer science department, and yet another is the management department. Breaking data into groups is a key part of designing an effective report.

While there may be many data field's on a report, usually there is only one field for which you are interested in grouping the data. To group data first select the field you want to group together. Once the field is chosen, specify the action you want to perform on each group of data from that field:

- If you want simply to group the data and take no other action, execute the Group command found in the Insert menu.

- If you want to subtotal a field for a chosen group, select Insert| Subtotal.
- Otherwise, select Insert|Summary if you want to average, count, or determine the maximum or minimum value.

Once you have selected the group field and the action, you can select another field that triggers a grouping whenever its value changes.

We define a simple group for the Class Teaching Assignments report. A simple group means breaking the data into groups without performing any additional action, such as totaling or averaging, on the grouped data. A group is recognized and formed whenever the faculty name changes. The formula field identifying the group is called @Faculty Name. We have created the group not to generate summary information to be printed for each group. Instead, we simply want to identify a group to provide a blank line between groups. Form a group based on the Faculty Name formula by executing these steps:

1. Select Insert|Group Section. The Insert Group Section dialog box appears.

2. In the top scroll box, select the field that you want to trigger a grouping whenever its value changes. Click the combo box to display all report fields and select the @Faculty Name field.

3. In the second scroll box, select the sort direction (Ascending or Descending). Click the combo box and select Ascending.

4. Click OK when you are finished. Or simply press Enter, because OK is the default, highlighted button.

You have formed a group that is based on the Faculty Name formula, a combination of an instructor's last name and first name. Notice that two new sections appear in the Report Editor surrounding the Details section (see Figure 6.16). The label "#1:@ Faculty Name" in the Report Editor left margin (above the Details section) indicates the field on which groups are formed. In this area or band of the report, you can place summary information or label the group. For example, you could move the @Faculty Name formula from the Details section to the group band. That way, the faculty name would print once, just above the several course rows listed for that faculty member.

The area below the Details section, also labeled "#1: @Faculty Name," is the traditional band where you place subtotals, counts, and so on that are related to the group whose rows have been placed on the report. For example, we could enter a function in that area to count the number of courses (Insert|Summary| Count). For the Class Teaching Assignments report, we omit any information in the summary bands. We leave the bands empty (they contain one line) to form a separation between adjacent groups. You can add more lines to any section— Details, Page header, and so on—by positioning the I-beam in the section and pressing Enter to add blank lines. Alternatively, you can position the mouse cursor over the line below the section. When the cursor changes to a double-headed arrow, drag the line down to add lines to the section above the line.

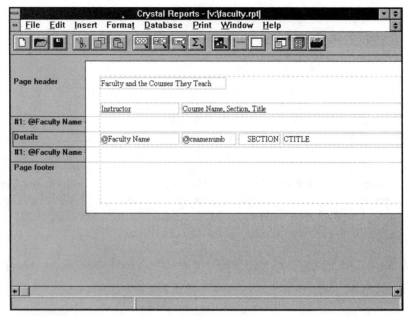

FIGURE 6.16
Forming a group based on the instructor's name

Just as it is easy to create an arbitrary number of report groups, it is also easy to eliminate them. Eliminate a group by executing the command Edit|Delete Section. The Delete Section dialog box displays the names of all sections. Select the section to be deleted from the list and click OK to remove it. That action will remove both section bands (preceding and following the Details section).

We have modified the report considerably since we last looked at an example of its output. Execute the Print to Window command once more to see how the report looks: Execute Print|Print to Window to view it on screen (no need to produce a printed copy yet). Figure 6.17 illustrates the Class Teaching Assignments report.

HIDING PARTS OF A REPORT

The report has improved, but it still needs more work. One obvious improvement would be to eliminate printing the instructors' names more than once. Additionally, there is too much blank space between adjacent instructors' courses.

First we eliminate the two blank lines between each group (instructors). There are two blank lines because one blank line is placed after a section (called the *group footer*) and one blank line is written just above the details section (called the *group header*). We can delete either the group header or the group footer, thereby eliminating one of the blank lines. Eliminate the group header by hiding it. The steps are as follows:

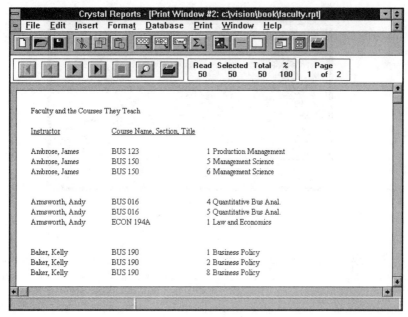

FIGURE 6.17
Window display of the modified report

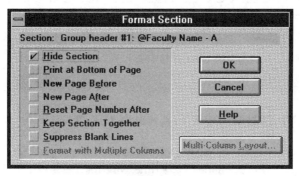

FIGURE 6.18
Format Section dialog box

1. Execute the Section command of the Edit menu (Edit | Section).
2. Double click the section show as `Group header #1: @Faculty Name - A`. The Format Section dialog box is displayed.
3. Click the Hide Section check box to hide the group header you highlighted previously (see Figure 6.18).
4. Click OK to complete the operation.
5. Double click the Control-menu box on the Report window to close it.

The group header is hidden and therefore not displayed or printed.

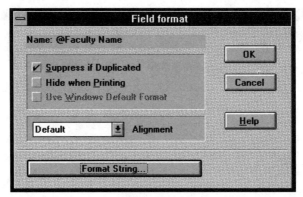

FIGURE 6.19
Field Format dialog box

Next we remove the multiple occurrences of an instructor's name within his or her group—once is enough. You cause repeated data for any column to print once by *formatting* it. Select the @Faculty Name column in the Report Editor (the instructor's name) and right click it. That displays a menu similar to the property inspector used in ObjectVision. Then do the following:

1. Select the entry Change Format (click the left mouse button to select it). The Field Format dialog box displays.

2. Check the Suppress if Duplicated check box (see Figure 6.19).

3. Click OK to finish the operation.

6.5 FORMATTING TEXT AND FIELDS

Crystal Reports makes it easy to alter and format text and fields in your reports. You can edit one or several fields at a time. Multiple fields can be edited by selecting (clicking) each one while holding the Shift key. Square handles surround each selected field. Whether you format one field or several, the process is the same:

1. Select the data you want to edit or format.

2. Click the right mouse button to display a pop-up menu containing editing and formatting options appropriate for the selected item or items.

3. Select any menu options and make changes in the dialog boxes that are displayed.

We illustrate altering field formats by changing the appearance of three report elements: the report page heading, the column headings, and the individual course titles. Here are the changes to be made:

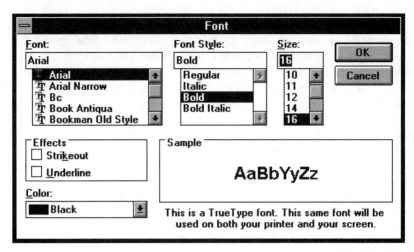

FIGURE 6.20
Font dialog box

- Change the font of the page title to Arial, bold, 16 point. Remove the underline that exists for the title.
- Change the two column heading fonts to Arial, bold, 11 point. Remove the underline automatically generated for the column headings.
- Change the course name titles so that they are italicized.

The report rows containing the instructors' names, course names and sections, and course titles all use the font Times New Roman, regular (not bold or italicized), 10 point. We leave those settings unchanged.

You can edit or format an object or collection of objects by selecting either the Edit or the Format menu. Having selected the Format menu, for instance, you can change a field's font by executing the Font command. An easier way is to select the fields to be altered and then click the right mouse button to display a pop-up menu that contains commands from the Edit and Format menus. First we format the page title located in the Page header section of the report:

1. Select the page title. Handles appear around the text field.
2. Click the right mouse button to display the Edit/Format pop-up menu.
3. From the menu select the Font command. The Font dialog box appears (see Figure 6.20).
4. Scroll and select Arial from the Font list, select Bold from the Font Style list, and select a point size of 16 from the Size list.
5. Make sure that the Underline check box (under the Effects label) is not checked. Click the box to deselect underline if needed.
6. Click OK to confirm your choices.

The page title reappears in a bolder, larger font.

Repeat the preceding steps for the two column titles. For those text fields, change the font to Arial, bold, 11 point. Remember to deselect the Underline check box to remove the underlines from both column headings. Finally, change the format of the Course Title field (named CTITLE) so that it is italicized. The font, Times New Roman, and point size, 10, do not need to be changed. Select CTITLE, right click the mouse button, select Font, and select Italic under the Font Style list. Click OK. Notice the column header text field boxes overlap when the Report Editor reappears. Do not worry about that because the information displayed in the fields is not as long as the boxes seem to indicate. Our next task is to bring the columns closer together, so we will be shrinking those text fields anyway. It would be a waste of time to size the fields and reposition them before font and point size have been established for each. These characteristics affect the length of each field.

Now shorten some of the fields and draw them closer together. Recall that the course section numbers, for example, are a bit too far to the right of the course names and numbers (see Figure 6.17). The process is iterative: you shrink fields, move them closer together, execute the Print to Window command, and view the results. Then you can refine your layout until the desired spacing is achieved. Using the process above, duplicate the text and data field layout shown in Figure 6.3. Observe that when you select a field—either a text column heading or a data field—its left and right end-point locations are displayed in the leftmost panel of the Report Editor status line. Those end points for each field are shown in Table 6.1. All metrics are in inches *relative* to the left margin, regardless of the actual left margin.

TABLE 6.1
Label and data placement in the report

Report Element	Left End Position (inches)	Right End Position (inches)
Page Heading	0.0	4.25
Instructor Column Heading	0.0	1.50
Course Name Column Heading	1.5	4.25
Instructor Name Field	0.0	1.50
Course Name and Number Field	1.5	2.17
Course Section Number Field	2.17	2.42
Course Title Field	2.54	4.25

The final element to add to our report is a graphic line at the top of each page, just below the column headings, to provide a clean, visual separation between the headings and the database fields. Add the line in the Page header area by following these steps.

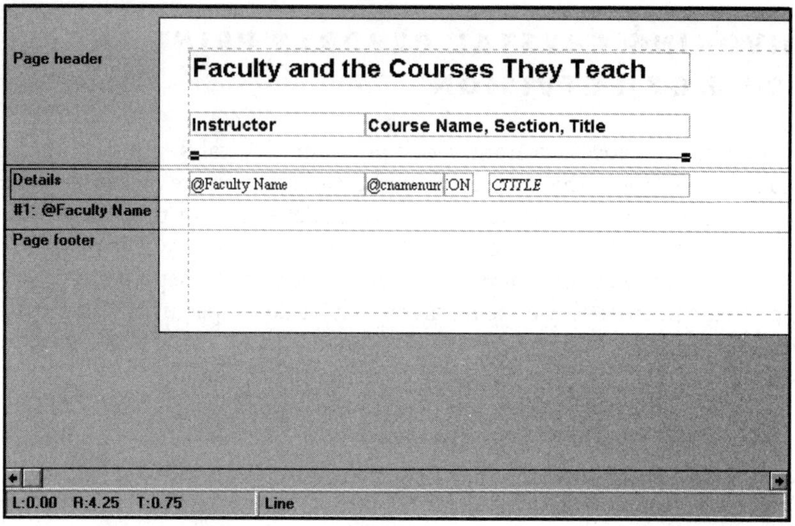

Page header	**Faculty and the Courses They Teach**		
	Instructor	Course Name, Section, Title	
Details	@Faculty Name	@cnamenum ON	CTITLE
#1: @Faculty Name			
Page footer			

L:0.00   R:4.25   T:0.75   Line

FIGURE 6.21
Inserting a line

1. Open up an additional line following the column heading text fields by placing the I-beam insertion point at the left margin of the column heading row. Then press Enter to insert a blank line.

2. Choose the Line icon from the Button bar. The pointer symbol changes to a pencil.

3. Move the pointer to the left margin of the blank line below the column headers and click the left mouse button.

4. Drag the line until it aligns with the right end of the rightmost column heading. Then release the left mouse button. The pointer changes back to an I-beam and the graphic line appears (see Figure 6.21).

One last task of setting the print margins and the Class Teaching Assignments report will be complete. By default, the report margins are set to the non-printing areas of your printer. For laser printers, that is typically one-quarter inch for top, bottom, left, and right margins. Set the margins to one inch for all margins by selecting the Set Printer Margins command of the Print menu. The Printer Margins dialog box appears. Enter 1 in each of the four text entry areas corresponding to the four margins and click OK.

That is it for our report. We have finished designing it! Before printing a copy of the report, print it to a window once more to make sure it looks satisfactory. Select the Print to Window command of the Print menu. Remember to save your report. (Save it as FAC.RPT, for example.) If you chose not to create the complete report, you can use the one named FACULTY.RPT on the disk supplied with this book or available from your instructor. The next section describes how to invoke the report you just created from within ObjectVision.

6.6 INVOKING CRYSTAL REPORTS PRINT ENGINE FROM OBJECTVISION

In addition to its use as a stand-alone program, Crystal Reports can be accessed and executed from other Windows applications. If you are developing Windows applications using ObjectVision, C, or other development tools that provide so-called DLL capabilities, you can add sophisticated report-writing capabilities to the finished applications. Your end users do not need a separate report-writing application in order to use the reports you have developed using Crystal Reports. You provide the Crystal Reports Print Engine facilities free of charge to your customers in addition to your ObjectVision application.

As an applications developer, create the report(s) you want using Crystal Reports Report Editor. Then add a button in your ObjectVision application that can be used to start the report-printing procedure. With the Crystal Reports Print Engine you can provide several report options. Users can print various reports to a window, to the printer, or both. You control which of these options and how many are available by encoding them in the event trees of the appropriately labeled ObjectVision buttons. You can set up multiple buttons, one for each report and preview/hard copy combination. Best of all, you need not be a programmer to provide the interface to the Crystal Reports Print Engine.

The mechanism for producing reports from ObjectVision is to provide several new functions (you *register* the functions) which perform all the necessary information exchange between ObjectVision and the Crystal Reports Print Engine. All the requisite functions are provided in the Crystal Reports Print Engine (CRPE) DLL provided with the Crystal Reports software. There are three steps that must be followed so that you can use Crystal Reports Print Engine as a developer:

1. With the Crystal Reports Report Editor, first create all the reports that you want your users to be able to produce (on screen or otherwise).

2. Next you must create the simple interface that allows your users to produce the reports you have developed (buttons that are clicked in Object-Vision to start a reporting process).

3. Finally, you must create an ObjectVision stack event tree that registers the required CRPE functions used in the buttons invoking the reporting processes (open a report, call the Print to Window program, and so on).

The first step—creating the report (FACULTY.RPT)—has been completed as described in the preceding sections of this chapter. All that remains is to implement the remaining two steps. They are described next.

REGISTERING CRYSTAL REPORTS FUNCTIONS

Reports are produced from ObjectVision by using functions that provide the interface between ObjectVision and Crystal Reports. In order to use these functions, you must first **register** them. When you register the Crystal Reports functions, they can be incorporated into ObjectVision applications just like any other function available with ObjectVision. Once registered, you can select the function from the scrolling list that is accessed when creating a conclusion node in an event tree.

Though you may not use in ObjectVision applications all the functions that are supplied by Crystal Reports, it is easy to register all of them at once. You register functions by using the ObjectVision function @REGISTER. All requisite Crystal Reports functions can be registered at once by calling the SelfRegister function as the open event in the stack event tree. It is a three-pass process in which you must enter a function, save the application, reopen the application, insert another function, save the application, and reopen it another time. The reason for the several save/open operations is that a function must be registered before it can be used. The catch is that you cannot even enter the function in the conclusion of an event tree unless it is already registered (known to ObjectVision). The following steps are the easiest way to register the required functions that provide report-producing capabilities for your ObjectVision application.

First we will register all the required Crystal Reports functions with the SelfRegister function. It is a function that is registered and, in turn, registers *all* the remaining Crystal Reports interface functions. We add a report-producing capability to the ObjectVision Faculty application developed throughout this text. Open FACULTY and enter edit mode. Then do the following:

1. Right click the application title bar (not the *form* title bar) and select Event Tree. (We are modifying the stack event tree for the open event.)
2. Select the OPEN event in the stack event tree (it already exists because we added the SETTITLE function sometime earlier).
3. Click the right mouse button and select Conclusion from the pop-up menu that displays. The Action for Application dialog box appears.
4. Position the cursor after the existing SETTITLE command by moving to the end of that line and pressing Ctrl+Enter.
5. Enter the following self-register function:
    ```
    @REGISTER("@REGISTER_CRPE","In","","C:\CRW\CRPE.DLL",
    "SelfRegister",1)
    ```
6. Click OK to close the dialog box.
7. Double click the Control-menu box of the event tree to close it.
8. Click the Enter icon on the Button bar.
9. Save the application by executing File|Save.

10. Finally, reopen the Faculty application. This last action triggers the registration of the self-registering Crystal Reports function, @REGISTER_CRPE (say that five times, fast!).

Be very careful in writing the self-registering function in step 5. Note that there are six arguments, and five of them are enclosed in double quotation marks. Capitalization is important, also. The third argument contains two double quotation marks in succession to indicate a null argument. The fourth argument is one you may have to change. It indicates the path on your computer to the function called `CRPE.DLL`. It is usually located in the same place in which Crystal Reports has been stored. But you may wish to simply enter CRPE.DLL so it will work from the current directory on your end-users' machines.

The next pass of the three-pass procedure is to add the Crystal Reports function registration itself, called @REGISTER_CRPE. When it is executed, it will register the remaining Crystal Reports functions. To summarize what we have done in pass one: We added the ObjectVision @REGISTER function to register the @REGISTER_CRPE so that it is known to ObjectVision when it is later executed. We cannot register that function *and* use it in the same pass, because it has not been registered yet (a sort of catch-22).

REGISTERING FUNCTIONS WITH @REGISTER_CRPE

After you reopen the Faculty application, the stack open event is automatically triggered. That causes the @REGISTER function we just added to register the @REGISTER_CRPE function. Next, we can add the @REGISTER_CRPE function, itself, to the list of stack open events that are executed. Reopen the stack event tree by executing the first three steps previously listed. Then add the @REGISTER_CRPE function by following these steps:

1. Place the I-beam on a new line: Position it at the end of the line containing the @REGISTER function and press Ctrl+Enter.

2. Type in this line:

   `@REGISTER_CRPE`

3. Click OK to close the event tree.

4. Click the Enter button on the Button bar.

5. Save the application (File|Save).

6. Reopen the Faculty application.

Following this second series of save- and open-application operations, the REGISTER_CRPE function is executed. That causes thirty Crystal Reports Print Engine functions to be automatically registered. (They all begin with the prefix PE and are easily recognizable in the function list.)

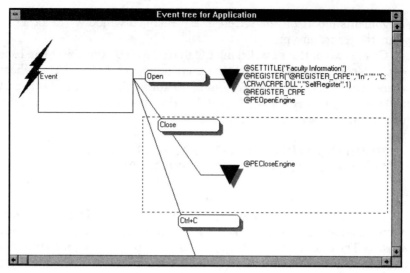

FIGURE 6.22
Stack open and close event trees

ENTERING THE OPEN AND CLOSE PRINT ENGINE FUNCTIONS

Like the preceding two passes, this third pass affects the stack event tree. Open the stack event tree as you did previously and add the following as the last line of the open event conclusion:

        @PEOpenEngine

Click OK to close the Conclusion dialog box, and double click the Control-menu box to close the stack open event tree. Create a close event and add the following function as the single line of the conclusion:

        @PECloseEngine

The final contents of both the open and close stack event trees are shown in Figure 6.22.

Close the stack event tree. Now you are ready to provide buttons that users may push to produce either printed or screen-displayed reports.

CALLING THE PRINT ENGINE TO PRODUCE REPORTS

Provide users with two report methods: viewing a report on screen (saving paper) or printing it on the printer. For this application, you have one report and two ways to print it, so you need two buttons. One button prints the Class Teaching

Assignments report on the screen in a predefined window. The other button prints the report on a printer.

Create two buttons by clicking the Button icon on the object bar. Label one button **Report/Window** and label the other one **Report/Printer**. Place them anywhere there is space near the bottom of the form with the other buttons. Open the button event tree for the Report/Window button and enter the following function in the conclusion node of the click event:

```
@PEPrintReport("FACULTY.RPT",0,1,"Faculty Teaching
Assignments",32768,32768,32768,32768,0,0)
```

Close the event tree in the usual way.

The preceding function calls the Crystal Reports Print Engine and causes the report name specified as the first argument to display its results on screen in a window. The characteristics of the window are specified by the several numeric arguments. Details about these arguments can be found in Chapter 10 of the Crystal Reports manual. There are no letter *o*'s in the function—they all are zeros. The second and third arguments indicate no (0) printed report and display (1) the results in a window. The fourth argument, Faculty Teaching Assignments, is the report title displayed on screen.

Open the button event tree for the Report/Printer button and enter the following function in the conclusion node of the click event:

```
@PEPrintReport("FACULTY.RPT",1,0,"Faculty Teaching
Assignments",0,0,0,0,0,0)
```

Close the dialog box and the event tree.

The preceding is similar to the window display function just described. The main difference is that the second and third arguments are 1 and 0, respectively. That means print on the printer and do not (0) display the report in a window. Obviously, if both those arguments were one (1), then both a hard copy and a screen display would be produced. Notice the last six numeric arguments are zeros, because these have to do with the characteristics of a window displayed on screen.

Try out the new buttons. They produce both printed copies and a window display at the click of a button. If you wish, you can use the application saved as FIG06-23.OVD on the enclosed disk to try these new buttons. Figure 6.23 shows an example of the report produced on screen in its own window that overlays the Faculty application.

PROVIDING CRYSTAL REPORTS RUNTIME MODULES

If you are a registered user of Crystal Reports, you are permitted to distribute a runtime version of the Crystal Reports Print Engine with your applications at no charge. In addition to your application (.OVD file), you must supply to your user

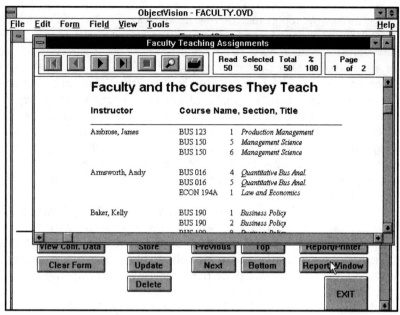

FIGURE 6.23
Example Faculty window report

population selected files from the Crystal Reports suite of runtime files in order for the report-invoking functions to work properly. A list of these runtime routines (called DLLs) is given in Appendix B of the Crystal Reports documentation. Consult that source to determine which modules you should supply with your application.

SUMMARY

Crystal Reports is a report-writing system that allows designers to create various summary and detail reports. Reports designed with the Report Editor and generated by Crystal Reports display information from databases and provide a simple means of sorting report rows into order by one or more key fields. In addition, related items can be grouped together and summary information, such as sums and averages, can be produced for each group. Statistics about all the groups can be displayed at the bottom of the report.

Report elements you can place in a report include database fields, text fields, and formula fields. Formula fields resemble the functions found in most popular spreadsheet products. With formulas, you can create expressions, including ones of arbitrary complexity that calculate values from database fields. Graphical elements such as lines, boxes, and imported graphics may be placed in the report.

Sections of the report include Page header, Page footer, and Details. The Details section is the report band containing the rows of fields that comprise the major portion of the report. Header and footer sections can contain elements that are printed once at the top or bottom of each page, respectively. Additionally, group sections can be created that bookend the Details line. Sections typically contain subtotal and summary information about the group they define.

Extensive report formatting is available. Elements in each report section can be individually formatted. You can select any of the Windows fonts, point sizes, and appearance features. Color and specialty effects such as drop shadows can be selected. You can suppress display of duplicate fields on the report, which is especially handy when listing repeating groups in which you want to display the grouping field only once.

Supplied with Crystal Reports are dynamic link library functions (DLLs). These Crystal Reports Print Engine functions provide the interface functions allowing ObjectVision programs to call on the services of the Crystal Reports reporting system. These functions are collectively known as the runtime modules. As a developer, you can place these functions in the appropriate places in ObjectVision so that users merely click an ObjectVision button to produce an on screen, windowed report or to produce a printed copy of it. The Crystal Reports licensing agreement you agree to as a registered user of Crystal Reports allows you to ship the runtime modules, free of charge, to your end users along with the ObjectVision applications you have created.

KEY TERMS

Alias An alternative name assigned to a database file. If a database is called CUSTOMER.DBF, you could assign the alias CUST, for example.

Concatenate To join two or more text strings together to form a single contiguous string.

Database field A Crystal Reports field whose value is drawn from a database linked to the report.

Foreign key A field in a database that either matches a primary key in another database or is null.

Formula field A report field that is a symbolic statement of the manipulations to be performed on certain data before it is displayed or printed.

Group A set of records that are related to each other in some way. In a customer mailing list example, a group might be comprised of everyone in the same zip code.

Page footer A small amount of text that appears at the bottom of a report page.

Page header A small amount of text that appears at the top of a report page.

Register (function) Registration of a function with ObjectVision makes that function known to ObjectVision and it subsequently appears in the Paste Function dialog box that can be displayed in any Event tree dialog box. All functions that are not part of ObjectVision external functions must be registered.

Status bar The bar at the bottom of the Report Editor. It displays valuable information such as the description of a selected Button bar icon, menu command descriptions, and field names.

Text field A report field whose contents is a text string.

REVIEW QUESTIONS

True or False Questions

1. **T F** Crystal Reports can read dBase, Paradox, and Foxpro databases.

2. **T F** When a new report is opened, Crystal Reports automatically creates two sections: Page header and Page footer.

3. **T F** It is not possible to link a primary key with a foreign key through Crystal Reports.

4. **T F** The command Print Report to Window prints a report in its own, on screen window.

5. **T F** It is possible both to create and to check the correctness of a formula with the Formula Editor dialog box.

6. **T F** Using a text field when adding a page title is equivalent to typing the text directly.

7. **T F** The only way to edit or format an object is by selecting the Edit menu.

8. **T F** Crystal Reports cannot be accessed or executed from other Windows applications.

9. **T F** Runtime modules can be provided to clients free of charge.

10. **T F** Crystal Reports is a report-writing system that allows end users to create various summary and detail reports.

EXERCISES

1. Using Crystal Reports, define and print a listing of all courses that appear in the database CLASSNME.DBF. For each course, list the course name, number, title, and credit hours. Make sure that the information is in ascending order by course name and number.

2. Create the same report as above and add a page title and appropriate column headings. Change the font of the page title to a value that is larger than the default point size. Likewise, change the point sizes of the column heading text fields to a larger-than-default value.

3. Create a report using the database labeled STOCKLST.DBF provided on a disk included with this text. The report should list the following information, left to right: client identification (ID) number, stock name, purchase date, purchase price, and number of shares purchased. Group the information on the client identification number. Individual stock purchase lines for each client should be sorted by stock name and then purchase date. Format the client ID numbers so no commas are used and do not print duplicate client ID numbers. Format purchase date as a date, and format the purchase price to display two decimal places and no dollar sign. The number of shares purchased are integer numbers. Print both a window report (check it for completeness) and a printed copy to hand in to your instructor.

4. Add a page heading that contains labels for each of the fields displayed in the STOCKLST report described in in exercise 3. Insert a graphic line in the group heading area so that it separates successive clients' stocks. Create headings such as Stock Name, Purchase Date, and Purchase Price, and place the two-word headings one over the other on two lines. In addition, insert a new field, a formula, in the rightmost position. It calculates the total price paid for each stock. Format the total price value with a dollar sign and two decimal places. Print a copy of the report.

5. The dBASE database ROSTER.DBF contains one thousand records. Each record represents a student registered in a particular course and section. A database record contains a student's last name (LNAME), first name (FNAME), course name (CNAME), course number (CNUMB), and section number (CSECTION). Produce a class roster for all accounting courses (the course name matches the abbreviation ACCT). Each course roster should be printed on a new page and should list the course name and section at the top. The roster should show the last and first names of each student.

6. Enhance the preceding report by concatenating each course name, course number, and section number into a single string with only one blank between the constituent parts and a comma preceding the section number. The string should resemble this example: "ACCT 101B, Section 1" where

ACCT, 101B, and the section number (1) are all retrieved from the database. Rosters should be in order by course name and section number, and the students should be listed in alphabetical order by last name and then first name. Insert a blank line just above the first of the student names, and indent each student name slightly from where the course name, number, and section are printed.

7. Produce a report showing the name, rank, office number, and phone number of each faculty member found in the database FACULTY.DBF.

8. Produce a printed report showing each course and the instructor who is assigned to teach it. List only courses that have been assigned an instructor. Order the report by class name and number. Indicate the section number of the course to the right of each instructor's name for those assigned to teach a particular course.

CREATING MENUS
AND PROTECTING
APPLICATIONS

OBJECTIVES

This capstone chapter describes how to integrate on one work surface several ObjectVision applications and Windows applications via a menu from which each application is invoked. In addition, you will learn the following:

- *How to create buttons that launch other Object-Vision applications*
- *How to create a button that launches another Windows application*
- *How to create custom menus for your applications*
- *How to protect your applications from end-user tampering*
- *How to include ObjectVision runtime modules with your applications*

7.1 INTRODUCTION

In this chapter we will create a new, simple ObjectVision application that is a main menu. From it users can select which of several ObjectVision applications are to be invoked. Functionally, the main menu—which we dub the Application Launch Pad—serves a function similar to the Windows Program Manager. Using the Application Launch Pad, you can click icons on the application work surface to execute the associated application. Applications can be either ObjectVision applications or any other DOS or Windows software application.

After we create the Application Launch Pad, we will turn our attention to making small modifications to the Faculty and Employee applications. Most of our efforts will be focused on the Faculty application. Faculty will receive a friendlier, customized menu, and the original ObjectVision menu will be eradicated. The next section will provide a detailed discussion of how to create a small, straightforward Application Launch Pad.

7.2 CREATING AN APPLICATION LAUNCH PAD

The Windows Program Manager provides an intuitive way for users to select both DOS and Windows applications to be executed. We will build a similar interface in which users can click buttons to launch either ObjectVision programs or commercial software packages. The menu choices available via the proposed Application Launch Pad make it easier for users to execute your ObjectVision applications. New users, particularly, will like the ease with which they can execute various ObjectVision applications from a central menu.

You will create a new ObjectVision application which contains buttons that invoke other applications. Giving action to the buttons will be two distinct ObjectVision functions. One will be used to execute ObjectVision applications. The other function will **launch** commercial software applications—non-ObjectVision applications. We will illustrate the concept of how to create a launch pad by establishing an ObjectVision application containing only three buttons. Two of the buttons will execute the ObjectVision applications you created in the preceding six chapters: Employee and Faculty. The third button will show you how simple it is to launch a Windows application, Terminal, found in the Windows Accessories group. Terminal is a communications application that can use a modem to dial into another computer. Figure 7.1 shows the new ObjectVision application—the Application Launch Pad.

Two buttons, labeled Employee Review and Faculty Information, contain ObjectVision functions that invoke the Employee and Faculty applications, respectively. The button labeled Data Communications contains a slightly different function that executes the Terminal program supplied with Windows. The Exit button provides a departure point that sends control back to the Windows Program Manager. We will create each of these buttons shortly. First, however, we will create a new form containing a text heading.

FIGURE 7.1
Application Launch Pad

CREATING A TEXT HEADER

The first step is to create a new application form, at the top of which you will insert the text "Application Launch Pad." Launch Windows, if necessary. Then click the ObjectVision icon. After the ObjectVision opening window is displayed, do the following:

1. Click Tools | Form.
2. Enter launcher in the Form Name dialog box and click OK.
3. Click View | Ruler and click the Characters radio button.
4. Click the Top and Left check boxes so that rulers are displayed on the top and left sides of the form.
5. Click OK to complete setting up a ruler.
6. Size the form to 55 characters horizontally and 14 characters vertically.

Next create the text across the top of the form. Click the Text button on the object bar. Then, enter the text Application Launch Pad into the Text Value dialog box. Position the text so that it extends the full width of the form near the top. Then, right click to invoke the property inspector and choose the text label font MS Sans Serif, 18 point, bold. Invoke the property inspector again, select the Alignment property, and click the Center radio button to center the text on the form. Finally, invoke the property inspector and choose Borders. Uncheck the Outline check box to remove the border surrounding the text.

CREATING BUTTONS

Buttons on the form will be used either to execute other ObjectVision applications and Windows programs or to exit the ObjectVision application. The first step is to create buttons. Then we will add an event tree to each button that either executes the associated program or exits the application. You create the four buttons by doing the following:

FIGURE 7.2
Positioning the buttons

1. Click the Button icon on the object bar.

2. Type the name Employee Review.

3. Click OK.

4. Drag the Button icon so that the outline is about 2 by 20 characters.

Repeat the preceding four steps for the other three buttons, entering the button names Faculty Information, Data Communications, and Exit. However, make the Exit button smaller. It should be about 2 by 10 characters. Position the buttons so that your form is similar to Figure 7.2.

ADDING AN APPLICATION TITLE

We now add an application event that displays the title Application Launch Pad in the application title bar. Because we want the title to be displayed each time the application is opened, we will create an event tree that responds to the application open event. The function we employ to establish a title is @SETTITLE. You have seen this function before. The steps needed to add an application open event tree are these:

1. Right click the application title bar.

2. Click the Event Tree property.

3. Click Conclusion on the object bar.

4. Type Open in the Event Name dialog box and then click OK.

5. Type @SETTITLE("Application Launcher") when the Action for Application dialog box appears. Then, click OK.

6. Close the event tree.

7. Save the application under the name LAUNCHER.OVD.

Remember that the application title *does not* change until the application is opened. You can test the new stack open event by reopening Launcher (LAUNCHER.OVD).

Next, button event trees are added to each of the four buttons so that they either execute applications or terminate the ObjectVision session and return to Windows.

ADDING APPLICATION AND BUTTON EVENT TREES

We create event trees for all four buttons in the same way. Each event tree will respond to the click condition. The response to that event will vary by button. For two of the buttons, Employee Review and Faculty Information, the event tree will execute a special function that invokes another ObjectVision application. For the Data Communications button, a different ObjectVision function is used in the event tree. Finally, the Exit button click event will contain the function @APPEXIT, which terminates the ObjectVision application and returns to Windows. First, we will construct the event trees for the buttons that launch other ObjectVision applications.

ObjectVision provides a built-in function that opens another ObjectVision application. The function is @APPOPEN, and it performs the same actions that occur when you execute File | Open and select an ObjectVision application name to be opened. First build an event tree for the Employee Review button. Follow these steps:

1. Right click the Employee Review button to display its properties and then select Event Tree.
2. Type `Click` in the Event name dialog box and then click OK.
3. Type the function `@APPOPEN("employee.ovd")` when the Action for Application dialog box appears.
4. Click OK. The completed event tree is displayed (see Figure 7.3).
5. Close the event tree.
6. Finally, close the Form tool.

It is a good idea to test the button before going on with the development. But first save the application so that you can reopen the latest version in case the newly added button event tree goes awry. Test the Employee Review button by simply clicking it. If you have the Employee application (EMPLOYEE.OVD) available in the same area where other ObjectVision applications are found, then the Employee Allowance form should display on the screen.

You will quickly notice a small difficulty has arisen: How do you return to the Application Launcher from the Employee Review application? There is no button on the Employee Review form to do so. Later in this section we will add

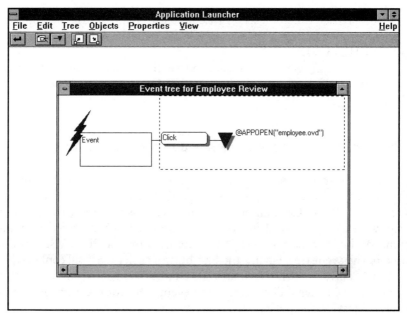

FIGURE 7.3
Event tree to invoke an ObjectVision application

a button—that was previously not required—which returns to the Application Launcher from any ObjectVision application. For now, you can return to the Application Launcher Pad by executing File|Open and selecting Launcher from the list.

Repeat the previous steps to create an event tree for the Faculty Information button. This time, enter the following function for the conclusion of the click event:

```
@APPOPEN("faculty.ovd")
```

Close the event tree and the tool. Save the application to preserve your work so far.

Next we build the click event tree for the Data Communications button. The steps are the same as before, except that you insert a different function. Follow the same steps you did for the previous two event trees. For step 3, however, insert this function:

```
@EXEC("terminal.exe",0)
```

The @EXEC function is used to execute non-ObjectVision applications. The name inside double quotation marks is the file name associated with the Windows Terminal application. Because the Windows programs, including TERMINAL.EXE, are on a path that Windows searches, you do not need to include the full DOS path (such as C:\WINDOWS\TERMINAL.EXE). The third argument is the value

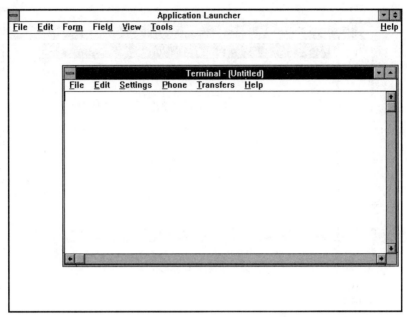

FIGURE 7.4
Executing a Windows program, Terminal

zero. That indicates the called program should be displayed in a standard size window. Two other arguments, 1 and 2, indicate the program should be displayed as an icon or as a full screen, respectively. When you execute File | Exit from Terminal, the Application Launch Pad form is redisplayed.

Complete the Data Communications event tree and save the application. Now try out the button: click Data Communications. The Terminal program is displayed in a window (see Figure 7.4). Notice that the Terminal window overlays the Application Launch Pad application. Only the ObjectVision title bar and menu are visible.

The last event tree to be inserted is for the Exit button. Follow the familiar steps above for the Exit button. Place this function,

    @APPEXIT

in the conclusion node of the click event for the Exit button. Once more, save the application. The APPEXIT function has no arguments. It terminates the Object-Vision application and returns to Windows.

MODIFYING APPLICATIONS TO RETURN TO THE APPLICATION LAUNCH PAD

To complete this part of the application, we must modify both the Employee and Faculty applications so that control returns to the Launcher application when a

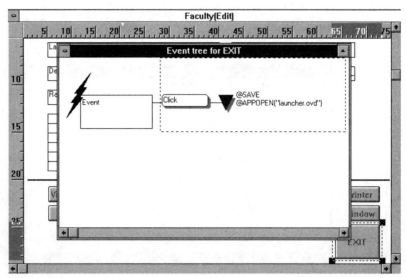

FIGURE 7.5
Modified Exit click event tree

user exits either application. Both applications can be modified in the same way. You will add an Exit button to the Employee application that returns to the Application Launch Pad application. The Faculty application will be modified. Faculty already has an Exit button. You will alter the Exit button's click event tree to return to the Launcher rather than to exit ObjectVision.

First open the Employee application. Add a button and label it Exit. Create an event tree for the Exit button that responds to the Click event. That one-line function is

```
@APPOPEN("launcher.ovd")
```

and is the conclusion of the click event. Save the Employee application to disk.

Next we will open the Faculty application and change the Exit button. First, open Faculty and use the Form tool. Because an Exit button exists, we will simply *modify* the Exit button by doing the following:

1. Right click the Exit button.

2. Click the Event Tree selection.

3. Right click the Click event.

4. Click the choice Conclusion from the displayed properties.

5. Replace the function @APPEXIT by dragging the mouse over it. Then type: `@APPOPEN("launcher.ovd")`. Figure 7.5 shows the modified Exit event tree.

6. Click OK.

7. Close the event tree.

8. Close the Form tool.

9. Save the application to disk.

Now both the Employee and Faculty applications will return to the Launcher application whenever you press the Exit button in either one. Of course, if you open either Employee or Faculty directly from ObjectVision, pressing the Exit button will always cause the Launcher application to be opened.

7.3 CREATING A CUSTOM MENU

ObjectVision applications you create can be further customized by adding your own individual menus. You can remove all or some of the standard ObjectVision menus, remove only selected commands from some menus, or place application-specific menus and commands on the menu bar.

Individual, **customized menus** can make your applications easier to use and provide additional security. Your end users will find it simpler to use your application if it has distinct, simple menu choices. Special menu selections protect your application by limiting what users can do. Implementing custom menus comprises two major steps. First, you create a new application menu by adding menus and menu items and removing existing ObjectVision menus and menu items through special ObjectVision **menu customization functions**. Second, you give custom menu items life by defining their actions with a series of stack event tree conditions and conclusions.

OBJECTVISION MENU CUSTOMIZATION FUNCTIONS

Among the many ObjectVision built-in functions are those that change the main menu. There are seven menu customization @functions. @ADDMENU and @ADDMENUITEM create a *menu* or a menu *item*, respectively. Two other menu customization functions, @DELETEMENU and @DELETEMENUITEM, delete an entire menu with all of its items or delete a single menu item, respectively. @CHECKMENUITEM and @UNCHECKMENUITEM places a check mark next to a menu item or removes it, respectively. Finally, @RESTOREMENU erases all menu changes and reinstates the original, standard ObjectVision menus.

Removing Selected Menu Items

You can remove some or all of the standard ObjectVision menus with the built-in functions @DELETEMENU and @DELETEMENUITEM. The @DELETEMENU function removes a single menu and all of its attendant menu items. It has the form,

```
@DELETEMENU("Menu-Name")
```

where Menu-Name is the name of an existing menu (such as File or Help). For example, you could eliminate the Tools menu completely by issuing the following

```
@DELETEMENU("Tools")
```

when the application is opened.

Similarly, you can remove a single menu item from a menu, leaving the parent menu in place, with the @DELETEMENUITEM function. It has the form,

```
@DELETEMENUITEM("Menu-Name","Menu-Item-Name")
```

where Menu-Item-Name is a menu selection found in the menu, Menu-Name. For example, instead of deleting the entire Tools menu, you could remove just the Form command of the Tools menu. That would prevent users from editing an application. You could execute the function

```
@DELETEMENUITEM("Tools","Form")
```

to remove the Form command, leaving the other Tools menu choices in place.

Creating New Menu Selections

Two ObjectVision functions allow you to create menu selections. If you wish to create a new menu, complete with new menu items, then you establish the new menu name with the @ADDMENU function. The function has the general form,

```
@ADDMENU("New-Menu-Name",Position)
```

where New-Menu-Name is the name you want for the menu command and Position is where you want the command to be placed in the menu bar. A position value of 0 places the menu in the leftmost position on the menu bar. To place new menus at the right end of the menu bar, you can use –1.

If you wish to underline a letter in the menu name, use an ampersand (&). By convention, an underlined letter indicates you can press Alt and tap the letter to invoke the menu.

Suppose you want to create a menu called "Reports" containing various commands that produce on screen and printed reports. It is to be the third menu from the left. Furthermore, the shortcut key Alt+P can be used to invoke the menu. You want to underline the letter p (that is, Reports) to indicate the menu's hot key. The prescribed new menu is defined by the following function:

```
@ADDMENU("Re&ports",2)
```

The name Reports appears in the third position (0 is the first, 1 the second, and 2 the third position) in the menu bar.

A related command, @ADDMENUITEM, defines a menu item (command) for an existing menu. It has the following form,

```
@ADDMENUITEM("Menu-Name","New-Menu-Item-Name",Position)
```

where New-Menu-Item-Name is the name of the item you want placed under the menu called Menu-Name. The third parameter of @ADDMENUITEM, Position, indicates the position, relative to the top of the drop-down list, where the new item is to be placed. The topmost position is 0, and a position value of –1 places the item at the end of the list. The following adds the menu item Print Report to the existing ObjectVision File menu. A user can select the item with the mouse or press Alt+R. The new item is placed at the end of the File menu list:

```
@ADDMENUITEM("File","Print &Report",-1)
```

Restoring the Default Menu

The @RESTOREMENU function reinstates the original ObjectVision menu structure. That is an "escape" option you may want to provide for yourself or your end users. The @RESTOREMENU function, having no arguments, does that. You can issue @RESTOREMENU when you are testing your new menus and find yourself in a bind. After the ObjectVision menus are reinstated, you can execute Tools|Form to edit the application to make needed changes.

Normally, you make @RESTOREMENU available through one of the menu items in the custom menu. For example, you might include a menu item called RESTORE in the File menu. On the other hand, you may want to exclude use of @RESTOREMENU if you desire absolute security for your application. By deleting the original ObjectVision menu, you eliminate the Form menu item. That prevents users from editing your applications. The form of @RESTOREMENU is simple:

```
@RESTOREMENU
```

It has no arguments, therefore there are no parentheses. We will illustrate exactly how to use @RESTOREMENU in this chapter's example.

Modifying the Stack Event Tree

Using the menu customization functions to create a unique application menu is only half of the process. You must add events and associated actions to the application's stack in order to define what each menu item does when it is invoked. For each item you add to each menu, you must have a corresponding event whose condition matches the menu name, including any ampersands. For example, we showed how to add a hypothetical command called Print Report to ObjectVision's File menu. The actions that Print Report performs must be contained in the

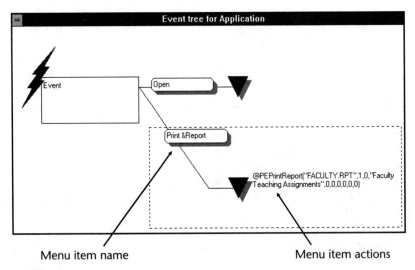

Menu item name   Menu item actions

FIGURE 7.6
Example menu item definition

application event stack. There must be a branch whose condition is "Print &Report" (without the quotation marks). Figure 7.6 shows part of the stack event tree defining the Print &Report actions. It prints a copy of the faculty roster, using the Crystal Reports functions shown in Chapter 6.

REMOVING EXISTING MENU ITEMS

Next we will add a custom menu to the Faculty application developed in Chapters 2 through 6. The custom menu will make the application easier to use and will protect it from being altered. Because users do not need all of the commands provided to application developers, the default ObjectVision menu will be erased. Then new menu selections will be created that facilitate generating faculty reports and searching the database.

If you want to create a custom menu that is displayed once the application is open, then you must place the menu creation functions in the stack event tree. In particular, you must place the menu customization functions in the conclusion node of the Open event condition. We will examine how to create custom application menus by first removing the default ObjectVision menus.

First invoke ObjectVision, if necessary, and open the Faculty application you last modified in Chapter 6. If you did not create or modify Faculty, the latest version of the Faculty application (as of the end of Chapter 6) is saved as the file FACULTY6.OVD on the data disk that accompanies this text. Follow these steps to begin modifying the application (stack) event tree:

1. Right click the application title bar (not the form title bar).

2. Click the Event Tree property displayed in the Stack properties list. The Faculty application event tree is displayed. It is shown in Figure 7.7.

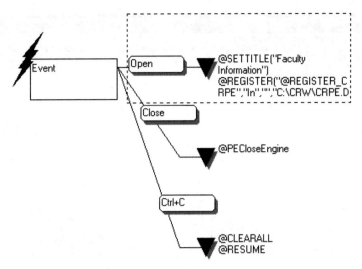

FIGURE 7.7
Faculty application event tree before change

For the best effect, we want the new menus to be displayed *immediately* after loading the Faculty form. Thus, any actions taken to change a menu must occur automatically upon opening an application. So, those menu-affecting instructions must be placed in the conclusion statements of the open condition. If an application does not yet have an open condition on its stack event tree, then you can create one. Otherwise, you can open the existing open event conclusion node and modify it. Follow these steps to modify the Faculty Open event conclusion node:

1. Click near the open event in the tree to select it. A dashed line will appear around the node when it is selected (see Figure 7.7).

2. Right click the open event node. Two properties are displayed: Condition and Conclusion.

3. Click the Conclusion property. The Action for Application dialog box appears (see Figure 7.8).

4. Position the cursor at the end of the last line of the script (following the function @PEOpenEngine) and move to a new line by pressing Ctrl+Enter.

5. Type the following functions, one after another, each on a separate line:

```
@DELETEMENU("File")
@DELETEMENU("Edit")
@DELETEMENU("Form")
@DELETEMENU("Field")
@DELETEMENU("View")
@DELETEMENU("Tools")
```

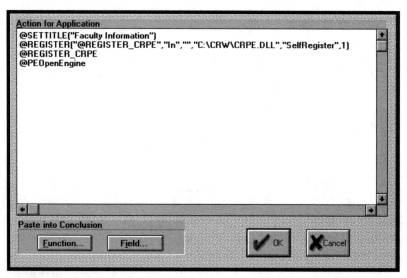

FIGURE 7.8
Action for Application dialog box

The preceding functions each remove one of the default ObjectVision menus. They can be removed in any order. We merely arranged the @DELETEMENU functions in the same order as the menus that appear on the menu bar.

After you have entered the preceding functions, the dialog box should look like Figure 7.9. Do not close the dialog box, because next we will be adding more lines that create new menus and menu items.

ADDING MENUS AND MENU ITEMS

The next step in the menu customization process is to add the new menus and the menu items, which appear in the pull-down menus. To illustrate adding useful, application-sensitive menus, we will add three menus: File, Database, and Report. The File menu will contain two items: Restore and Exit. Restore can be selected to reinstate the ObjectVision default menus. Exit leaves the ObjectVision program and returns to the Windows Program Manager. In the Database pull-down menu are these items, initially: Top and Bottom. Top is selected to position the database on the first faculty record. Bottom is selected to position the database on the last faculty record. Finally, the Report menu provides two choices in its pull-down menu: Roster/Window and Roster/Printer.

We continue to modify the Action for Application dialog box and now will add the File, Database, and Report menus. We will add the items appearing in pull-down menus in later steps. Follow these steps to add the menus:

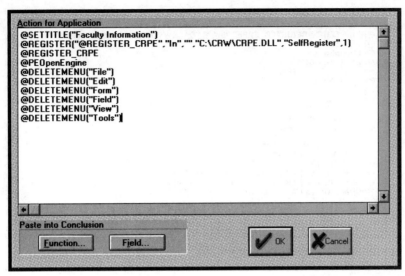

FIGURE 7.9
Functions to delete ObjectVision menus

1. On a new line in the open event conclusion, add the following line:

   `@ADDMENU("&File",0)`

2. Press Ctrl+Enter to go to a new line and add the following function:

   `@ADDMENU("&Database",1)`

3. Finally, move to a new line and add the last menu with the function:

   `@ADDMENU("&Report",2)`

The ampersands before the initial letters of File, Database, and Report indicate which letter is to be underlined in the menu, and that indicates the speed key which activates the menu. Pressing Alt+D, for example, will invoke the Database menu. The second argument of each function indicates where the menu item appears in the menu bar, left to right. The File menu is first (0), followed by Database (1), and then Report (2). (Because we did *not* delete the ObjectVision Help menu, it remains rightmost in the menu bar.)

Next we add the menu items that appear in each of the pull-down lists. Continue adding lines to the Action for Application dialog box, part of the conclusion node of the open condition. Do the following:

1. Add the following two lines to place menu items in the File menu pull-down list:

   `@ADDMENUITEM("&File","&Restore",0)`
   `@ADDMENUITEM("&File","&Exit",1)`

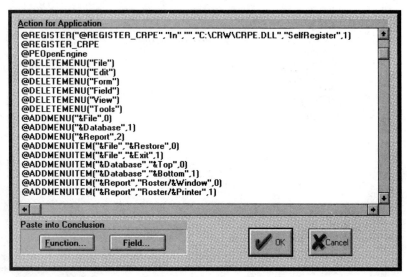

FIGURE 7.10
Completed menu customization commands

2. Add the following two lines to create the Database menu pull-down list:

```
@ADDMENUITEM("&Database","&Top",0)
@ADDMENUITEM("&Database","&Bottom",1)
```

3. Add the following two lines to create the Report menu pull-down list:

```
@ADDMENUITEM("&Report","Roster/&Window",0)
@ADDMENUITEM("&Report","Roster/&Printer",1)
```

Figure 7.10 shows the completed Action for Application conclusion statements for the open event. Complete this process by clicking OK to close the dialog box. Close the application event tree. Finally, close the Form tool by clicking the Return icon on the left end of the object bar.

ADDING EVENT RECOGNITION LOGIC TO THE STACK

Once you have created a set of new menus and menu items, you will need to add action statements that bring life to the menus. A menu has the power to do something—produce some result or cause something to change—when the stack event tree contains branches whose *condition names* match the menu *item names*. The relationship between menu names and stack event tree branches works like the following.

When you select a menu item from a drop-down menu, an event, or signal, is sent to the application stack. That event name matches the menu item name.

The stack event tree is searched to see if there is a branch whose condition name matches the event name just received. If so, then the conclusion node of the matching event tree branch is activated. For example, suppose you select the item Roster/&Window from the Report menu. In order for the menu item to cause something to happen, the application (stack) event tree must have a branch whose condition is spelled exactly the same: Roster/&Window. Once located, the statements in the event conclusion are executed—the report is printed in a window.

Thus, for every menu item (*not* every menu), there should be a condition whose name matches the menu item. Menu items with no matching branch in the stack event tree are powerless. They are, in effect, commentary.

The process empowering a menu item is best understood if we create two event tree branches for two new menu items. Then you can repeat the steps for the remaining menu items. In the steps that follow, we will implement the Restore and Exit menu items. Both are choices displayed in the File menu pull-down menu.

1. With the Faculty application open, select Tools|Form to enter edit mode.
2. Right click the application title bar and select Event Tree. The Faculty application's event tree should be displayed and should resemble the one shown previously in Figure 7.7.
3. Maximize the event tree to make viewing easier.
4. Select the last node in the tree, Ctrl+C. A dashed line surrounds that branch.
5. Create a new conclusion by clicking the Conclusion icon on the object bar.
6. For the event condition, type **&Restore**. (Be sure to include the ampersand so the condition's spelling exactly matches the menu item name spelling in the @ADDMENUITEM function.)
7. For the event conclusion, type **@RESTOREMENU**.
8. Repeat steps 5 through 7, but type **&Exit** for the condition and type **@APPEXIT** for the event branch conclusion.

Figure 7.11 shows the application event following the addition of the Restore and Exit event tree branches.

Create event tree branches to implement the four remaining menu items. Repeat the preceding steps 5 through 7, substituting the condition names and conclusions shown in Table 7.1. Be careful to include the ampersand in the same position as in the associated @ADDMENUITEM menu item name.

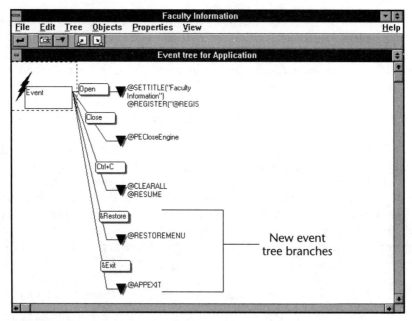

FIGURE 7.11
Restore and Exit menu items on the event tree

TABLE 7.1
Menu item condition names and conclusions

Condition Name	Conclusion Statement
&Top	@TOP("faculty")
&Bottom	@BOTTOM("faculty")
Roster/&Window	@PEPrintReport("FACULTY.RPT",0,1,"Faculty Teaching Assignments", 32768, 32768, 32768, 32768, 0, 0)
Roster/&Printer	@PEPrintReport("FACULTY.RPT",1,0,"Faculty Teaching Assignments",0,0,0,0,0,0)

Now the menu customization process is complete. You have created new menus and menu items and their corresponding actions implemented by application event tree branches. Complete the process by closing the event tree. Then close the Form tool to return to form completion mode. Save the application (save it under a new name, if you wish, or save it under the original name, FACULTY).

Try out the new menus. After saving the altered Faculty application, execute File|Open and select Faculty (or whatever name you called it). Instead of the usual ObjectVision menu names, your customized menus should be displayed. Try out the Report|Roster/Window command:

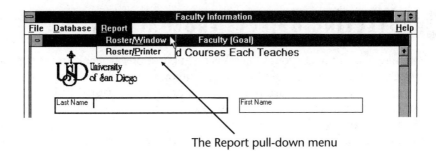

The Report pull-down menu

FIGURE 7.12
New menus with Report menu choices displayed

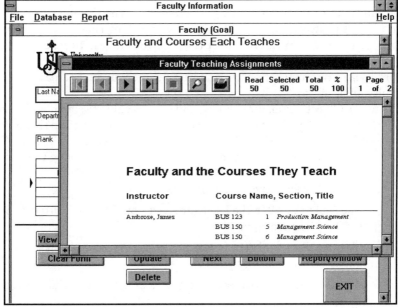

FIGURE 7.13
Test of the Report|Roster/Window command

1. Click the Report menu. Figure 7.12 shows the new menus with the Report pull-down menu choices displayed.

2. Click the Roster/Window command.

A faculty report should be displayed in its own window. Your display should match Figure 7.13. Close the Report window by double clicking its Control-menu box.

Make sure you can restore the original ObjectVision menus before going on. Execute the new command, File|Restore. The original ObjectVision menus should be displayed on the menu bar.

7.4 PROTECTING OBJECTS FROM ALTERATION

You may want to make your ObjectVision applications available to other people in your organization who use Windows. Or you may wish to sell selected applications to others. ObjectVision helps you protect your investment by providing a royalty-free runtime version. In any case, you probably will want to use password protection so that your applications are difficult for others to alter. This section describes how to save applications with passwords and illustrates the two ways to load password-protected applications.

SAVING APPLICATIONS WITH PASSWORDS

You can supply a password of up to 16 characters when saving a completed application. A password does not preclude your making changes to your application. However, you must remember the password for each application in order to make changes to an application. Users need not know an application's password to *use* your application. As an example, we will apply a password to the Faculty application.

Invoke ObjectVision, if necessary, and open Faculty. (Remember, a new, custom menu is displayed because we created the custom menu and then saved the changed Faculty application.) Click File|Restore to display the default Object-Vision menu. Save the application with a password by following these steps:

1. Execute the File|Save As command.
2. Type FACPASS.OVD in the File Name text box. (We use a different name to test the password facility.)
3. Select the Password text box and enter the password, SHERLOCK. Notice that asterisks display as you type.
4. Click OK. Another dialog box requests you to verify the password (see Figure 7.14).
5. Carefully, type SHERLOCK again. Be careful to spell it exactly the same way, including capitalization.
6. Click OK to save the application with its newly assigned password.

It is important to remember the password you assign to an application when you save it because it is impossible to determine a password from an application's contents if you forget it! Write down the passwords and secure the log of application names and their passwords, if necessary.

Next we examine the affect of assigning a password. That is, what good is a password? How does it protect an application?

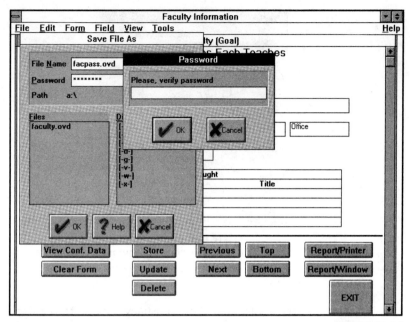

FIGURE 7.14
Verifying a password

RETRIEVING PASSWORD-PROTECTED APPLICATIONS

You can open a password-protected application without knowing its password. However, if you do not supply a password or if you give an incorrect password, ObjectVision omits the Tools menu. Without the Tools menu, neither you nor any other user can alter the application. Anyone may *use* the application without knowing the password, though. Passwords protect your applications from tinkering and alteration. Consequently, you should always save your finished applications with a password prior to distributing them. Let us see what happens when the FACPASS.OVD application is opened without supplying a password. Does the password protection really work? Follow these steps to test password protection:

1. Execute File|Open.
2. Select FACPASS.OVD from the list of application names or simply type that name in the File Name text box.
3. Click OK (do *not* enter the password).
4. Select File|Restore to reveal the default ObjectVision menus.

FIGURE 7.15
Entering an application's password

You will notice that the Tools menu, which usually appears to the right of the View menu, is missing. Thus, users cannot alter password-protected applications because the entry gate—the Tools menu—is unavailable. They must supply a correct password to have access to the Tools menu.

Of course, you can alter your password-protected applications by supplying the correct password when you open them. Figure 7.15 shows an example of entering the password SHERLOCK prior to pressing OK (asterisks appear in place of each letter).

REMOVING PASSWORD PROTECTION

You may wish to remove an application's password, either temporarily or permanently. To remove a password, simply open the application, supplying the current password. Then execute the command, File|Save As. Either click OK to save the application under the same name or enter a new name. In either case, no password has been supplied, so the application's password is removed.

7.5 SHIPPING RUNTIME MODULES

We have described how to develop Windows applications and produce reports using two products. These products are ObjectVision and Crystal Reports. Both products come with separate **runtime** versions of the software. If you are a registered owner of ObjectVision, you may ship the runtime modules free of charge to your customers. Similarly, Crystal Services, the publisher of Crystal Reports, allows registered users to distribute a runtime version of the Crystal Reports Print Engine with your applications at no charge. Of course, you must have a development version of Crystal Reports to *create* or *modify* reports such as those we produced in Chapter 6. Here we briefly describe which files of both runtime products you will want to distribute together with your finished ObjectVision and Crystal Reports applications.

INCLUDING THE OBJECTVISION RUNTIME SYSTEM

A separate ObjectVision runtime disk is included with ObjectVision. Make the runtime disk available to your users by duplicating it. Then you can copy your application(s) to the same disk. The runtime disk contains an install program that will install the runtime version ObjectVision modules and will copy your programs from the runtime disk to the user's disk. However, you must copy your *applications* to the runtime disk directory VISIONR for them to be automatically installed on the user's own disk. If you need more space on the runtime disk, you can delete the two sample files called OVPEXAMP.PAK and RTSMP.PAK.

You can modify the runtime disk file README.TXT to contain any special instructions for your users. (The last installation step asks the user if she or he wants to read the README.TXT.)

INCLUDING THE CRYSTAL REPORTS RUNTIME MODULES

If your ObjectVision allows users to produce reports—either on screen or printed—with Crystal Reports, then you will want to include the Crystal Reports Print Engine on the distribution disk. How many and which of the modules you include on the distribution disk depend on the requirements of your applications. Some Crystal Reports files are always included, such as CRPE.DLL, COMMDLG. DLL, and CRXLATE.DLL. Other Crystal Reports files are included if your applications open files that are stored in one of several database formats. In all cases, the files should be installed where Windows can find them. That is, they should be in one of the Windows directories or on the directory search path.

If your applications make use of Paradox, dBASE, or Btrieve database formats, then additional files must be included. Applications using Paradox database data require PDBPDX.DLL and PXENGWIN.DLL. Applications using dBASE format files should include the file PDBXBSE.DLL on the runtime distribution disk. Include the following files if your application accesses Btrieve databases: PDBBTRV.DLL, PDCTBTRV.DLL, WBTRCALL.DLL, and WDDLSVCS.DLL.

SUMMARY

You have learned that you can create buttons to launch either ObjectVision applications or other DOS or Windows programs. The @APPOPEN function is used to execute another ObjectVision application. The function is placed in the conclusion of a button's click event. Similarly, you can execute DOS or Windows applications by specifying the path and application name as an argument of the @EXEC function. The function is the click event conclusion node.

You have also learned how to create custom ObjectVision application menus. You can delete entire menus or selected menu items. New menus can be added to the menu bar. You can place menu items in drop-down menus. The functions that delete and add menus and menu items should be placed in the stack open event tree branch. Associated action branches must be placed in the stack event tree to implement the new menu items you create.

You can protect your applications from inadvertent alteration by saving each one with a password up to 16 characters. ObjectVision omits the Tools menu whenever users load any of your password-protected applications—even users having the full development version of ObjectVision. Runtime ObjectVision modules do not display a Tools menu option at all. You can remove password protection by opening an application with a password and subsequently saving it under a new name without a password.

ObjectVision and Crystal Reports both provide runtime versions of their developmental systems (collectively called the *runtime system*). As a registered user, you are permitted to distribute runtime versions of both software packages free of charge to your clients and customers. Of course, you should include your applications on the disks you distribute.

KEY TERMS

Customized menu A menu that you create which replaces, in part or in whole, the ObjectVision menu found in the menu bar.

Launch Commencing execution of another ObjectVision or Windows application from an ObjectVision application.

Menu customization function One of the several ObjectVision functions that allow you to add or delete menus and menu items. Included in these functions is @RESUME, which restores the original ObjectVision menus.

Password protection The ability to provide a password prior to saving an ObjectVision application on disk. Without supplying the correct password, a user can run an application but cannot change it.

Runtime system The collection of files that comprise both the royalty-free ObjectVision and Crystal Reports systems. These files may be distributed to permit other users to run your applications without requiring them to be registered ObjectVision or Crystal Reports users.

Stack open event The event on the application event tree that is triggered whenever the application is opened. The open condition is found on the stack event tree.

REVIEW QUESTIONS

True or False Questions

1. **T F** You cannot delete the Help menu from the ObjectVision menu bar.

2. **T F** Any menu customization functions *must* appear only in the conclusion node of an open event on the application (stack) event tree.

3. **T F** Other Windows applications cannot be executed from an ObjectVision application.

4. **T F** Once any of the default ObjectVision menus have been deleted, none can be reinstated.

5. **T F** A menu item appearing in the menu bar is not enough to create a custom menu that does something. There must be a corresponding event condition on the stack that takes action when the menu item is selected.

6. **T F** Once you save a password with an ObjectVision application, you cannot remove it.

7. **T F** Passwords prevent unauthorized users from running your applications.

8. **T F** You can freely distribute *any* of your ObjectVision program files to others along with your applications.

9. **T F** Crystal Reports runtime files must always be distributed with any of your applications.

10. **T F** Crystal Reports runtime files allow users to develop (create) reports as well as run them.

Multiple Choice Questions

1. You use the @APPOPEN function to execute what type of application?
   a. DOS
   b. Windows
   c. ObjectVision
   d. Crystal Reports
   e. none of the preceding

2. Which function creates a new menu called *Search* and places it in the left-most (first) position on the menu bar?
   a. @ADDMENU("Search",1)
   b. @ADDMENUITEM("Search",1)
   c. @ADDMENU("Search",0)
   d. @ADDMENU(Search,left)
   e. @ADDMENU("Search",–1)

3. Which function deletes only the New menu item from the File menu?
   a. @DELETE("File")
   b. @DELETEMENUITEM("New","File")
   c. @DELETEMENU("New")
   d. @DELETEMENUITEM("File","New")
   e. @DELETEMENU("File","New")

4. What function restores the default ObjectVision menu?
   a. @RESTOREMENU
   b. @REVIVE
   c. @RESTORE
   d. @EXECRESTORE
   e. none of the preceding

5. When do you have the opportunity to create a password for an application?
   a. When the application is first opened
   b. Following execution of Tools|Form
   c. While you execute the File|Save command
   d. While you execute the File|Save As command
   e. By executing the ObjectVision command, Edit|Password

6. Users can _____ your password-protected application if they supply an incorrect password or no password at all.
   a. execute (use)
   b. execute or alter
   c. do nothing with
   d. passively view
   e. execute, alter, or delete

7. The event tree *condition* attached to a button to execute another Windows program contains the condition
   a. open
   b. close
   c. select
   d. unselect
   e. click

8. Suppose you want to select the <u>S</u>earch command found in the <u>D</u>atabase menu (both the S in Search and the D in Database are underlined in the displayed menu). You could press what to invoke the Database menu?
   a. Alt+D
   b. Ctrl+Shift+S
   c. Alt+Shift+S
   d. Ctrl+D
   e. none of the preceding

9. Assume you want to write the stack event tree condition to take action when a user selects the Search menu item from the menu described in question 8 above. What would you type for the condition when you create the new branch for Search command?
   a. Search
   b. &Search
   c. S&earch
   d. SEARCH
   e. &Database &Search

EXERCISES

---

1. Open the Employee Allowance form you worked with in Chapters 1 and 2. You may recall you saved the finished application in the file called EMPLOYEE.OVD. You will create a custom menu for Employee. First add a new menu item called Options that contains two menu items: Restore and Exit. The Options menu should appear to the right of the Tools menu. The Restore menu item restores the default ObjectVision menu. Exit exits ObjectVision, returning to Windows. Be sure to add the required action statements to the stack event tree in addition to the menu customization statements. Save the modified application in the file EMPLOY2.OVD to preserve the original application.

2. Open EMPLOY2.OVD and further modify the Employee Allowance application. This time, change the stack Open event to remove *all* the original ObjectVision menus. Modify the Options menu so that it appears first in the menu list. Then add two new menus and their corresponding actions. To the right of Options is the menu Database. It contains the commands Store and Delete, which perform functions identical to the Store and Delete buttons already on the form. To the right of the Database menu, in the third position, create the new menu Search. Search contains two menu items, Previous and Next, which perform the same duties as the buttons on the form by the same name (look at the event trees for all buttons). When you have successfully created the new menus and menu items, remove the four buttons from the form. Then save the application in the file called EMPLOY3.OVD. Test the form to make sure the menu works correctly.

3. Modify the Faculty application so that none of the buttons on the first form are required. That is, place the actions from the buttons into menu items. You have complete freedom to design the menus any way you want. However, when you are done, be sure to delete all the buttons on the form. Save the modified Faculty application in a new file such as FACULTY2.OVD. Test all menu items thoroughly.

APPENDIX
ObjectVision Built-in Functions

MATHEMATICAL FUNCTIONS

Function	Value Returned or Action
@ABS(X)	Absolute value of X.
@ACOS(X)	Arc cosine of X.
@ASIN(X)	Arc sine of X.
@ATAN(X)	Arc tangent of X (two quadrant).
@ATAN2(X)	Arc tangent of Y/X (four quadrant).
@AVG(List)	Average of List.
@COLUMNAVG(ColumnName)	Average of all displayed values in ColumnName.
@COLUMNCOUNT(ColumnName)	Number of items displayed in ColumnName.
@COLUMNMAX(ColumnName)	Maximum value displayed in ColumnName.
@COLUMNMIN(ColumnName)	Minimum value displayed in ColumnName.
@COLUMNSUM(ColumnName)	Sum of displayed values on ColumnName.
@COS(X)	Cosine of angle X.

`@DEGREES(X)`	Number of degrees in X radians.
`@EXP(X)`	e raised to the Xth power.
`@INT(X)`	Integer portion of X.
`@LINKAVG("LinkName","Datafield")`	The average of all values in the current range of Datafield.
`@LINKCOUNT("LinkName")`	The number of records in the current range.
`@LINKMAX("LinkName","Datafield")`	The maximum value of Datafield in the current range.
`@LINKMIN("LinkName","Datafield")`	The minimum value of Datafield in the current range.
`@LINKSUM("LinkName","Datafield")`	The sum of all values in Datafield.
`@LN(X)`	Log base e of X.
`@LOG(X)`	Log base 10 of X.
`@MAX(List)`	Maximum value in List.
`@MIN(List)`	Minimum value in List.
`@MOD(X,Y)`	Remainder of X/Y.
`@PI`	The value pi (.314159).
`@RADIANS(X)`	Number of radians in X degrees.
`@ROUND(X,Num)`	X rounded to the number of digits. Specified with Num (up to 15).
`@SIN(X)`	Sine of angle of X.
`@SQRT(X)`	Positive square root of X.
`@SUM(List)`	Sum of values in List.
`@TAN(X)`	Tangent of angle of X.

DATE AND TIME FUNCTIONS

Function	Value Returned or Action
`@DATE(Yr,Mo,Day)`	Date serial number.
`@DATEVALUE("DateString")`	Date serial number.
`@DAY(DateTimeNumber)`	Day of the month (1–31).
`@HOUR(DateTimeNumber)`	Hour of the day (0–23).

@MINUTE(DateTimeNumber)	Minute of the hour (0–59).
@MONTH(DateTimeNumber)	Month(1–12).
@NOW	Current date/time serial number.
@SECOND(DateTimeNumber)	A second (0–59).
@TIME(Hr,Min,Sec)	Time serial number.
@TIMEVALUE("TimeString")	Time serial number.
@TODAY	Current date serial number.
@WEEKDAY(DateTimeNumber)	Day of week (1–7).
@YEAR(DateTimeNumber)	Year (1800–2099).

STRING FUNCTIONS

Function	Value Returned or Action
@CHAR(Code)	Character for ANSI decimal number Code.
@CODE("String")	ANSI decimal code for the first character in String.
@EXACT("String1","String2")	Yes if String1 and String2 are identical; otherwise, No.
@FIND("SubStr","Str",Start)	Character position of the first SubStr found in Str.
@LEFT("String",Num)	First Num characters in String.
@LENGTH("String")	Number of characters in String.
@LOWER("String")	Lowercase letters of String.
@MID("String",StartNum,Num)	Num characters of String, beginning with StartNum character position.
@PROPER("String")	Text in String with the first letter in each word capitalized.
@REPEAT("String",Num)	String, repeated Num times.
@REPLACE("String",StartNum,Num, "NewString")	Removes Num characters from String, beginning with StartNum, inserts NewString in its place.
@RIGHT("String",Num)	Last Num characters in String.
@TRIM("String")	String without leading, trailing, or consecutive spaces.
@UPPER("String")	String in uppercase characters.

LOGICAL FUNCTIONS

Function	Value Returned or Action
@AND(LogicalList)	Yes if all arguments in LogicalList are true; otherwise, No.
@IF(Cond,TrueExpr,FalseExpr)	TrueExpr if Cond is Yes; FalseExpr if Cond is No.
@NOT(Logical)	Yes if Logical is false; otherwise, No.
@OR(LogicalList)	Yes if any argument in LogicalList is true; otherwise, No.

FINANCIAL FUNCTIONS

Function	Value Returned or Action
@CTERM(Rate,Fv,Pv)	Number of compounding periods (kept for compatibility—see @NPER).
@DDB(Cost,Salvage,Life,Period)	Double-declining depreciation allowance.
@FV(Pmt,Rate,Nper)	Future value of an annuity (see @FVAL).
@FVAL(Rate,Nper,Pmt,Pv,Type)	Future value of an annuity (an improved version of @FV).
@IPAYMT(Rate,Per,Nper,Pv,Fv,Type)	Interest portion of a payment amount for a loan.
@IRATE(Nper,Pmt,Pv,Fv,Type)	Periodic interest rate (an improved version of @RATE).
@IRR(Guess,ColumnName)	Internal rate of return.
@NPER(Rate,Pmt,Pv,Fv,Type)	Number of period (an improved version of @CTERM and @TERM).
@NPV(Rate,ColumnName,Type)	Present value of future cash flow.
@PAYMT(Rate,Nper,Pv,Fv,Type)	Payment amount for a loan (an improved version of @PMT).
@PMT(Pv,Rate,Nper)	Present amount for a loan (see @PAYMT).
@PPAYMT(Rate,Per,Nper,Pv,Fv,Type)	Principal portion of a payment amount for a loan.
@PV(Pmt,Rate,Nper)	Present value of an annuity (see @PVAL).

`@PVAL(Rate,Nper,Pmt,Fv,Type)`	The present value of an annuity (an improved version of @PV).
`@RATE(Fv,Pv,Nper)`	Periodic interest rate(see @IRATE).
`@SLN(Cost,Salvage,Life)`	Straight-line depreciation allowance.
`@SYD(Cost,Salvage,Life,Period)`	Sum-of-the-years digits depreciation allowance of an asset.
`@TERM(Pmt,Rate,Fv)`	Number of payment periods of an investment (see @NPER).

VALUE MISCELLANEOUS FUNCTIONS

Function	Value Returned or Action
`@BLANK`	Assigns a blank value to a field.
`@CHOOSE(Number,List)`	The value in List in the position of Number.
`@CURRENTFILE`	The name of current files.
`@CURRENTPATH`	The name of current path.
`@ERR`	The value ERR (error).
`@FORMAT(Num,Format,Places)`	Formats the number so it can be saved or sent to another application in that format.
`@ISBLANK(FieldName)`	Yes if FieldName is blank; otherwise, No.
`@ISCOMPLETE("FormName")`	Yes if FormName is complete; otherwise, No.
`@NA`	The value NA (not available).
`@SELECTEDFIELD`	The name of the currently selected field.
`@SELECTEDFORM`	The name of the currently selected form.
`@TYPE(Value)`	A number (1, 2, 4, or 16) indicating the data type of Value.
`@VERSION`	The version number of ObjectVision.

LINKING FUNCTIONS

Function	Value Returned or Action
@ASCIIOPEN("LinkName","FileName", "OVFields",Option)	Opens the LinkName link between an ASCII file and ObjectVision OVFields.
@BOTTOM("LinkName")	Moves to the last record in the open database.
@BTRVOPEN("LinkName", "DictionaryPath","TableName", "DataFields",OVReadFields", OVWriteFields",IndexNo,Option)	Opens the LinkName link between the Btrieve table, TableName DataFields and the ObjectVision fields.
@CLEAR("LinkName")	Clears the associated link fields in preparation for writing a new record.
@CLOSE("LinkName")	Closes and disconnects the associated link fields and dissolves the link.
@DBOPEN("linkName","FileName", "DataField","OVReadFields", "OVWriteFields", "IndexFile",Option)	Opens a db link between the db data file's DataFields and ObjectVision's fields.
@DDEEXECUTE("LinkName","[Commands]")	Sends commands to the linked DDE application.
@DDEOPEN("LinkName","Application", "Document","RemoteNames","OVFields")	Opens a DDE link between Application Document DataFields and OVFields.
@DDEPOKE("LinkName","RemoteName", Value)	Sends values to an opened file in a Window application.
@DELETE("LinkName","RemoteName", Value)	Deletes current database record.
@FILTERACTIVATE("LinkName", "FilterName")	Activates the filter to LinkName.
@FILTERDEACTIVATE("LinkName")	Deactivates the filter to LinkName.
@INSERT("LinkName")	Inserts the current ObjectVision values into the data file at the current record.
@LINKVALUE("Datafield")	The current value of Datafield.
@LOCATE("LinkName",InexactFlag, IndexValues)	The record in LinkName that matches IndexValues.
@NEXT("LinkName")	Moves to the next data file record in the open link.
@PAGEDN("LinkName")	Moves down the database table by one page.

`@PAGEUP("LinkName")`	Moves up the database table by one page.
`@PREVIOUS("LinkName")`	Moves to the previous record in the open database.
`@PRINTLINK("LinkName")`	Prints the current form once for each value in the current range of LinkName.
`@PXOPEN("LinkName","TableName", "DataFields","OVReadFields", "OVWriteFileds","SecIndexField", Option)`	Opens the LinkName link between the Paradox Filename DataFields and the ObjectVision field.
`@STORE("LinkName")`	Appends a new record or updates an existing record in the open database.
`@TOP("LinkName")`	Moves to the first record in the open database or ASCII file.
`@UPDATE("LinkName")`	Updates a record in the open database with the current ObjectVision values.

MENU CUSTOMIZATION FUNCTIONS

Function	**Value Returned or Action**
`@ADDMENU("MenuName",Position)`	Adds a command MenuName to the application's menu at Position.
`@ADDMENUITEM("MenuName","Item",pos)`	Adds Item to the menu command MenuName.
`@CHECKMENUITEM("MenuName","Item")`	Places a checkmark next to the item.
`@DELETEMENU("MenuName")`	Deletes the menu command MenuName.
`@DELETEMENUITEM("MenuName","Item")`	Deletes the item from the menu command.
`@RESTOREMENU`	Erases all menu changes and returns to normal ObjectVision menus.
`@UNCHECKMENUITEM("MenuName","Item")`	Removes the checkmark from the item.

MENU EQUIVALENTS FUNCTIONS

Function	**Value Returned or Action**
`@APPEXIT`	Exits the application without saving.
`@APPNEW`	Creates a new application.

@APPOPEN("AppName")	Opens the application AppName.
@CLEARALL	Clears all values in an application except linked values.
@FIELDCALCULATE(FieldName)	Calculates the value of FieldName.
@FIELDCLEAR(FieldName)	Clears the value from a field except protected fields.
@FIELDFIND(FieldName)	Finds FieldName in the current application.
@FORMCLEAR("FormName")	Clears values in FormName except linked values.
@FORMCLOSE("FormName")	Closes FormName.
@FORMSELECT("FormName")	Makes FormName the selected form.
@PRINTFORM("FormName")	Prints FormName.
@PRINTALL	Prints all forms in the application.
@RESUME	Resumes guided completion.
@SAVE	Saves the current application.
@SAVEAS("FileName")	Saves the current application as FileName.

EVENT MISCELLANEOUS FUNCTIONS

Function	Value Returned or Action
@ASSIGN(FieldName,Value)	Gives FieldName the Value.
@EVENT("Item","Event")	Sends a user-defined Event to an Item (an object, form, or stack).
@EXEC("Commandline",ShowOption)	Opens a Windows application.
@MESSAGE("String")	Puts the String message in a pop-up dialog box.
@REGISTER("OVAlias","ArgTypes", "ArgHelp","LibName","FuncName",Type)	Registers a function from a DLL.
@SETTITLE("Title")	Changes the window title from ObjectVision to Title.

MULTIMEDIA FUNCTIONS

Function	Value Returned or Action
@MMEXECUTE("MCIString")	Sends MCI strings to any multimedia device installed on your machine.
@MMNOTIFY(flags)	Lets you turn error messages on or off.
@MMPAUSE("Device")	Pauses the currently playing device.
@MMPLAY("Filename","Driver")	Plays a sound file that is one of .WAV, .MID, or a CD sound file.
@MMPLAYFROMTO("Filename","From", "To","Driver")	Plays specified segment of a sound file.
@MMRECORD("Filename",Flags,Time)	Records a .WAV file.
@MMRESUME("Device")	Resumes playing the device from its currently paused position.
@MMREGISTER	Registers all the multimedia functions listed here.
@MMSTATUS("Media",Flags)	Returns the status of a device (position in the file, length, etc.).
@MMSTOP("Device")	Stops playing a device.

SQL FUNCTIONS

Function	Value Returned or Action
@SQLBOTTOM("Link")	Moves to the last record in the open database.
@SQLCLEAR("Link")	Clears the buffer and all read-linked values.
@SQLCLOSE("Link")	Closes a database link.
@SQLDELETE("Link")	Deletes a record from the linked database.
@SQLERROR(Errorflag)	Enables or disables error messages.
@SQLEXEC("ConnectName", "SQLStatement")	Moves the last record in the open database.
@SQLINSERT("Link")	Inserts a new record in the open database.
@SQLLOCATE("Link","Condition", "Fieldlist")	Finds a record in the database.

`@SQLLOGOFF("ConnectName")`	Disconnects the connection and extant links created using the connection.
`@SQLLOGON("ConnectName","Username",` `"Password","Server","Database")`	Connects to a database server.
`@SQLNEXT("Link")`	Moves to next record in linked database.

`@SQLOPEN("ConnectName","Link",`
`"DBObject",Bufsize,Initializer,`
`"Datafields","OVReadFields",`
`"OVWriteFields","OrderBy")`
	Links database fields to ObjectVision fields.

`@SQLPAGEDN("Link")`	Moves down a page of records in database.
`@SQLPAGEUP("Link")`	Moves up a page of records in database.
`@SQLPREVIOUS("Link")`	Moves to previous record in database.
`@SQLREFRESH("Link")`	Clears buffer; moves to top record in database.
`@SQLREGISTER`	Registers all the SQL functions listed herein. This function must also be registered (@REGISTER).
`@SQLSTORE("Link")`	Saves values to current record in database.
`@SQLTOP("Link")`	Moves to first record in database.
`@SQLUPDATE("Link")`	Saves changes to record into the database.

INDEX